WONG PING

WONG PING
Your Silent Neighbor

Edited by Gary Carrion-Murayari

NEW MUSEUM

Contents

Page 6   Foreword
              Lisa Phillips

Page 10   Happiness is Only Real When Shared
              Gary Carrion-Murayari

Page 24   Wong Ping in Conversation
              with Tobias Berger

Page 38   A conversation between Wong Ping
              and David Horvitz with Chris Burden and
              Nam Jun Paik, facilitated by medium,
              Shirley Lipner

Page 172   List of Illustrated Works

Page 175   About the Artist

Foreword

—

Lisa Phillips

Wong Ping's animated videos, created regularly over the last ten years, paint a colorful, chaotic portrait of life in contemporary Hong Kong. Their painfully bright palette and grotesque human and animal protagonists suggest a cartoon fantasy world, but their narratives draw from very real anxieties, frustrations, and traumas of life in a global metropolis. The artist's early films depicted tortured romantic entanglements and outlandish sexual fantasies, while more recent works capture the social pressures experienced by the young Hong Kong generation affected by the political and economic influence of mainland China. These tales are funny and alarming and offer unique insight into lives lived and contested simultaneously online and in public space.

Wong Ping was included in the 2018 New Museum Triennial and joins a long list of artists who first rose to prominence in the museum's signature survey exhibition of young contemporary art. Both the Triennial and this current solo exhibition demonstrate the museum's long-standing commitment to debuting some of the most exciting young artists from around the world. We are confident that Wong Ping's work will prove to be some of the most strange, compelling work to emerge out of this moment of upheaval.

I would like to thank the curator of the exhibition, Gary Carrion-Murayari, Kraus Family Curator, for his work in bringing this exciting exhibition to the New Museum. I would also like to thank David Hollely, Director of Exhibitions Management, and his entire team for their work in realizing such an ambitious installation: in particular, Abby Lepold, Senior Registrar; Carlos Yepes, Registrar; Patrick Foran, Chief Preparator; and Arkadiy Ryabin, Audiovisual Preparator. I would also like to thank Karen Wong, Deputy Director; Diane Vivona, Director of Development; Dennis Szakacs, Chief Operating Officer; and their teams for their support in making this exhibition possible.

This catalogue was designed by Nicholas Weltyk. It includes a new monographic text surveying Wong Ping's hallucinatory videos and sculptures by Carrion-Murayari and an interview between the artist and curator Tobias Berger. I am also thankful to past New Museum alumni artist David Horvitz for his unique contribution to the catalogue.

The New Museum gratefully acknowledges our Board of Trustees and generous sponsors for their support of "Wong Ping: Your Silent Neighbor." Major support for this exhibition is provided by the International Leadership Council of the New Museum. Support for this exhibition is provided by the Toby Devan Lewis Emerging Artists Exhibitions Fund. Artist commissions are generously supported by the Neeson / Edlis Artist Commissions Fund. Artist support is provided, in part, by Laura Skoler.

We extend our special thanks to the Friends of Wong Ping: Kiang Malingue, Tanya Bonakdar Gallery, Nelson Leong, Evan Chow, Andrew Xue and Ruoqi Amy Zhou. Education and community programs are supported, in part, by the American Chai Trust. This publication was made possible, in part, by the J. McSweeney and G. Mills Publications Fund at the New Museum.

This exhibition would not have been possible without the support of Wong's two galleries, Edouard Malingue Gallery, Hong Kong/ Shanghai, and Tanya Bonakdar Gallery, New York/Los Angeles. In particular, I would like to acknowledge Edouard Malingue, Lorraine Kiang Malingue, and Ryan Lai from Edouard Malingue Gallery, and Tanya Bonakdar and Megan Bedford from Tanya Bonakdar Gallery.

Finally, I would like to thank Wong Ping for his colorful portrayals of contemporary life, as surreal and terrifying as they may be.

Happiness is Only Real When Shared

—

Gary Carrion-Murayari

Wong Ping creates short, animated videos that provide a night-marish vision of what it means to live online and alone in the world today. In less than a decade, he has built an unsettling, often hilarious, universe rendered in bright colors using an intuitive economy of means that serves as a mirror of the dystopian landscape of contemporary Hong Kong. As his work has migrated from short videos produced primarily for an audience of friends or anonymous internet viewers to presentations in museums, galleries and art fairs witnessed by a global contemporary world, Wong Ping has become increasingly adept at analyzing the ways in which technology has accelerated organic forms of isolation and repression. Self-taught, his seemingly naïve style of animation belies the complexity of his narrative scenarios and operates within a long history of popular animation and caricature in which human physiognomy, psychology, and behavior are distorted and abstracted for the purpose of social commentary.

An Emo Nose (2015) captures Wong Ping's elastic approach to the human form as it can be applied to his own bodily anxieties. The five-minute video tells the story of a man who gradually grows emotionally and physically apart from his anthropomorphic nose. Over the course of the video, the heart-shaped nose (which in other videos appears again as the head of a penis) extends further out into the world with every negative thought expressed by its sullen, introverted owner. A relationship that begins as an alternative to boring, anxiety-inducing interactions with real life friends ends up encouraging the narrator to become even more isolated and self-loathing than at the start. His own body eventually becomes a stranger as his nose lives a more exciting life than his own. *An Emo Nose* deliberately invokes the story of Pinocchio, but has more in common with Carlo Callodi's original tale of body horror where Pinocchio is burned and hanged rather than the sanitized version crafted by Walt Disney. The body in Ping's work is similarly vulnerable and its gradual fragmentation reflects the main character's inability to integrate into a larger social body.

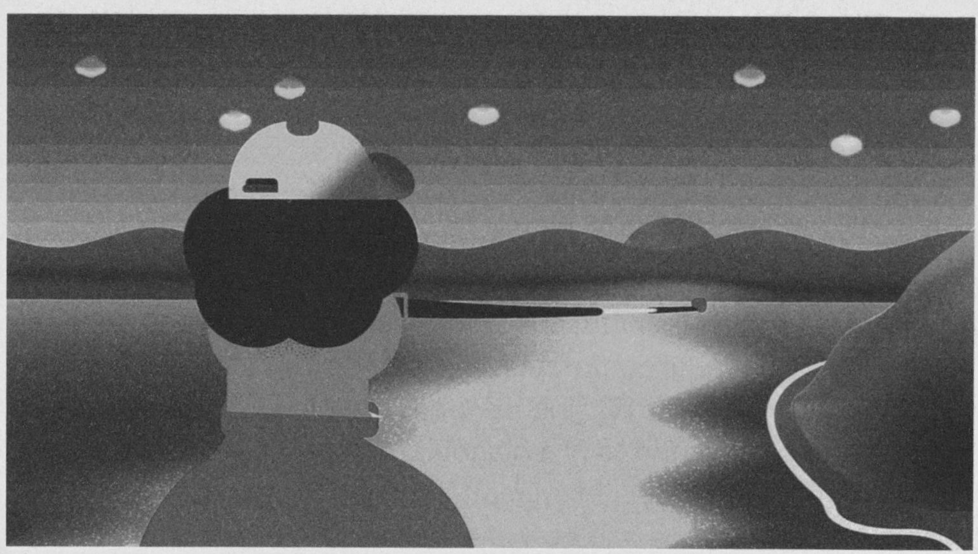

An Emo Nose, 2015

Sexual desire and frustration also dominate much of Wong Ping's work. He is often deliberately provocative in the way he depicts his characters' animated erotic exploits. *Slow Sex* (2013) is, as it sounds, a scene of a couple engaged in a marathon session of rhythmic sex until the head of the male partner's penis falls off. *Doggy Love* (2015) is a more complex tale in which a male student lusts after a female classmate whose breasts have grown on her back instead of her front. When the two finally consummate their relationship, the young man finds that his obsession has turned into true love. In both cases, Wong Ping uses animation to exaggerate and satirize the mechanics of desire and fulfillment. Although the disjunction between the raw content of the work and the cartoonish forms of the figures is initially shocking, it also helps the work tap into an erotic subconscious within the history of animation, which from its earliest days has inserted both coded and explicit sexual imagery, using the plasticity of animation to express desire, gender transgression, and sexual taboo.

By the time Wong was growing up in the 1990s, adult-themed cartoons were easily accessible, both in mainstream series from the United States and the infinitely diverse genres of Japanese anime from robot themed mecha to erotic ecchi. Wong's earnest,

12

confessional tone, however, separates him from these contemporaneous forms. His accounts of frustration and alienation have more direct roots in the Japanese mangas he would regularly read as a teenager. He has often cited Minoru Furuya, a popular Japanese manga author, as an inspiration. Furuya's works from the late 1990s typically focused on the misadventures of depressive young men who fall into and then self-destruct their romances with girlfriends far beyond their status. The parallels with Wong Ping's work are easy to see: from their shared stream-of-conscious narratives and self-deprecating first-person points of view to their frank expression of adolescent sexual fantasies. Although not a direct source of inspiration, another precursor to Wong's work is that of American underground comix legend Robert Crumb. Both Wong Ping and Crumb rely on the amplification of the artists persona and over-the-top sexual imagery that is often deliberately provocative, if not downright offensive. Crumb once described the effect of LSD on his drawings as creating "a grotesque kaleidoscope, a tawdry carnival of disassociated images [that] kept sputtering to the surface" [1] and Ping's discovery of computer motion graphics may have had a similar effect in his ability to transform private emotions into bizarre spectacles.

Part of what makes Wong Ping's narratives more awkward, while at the same time more relatable, than some of his predecessors is the fact that they are really translations of more intimate forms of writing that were initially posted digitally in the forms of blogs. Like most of his generation, the internet emerged as a critical space for creative experimentation with forms of identity construction and sexual fantasy, while offering the potential for possible social connections and community. The fact that his ribald tales found an enthusiastic audience in an online space before moving into the more buttoned-up art world is not a surprise. As the artist has stated:

> "If you take a look at the various behaviors on the internet, you will see our clothed bestiality is being exposed all at once. It is not that the society is going backwards, but that humanity has always been primitive."[2]

As bizarre as the exploits in his videos may seem, they could never reach the heights of the most extreme content that could be found with an even cursory internet search. At the same time, the main characters in his video are expressing genuine desires for connection and intimacy, and the impossibility of achieving these goals both online and in the real world are some of the strongest themes that have evolved in Wong Ping's work over the past several years.

Wong's characters are constantly trying and failing to find a liberatory space for themselves within their dystopian environments. They are often prisoners of their own desires even within their own homes. Philip Maughan has astutely described the universe these characters inhabit:

> "Tinder, internet pornography, sexual liberation: both signs of unrestricted freedom and drivers of atomization. And what better location than the dense, technologically-wired high-rises of Hong Kong to serve as a visual laboratory from which themes of alienation and urban loneliness emerge." [3]

This state of atomization is captured clearly in *Stop Peeping* (2014), where the main character spies on his next-door neighbor during a particularly hot Hong Kong summer, eventually sneaking into her apartment to make popsicles from the sweat collected from her exercise clothes. In the film, as in real life, the residential landscape of Hong Kong clusters residents together in densely packed, but impenetrably isolated, units. The narrator in the work describes how he works two jobs and 16 hours a day with no hope of escaping his tiny apartment. He further recounts how he previously used the peep hole between the two units to check in on an elderly neighbor, but now uses it to spy on and fantasize about the young co-ed. In both cases, there was no possibility of genuine connection between neighbors. In the end, the only bridge between the narrator and his neighbor was through a violation of privacy and an ultimately exploitative transformation of his desire into something he could consume.

In a more recent, non-animated work, *The Modern Way to Shower* (2019), Wong is again frustrated in his desires, even in a monetized, digital realm. In the video, Wong documents his struggle to come up with a new idea for a piece, eventually deciding to use his production money to commission a bondage performer for an online session. However, over the course of the work, their filmed interactions are gradually infected by encroaching phone notifications and the artist's own creeping thoughts about the social and political situation in Hong Kong. At one point, the artist requests a shower scenario using the same color blue liquid as that used by police to spray participants the in pro-democracy protest in which his generation had been leading. In both of these works, sexual intimacy is misguided as a strategy for liberation when the reality of life in a global metropolis like Hong Kong is increasingly engineered to prevent it through constant authoritarian encroachment into all aspects of life and the crushing demands of capitalism that have structured the way individuals live.

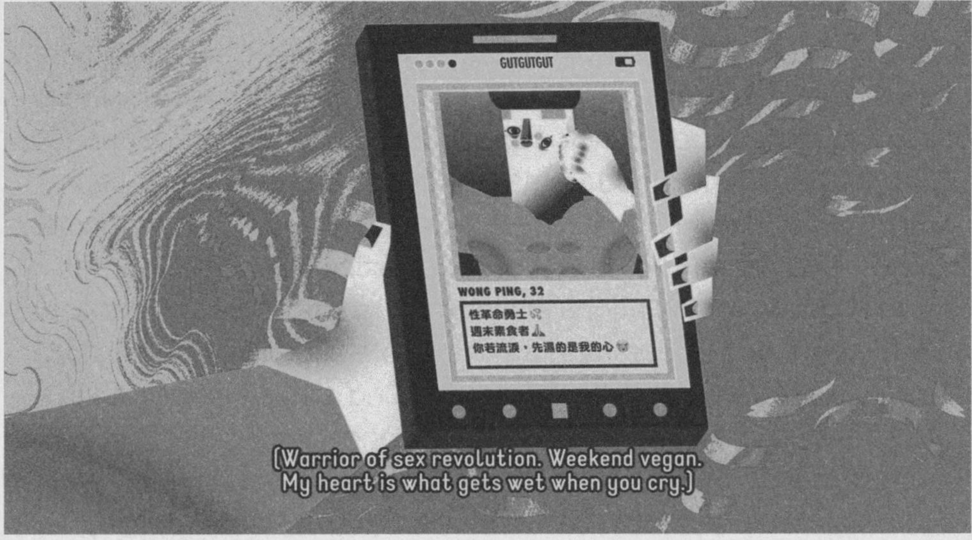

Who's the Daddy?, 2017

Who's the Daddy? (2017) explores this psychological condition in even more detail. In the work, the main character, again a fictionalized version of the artist, begins by trying to find love on a dating app but misunderstands the program as a tool for identifying political identity rather than one for judging and acting on a subject's attractiveness. He meets and has a brief, sexual relationship with an especially religious woman. Their sexual encounters are inflected by their respective, confused moral positions and the narrator's submissiveness and neuroses tied to his childhood memories of his father. After the couple fall out and the woman blinds the narrator in one eye using her high heel, she eventually returns to gift him an aborted baby to raise as his own child.

Much of the commentary of this and other examples of the artist's work has focused on seemingly oppositional positions between men and women with one exercising power and control over the other. Given the explicit sexual scenarios depicted, it would be easy to assume that the works are simply expressing a sort of lament for a masculinity under threat, but in reality, the power dynamics between genders in his videos are constantly shifting and any perceived imbalances and grievances are often extensions of larger psychological pressures, whether they be familial, cultural, or socio-political. In *Who's the Daddy?*, the romantic and physical relationship between the two characters becomes clearly analogous to generational differences in Hong Kong between those who hold conservative and liberal values and those who support or oppose the imposition of mainland China into the governance and culture of Hong Kong. As curator Yung Mas has observed, "the deployment of patriarchal power recurs in Wong's practice, rendered through sexual acts and observations of Hong Kong's politicized landscape" and the narrator's understanding of the role of parent, child, lover, citizen, and state are constantly overlapping and confused. As in *The Modern Way to Shower*, the use of bondage and discipline is a clear metaphor for the relationship between Hong Kong and China. The film ends with the narrator singing to his child a popular Cantonese nursery rhyme where the child is encouraged to kiss their father passionately in order to make sure the world doesn't end. Through this childhood memory, the narrator finally understands his "fetish for being harassed by power" and is capable of being a happy father himself.

Alongside a more complex understanding of desire and control in his work, Wong Ping's videos also grew more willing to directly address the realities of daily life in Hong Kong. *Jungle of Desire* (2015), the work that first drew larger attention to Wong's work from the artworld, is based on true stories of women practicing sex work out of their homes and of abuses of power by Hong Kong police towards them. In the video, the main character's wife begins seeing more clients to make money and to satisfy her unfulfilled desires. The husband/narrator hides inside a closet to observe his wife's sessions, becoming particularly obsessed with a corrupt cop who both blackmails the wife into unpaid sex and at the same time, satisfies her in a way in which her impotent husband has failed. Over the course of the video, the husband fantasizes about his rival with a mixture of desire, hatred, and disgust.

Throughout the video, Wong mixes in allusions to his own personal anxieties and to the pressures of life in Hong Kong. The husband justifies his passive acceptance of his wife's activities by citing his lack of income, echoing the artist's own struggles to get work in a production house after studying in Australia and his insecurity as a burgeoning contemporary artist. Eventually the voice-over collapses the distinction between narrator and artist by asking the viewer if they think he could make money from his animations. At one point, the artist's own business card scrolls down the screen in an attempt to use the visibility of the video, which was being shown in a smart Hong Kong alternative space, Things That Can Happen, as a promotional opportunity.

This feeling of economic insecurity is also reflected in the work's depiction of the increasingly authoritarian control of Hong Kong's physical geography. Early in the work, the narrator describes the landscape of Hong Kong as one in which public space has been made inhospitable to loiterers, including the unhoused population of the city, or even to anyone wishing for a moment's rest. As he states, "the city doesn't want you to stop…people even wake you if you fall asleep in the park. As if resting is a sin." Both the streets and the majority of the home have been colonized by the

pressures of capitalism, leaving the narrator to conclude that:
"Hiding in the closet at home becomes my only option. At least there
is A/C and Wifi." With no physical or mental space of his own and
unable to protect or satisfy his wife, Wong/the husband is over-
whelmed by the uninhibited expression of state power in the form
of the corrupt cop. Any resistance mounted exists only in the
husband's own closeted fantasies. He desires intimacy with the
cop and at the same time imagines humiliating or killing him.

Jungle of Desire was created in 2015, shortly after the 2014
Umbrella Revolution. Following the Chinese government's moves
to restrict Hong Kong's electoral freedom, these protests galva-
nized a younger generation, and the subsequent violent crackdown
on protests only further motivated their political engagement. More
election reforms, a new extradition law, and cultural restrictions
by the government have triggered continued protest up to the
present. Throughout this period, technology has played a central
role in both organizing and facilitating communication between
protestors and in the increasingly sophisticated methods of sur-
veillance employed by the government. Sociologist Zeynep Tufekci
identifies the "techno-evolutionary arms race between authorities
and protestors,"[4] as protestors use smartphone apps to quickly
amass, demonstrate, and evade the attention of the police, even as
authorities likely track them through these same devices. The government's installation of series of new smart lampposts capable
of recording and transmitting sophisticated data have drawn new
waves of unrest. In demonstrations that later circulate as viral
videos, protestors dismantle lampposts with electric saws while
shielding their own identities from the embedded cameras using
umbrellas. Wong Ping's anxiety around the control of governmental authority over public space and even domestic space reflects
a public unease sublimated into the escalation of paranoia in
the minds of his videos' subjects.

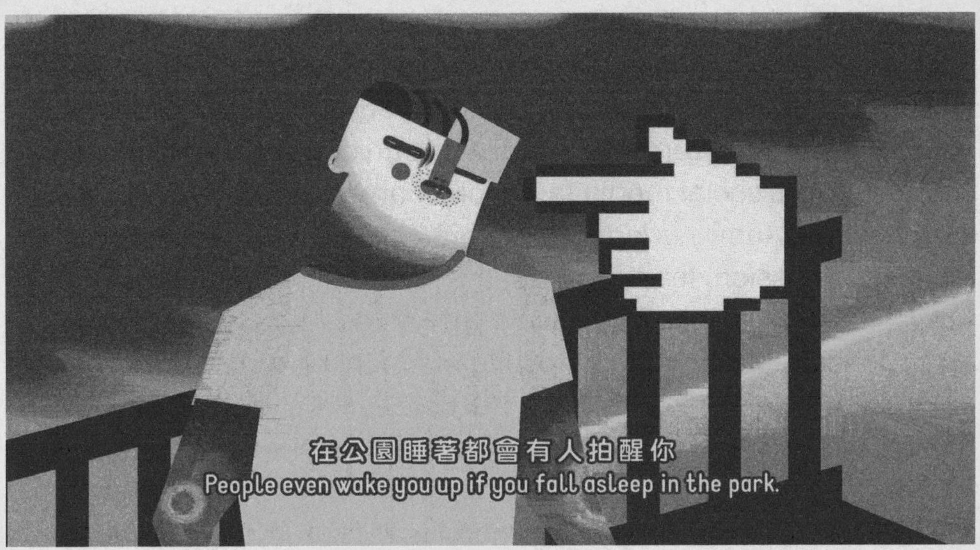

Jungle of Desire, 2015

The gradual loss of private space and individual autonomy in Hong Kong has provoked a crisis for young people of Wong's generation, many of whom are deciding to move elsewhere. The two-channel video installation *The Other Side* (2015) expresses complex feelings about emigration and immigration in the form of a mystical journey. The main character chooses to leave the comfort and familiarity of home and family, visualized as a monumental representation of his mother's womb, to journey across an ocean to a seemingly more utopian "other side." Instead of freedom and peace, he finds that things are mostly the same and is eventually lured back by memories and regret. *The Other Side* is work that accurately reflects the anxiety experienced by a younger generation who finds the freedom of the Hong Kong they have known gradually disappearing and are left with a feeling of loss whether they leave or stay.

For those who have chosen to remain, the pressures of life have only been heightened through a combination of political upheaval, economic pressure, and the alienating effects of technology. In recent work, Wong Ping has tried to document this increasingly apocalyptic landscape and offer his own commentary on how to potentially survive. *Wong Ping's Fables 1* (2018) and *Wong Ping's Fables 2* (2019) take the form of fairy tales intended to offer morals reflective of today's realities. In the short episodes, anthropomorphic animals have failed relationships, face familiar societal pressures, and live lives where the online and physical worlds have lost distinction. *Inspector Chicken* from *Fables 1* follows an overachieving chicken who trades his social media fame for a career as a police officer. Eventually his family is kidnapped, but his desire for likes sabotages his rescue mission, leading to deaths for hostages, kidnappers, and fellow officers alike. In *Tree*, also from *Fables 1*, the titular character watched a pregnant, unknowing elephant on a public bus as a cockroach slowly impedes upon her space. Paralyzed by his own anxieties, the tree retreats to the upper deck of the bus rather than muster up the courage to warn the elephant. Both works question the motivations of public-facing morality in Hong Kong and reflect the artist's skepticism that his generation's efforts to arrest the creeping restrictions and injustices at the hands of authorities will ultimately succeed.

Fables 2 is even more attuned to the challenges of navigating the professional pressures of contemporary life from the hurdles that must be overcome to the emptiness that potentially awaits once success is achieved. *Cow the Super-Rich*, from *Fables 2*, follows a globular bovine on a journey from activist, jailed for goring a police office to death during a demonstration, to mega-rich capitalist, wealthy from selling a fashionable line of protest-inspired jeans. As he grows more and more wealthy, the cow becomes increasingly isolated in his underground gold bunker, eventually accidentally roasting himself to death and transforming into a Chinese version of slow-cooked Wagyu beef. It is only at this moment that the cow achieves the connection to others that his wealth was unable to afford him, as the film's end proverb states "happiness is only real when shared." In the second tale of *Fables 2*, *Judge Rabbit*, a group of 3-conjoined rabbits meets a tragic end as one brother chooses to murder and imprison the other two on his way to a career as a powerful judge. The "moral" of this work is "striving for your own happiness by all means is already better than suffering together with your family."

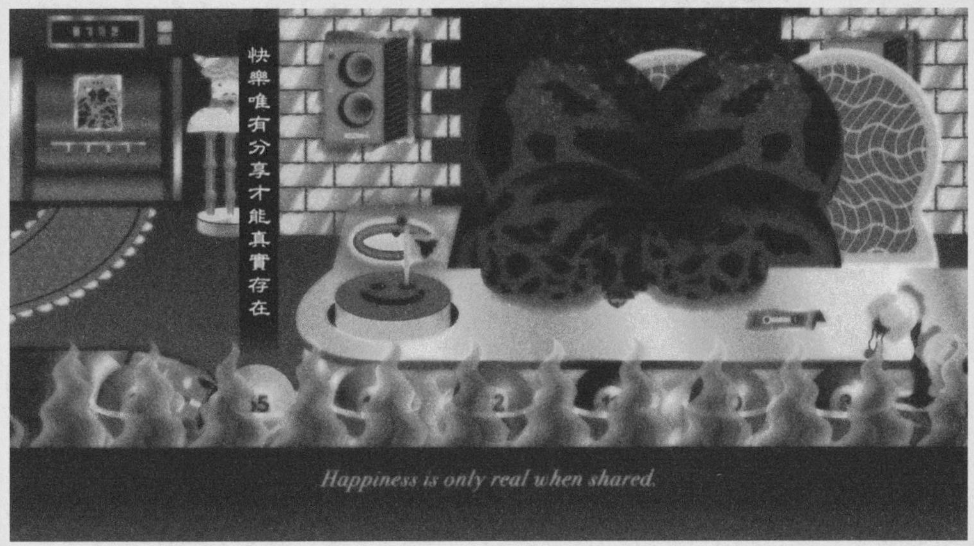

Wong Ping's Fables 2, 2019

In these recent works, Wong Ping displays a cynicism about finding happiness and human connection that can seem somewhat bleak, but feels disturbingly apt during these challenging times. In the past year and a half prior to this exhibition, Hong Kong endured lockdowns in response to the Covid-19 pandemic that only exacerbated the conditions which his work previously so accurately depicted. The psychological isolation of life in a city like Hong Kong became literalized into a state of extreme physical isolation. In the magnified space of the home, the fragility and vulnerability of the body, as well as of the already tenuous bonds with family and friends, has been amplified to a state of crisis. Outside, governmental authorities have taken advantage of the crisis to erode democratic freedoms and the possibility of public spaces for dialogue and dissent seems to have disappeared. The digital space of phones and laptops have become the primary environment in which communication and expression takes place. It is literally a nightmarish world that we have come to inhabit. Wong Ping's work does not offer any easy solutions for living in such an environment. At its best, however, it gives models for how to adapt our bodies and our minds to an ever-encroaching world of terrors through humor, fantasy, and honest confrontation of our demons.

1. Robert Crumb, "Minds are Made to be Blown" The Complete Crumb Comics—Volume 4 (Fantagraphics, 1988). https://www.crumbproducts.com/Minds-Are-Made-To-Be-Blown-1966-67_ep_77.html
2. "Inside the Cover: Wong Ping in conversation with Yung Ma," *Cura Magazine*, October 2019, 70.
3. Philip Maughan, "Wong Ping's Golden Shower," *032C*, February 2019.
4. Zeynep Tufecki, "In Hong Kong, Which Side is Technology on?," *Wired*, October 22, 2019.

Wong Ping
in Conversation
with Tobias Berger

Tobias Berger: Let's talk about what inspired you before you accidentally became an artist.

Wong Ping: I think manga comics were one of my only hobbies growing up because my parents were quite strict. They didn't allow me to watch TV or go out with friends, so I just spent time in my room reading comics—I didn't even watch many cartoons. Later, I became interested in stand-up comedy and jokes that felt like pre-internet memes.

TB: This was a time when certain stand-up comedians, regardless of gender, became famous by talking about sex or masturbation, especially in America. Was there a similar phenomenon in Asia, as well?

WP: To be honest, I haven't found any great comedians in Hong Kong yet. There is one successful comedian here who talks about political and social issues, but I don't know many who speak about sex. Maybe there are some performing in small clubs and bars, but the big comedians in Hong Kong don't speak much about it.

TB: There are some Asian Americans that talk about their sexuality in graphic terms.

WP: But they are famous in America, not in really in Hong Kong. I have only been interested in comedy for three or four years— before that, I didn't really have access to Western stand-up. There aren't many comedy clubs in Hong Kong, and there was no Netflix.

TB: But there is YouTube.

WP: YouTube, yes, but that was later. Also, my English wasn't very good then. Now I watch more with subtitles and when I travel, I see shows in small, local clubs, and ninety percent of them talk about their sexual experiences in a self-deprecating way. I think comedians are the best performance artists. I admire their honesty.

TB: It's funny that a self-deprecating attitude is rare in art and music. Musicians never make fun of themselves.

WP: What about artists?

TB: No, most artists don't make fun of themselves either. That's why I started to think about Surrealism in relation to your work. They were the first ones that explicitly talked about sex from a Freudian perspective, with the humor that implies, but you probably didn't even know the Surrealist films when you started.

WP: I kind of knew Buñuel's *Un Chien Andalou* (1929).

TB: The one where they cut the eye…

WP: Yes. A teacher showed us that specific shot in college, but I didn't see the whole thing. I didn't grow up knowing a lot about art or design, but that was the best class. I still remember the excitement when she showed us music videos or experimental films—my mind was blown. She showed stop-motion works by Jan Švankmajer, Charles and Ray Eames's *Powers of Ten* (1977), and works by Michel Gondry. I wondered how it was possible to make something so simple in video. At that time, I was only inter-ested in watching, rather than making something of my own. I viewed making work as purely fulfilling an assignment, instead of a way to express myself. I was doing poorly at university, not just because of the language barrier, but also because I hated the subject matter I was studying. It was a time when 3D animation was popular, but I found the software needed to make it too complicated and I failed the course twice. Since then, I've hated making anything too technical. There was another course I took about color theory in graphic design. I was confused and bored by the different rules that we have for colors.

In the first class, we were told to pick any color combination we liked and the class voted blindly for the one that they preferred. My combination had the most votes, but when everyone found out

it was mine, they looked at me with disappointment. I felt ashamed
and never went back to that class again.

TB: Where does the sense of humor come from in your work?

WP: My experience of humor was more connected to my family.
I hung out a lot with my father, who was a cook. Sometimes he
would have gatherings with friends, and I remember they made
lots of jokes that I found funny. I picked up their sense of humor
and became a loud, class clown. One time in high school, a teacher
asked us to gather around him in a circle so he could speak.
I ran up to his face and kept pushing him while I rotated around
him. He was mad and shouted at me "Why are you doing this?"
"To form a circle around you by myself," I replied.

Later on, when my parents sent me to Australia, the language barrier
made me feel embarrassed. I just stayed in my bedroom a lot and
didn't go to class. I graduated in the end, but I don't know how.
Then I found that I had changed—I had become really introverted
and was embarrassed to express my thoughts. I didn't make fun
of things. Socially, I became quiet, but later on, I found myself in
my work.

TB: When you came back from Australia and started making videos,
you took a lot of inspiration from everyday life in Hong Kong. You
see it in the work when you look at people on buses or in apartments
and so on. How observant are you about the reality of everyday life
in Hong Kong entering your stories?

WP: Since my writing is mostly from my diary, it consists of details
that I observe and remember. When I'm writing in Hong Kong,
it's quite obvious and natural to have that as an inspiration. For
example, in the bus story in *Wong Ping's Fables 1* (2018), I didn't
invent much—it was from my personal experience: I saw the cockroach crawling over a pregnant lady on the bus. I agonized over
whether I should tell her about it or not, until I finally decided to just
move to the upper deck because my brain could not take it anymore.

I felt pathetic as I sat alone. I asked myself whether thinking about doing something or the actual outcome of that action was more important. I had no idea. This happened at a time when Hong Kong was going through an intense period of daily protests. My questioning and feelings of being pathetic felt connected to this moment.

This story illustrates my writing process and how Hong Kong enters the work. I'm just sitting on the bus waiting for another cockroach to come along.

TB: Do you think that going to Australia and being an outsider there and then coming back has given you this bird's-eye view in telling your own stories? On the one hand, your work is deeply personal, but on the other, you are also the external narrator. Did it help in rediscovering Hong Kong in a new way?

WP: I think so. I felt like an outsider in Australia for four years, and when I came back to Hong Kong, I still felt the same way. I had studied multimedia design and couldn't find any jobs. I saw friends who studied similar things in Hong Kong having more success because the educational system back home was much more practical to serve the market. They were able to get work in the creative design industry quite easily, but I had to go to the library to teach myself so I could catch up. Later in my twenties when I started to make random videos on my own, I didn't have basic knowledge of or references to art. I felt isolated and had too many questions for anyone to answer, so I just decided to do my own thing.

The work is intensely personal. I hate listening to my own voice, but as a solo animator and editor, I have to listen to it over and over again. It's karma, but I know I am the best one to tell my own story, so I play with this perspective. It's still very interesting to me that people can't tell what is real and what is not in my work. This gives me the space to reveal more of my own fetishes or my evil side. It reminds me of when you use the laugh-cry emoji after every text and people don't know how to read it.

TB: I wouldn't say that it is an evil side that you reveal. It's just an honest side, right? You've said that sixty percent of your work is real feeling. What is the mixture between true ideas, fetishes and desires, and things external to yourself?

WP: The mixture? I think it shifts from work to work, but at this point, I put less personal stuff in—because how much personal stuff can you…

TB: … Yeah, how many fetishes can you have? [*laughter*]

WP: It's not like I'm trying new fetishes every day or that my hobby is to constantly try different things, but in general, it's hard to separate social observations from my personal experience. Let's say I go on a Tinder date. That turns into an observation of a social phenomenon, but it's also my personal experience. Now I do things for the purpose of making the work, so it has become kind of blurry. It's hard to get new experiences these days. I really need to push myself. But how far can I go to do something that is not me? I might want to have a kid just to feel how much it would change me inside. I want feelings. Like how many new friends can you make these days? It was one or two a month when I was younger. Maybe it is one or two a year now?

TB: So, if you meet a Tinder date, do you tell them who you are? Do you use your real name?

WP: Yeah, sometimes. I find that people have strong stereotypes about artists. They think that we are moody or crazy, or that we have an attitude, and so on. Using a dating app in a small city like Hong Kong is very weird, because everyone you swipe knows someone that you know. In Hong Kong, six degrees of separation should be three degrees with Tinder.

TB: Because Tinder is very much site-specific.

WP: Yeah, but there are also new things I've discovered from it. Recently, I found that many of my female friends are in relationships with Westerners they have met through Tinder. I've known them for ten, twenty years, and they don't have any Westerners in their social or professional circles, but now they are in relationships with people from the West. If this continues, I think Tinder is going to change the human genetic makeup (at least in Hong Kong) by giving people a chance to mix in ways they wouldn't have before dating apps. Tinder should get the Nobel Prize.

TB: In terms of your other influences, I was wondering about Stephen Chow and his movies. They were very important for Hong Kong in the '90s. Did they inspire you? They are basically Western.

WP: I like them and have seen many. He is one of the most iconic Hong Kong comedic movie stars. The jokes are really "local," so I don't know if an outsider would understand. It would be interesting to find out. Anyone from my generation can probably name them all and quote lines from them, but I don't think they directly influenced me. My sense of humor comes more from Japanese comics.

TB: You mentioned that you were inspired by Minoru Furuya comics about a sort of conflicted guy…

WP: Yes, his works were one of the few things I would look forward to as a kid. The main character in his works was always an otaku, a nerdy high schooler with no talent, always alone and talking to himself. Then some dream girl who was out of his reach would somehow become his girlfriend and he would start to doubt himself and think about how much he didn't deserve her. The tone and mood of the work really overlapped with my own interests.

Furuya has published a few works in recent years, but they had a very different tone. They had a much more positive aura. I checked online to find out what made him change and I found out that he has a kid now.

TB: When people speak about your aesthetic, they don't necessarily mention comics, but they do compare it to a style of animation from the 1980s and '90s. To me, it also recalls early MTV music videos, but the stories you tell are obviously reflecting the lives of a post-millennium generation rather than something retro. I couldn't imagine your work without YouTube or porn sites. So, for me, it's basically MTV meets YouPorn. Is that how you would describe it?

WP: [*Laughs*] That's the best description. It is true that I grew up with things like MTV, video games, and the internet, but I never tried to "design" my aesthetic to evoke these sources. The aesthetic in my work is basically things that I like divided by my limited skill set. It was there from day one and has only evolved very slowly. I've realized that my early failures at 3D animation have encouraged me to adopt an anti-technical attitude towards my own work. My videos really reflect the moment when motion graphics came along because, they were the new thing in video production when I graduated. You would see it in videos on YouTube or Vimeo and in music videos. I wouldn't say that my work draws on animation, but instead from commercial motion graphics. It's way easier to do that than traditional animation, so I was able to teach myself.

Since I found this way of working, I've only really tried to push the boundaries within the limitations of my modest skills rather than actually expanding my skillset. This has been an excuse for me to be lazy, but I have also realized I would rather spend more time on writing and push the narratives of the stories themselves. The visual or aesthetic portion of my videos feels like my luxury holiday during the production process —a time when I don't have to really think.

TB: One of your first videos was a music video in 2011, right?

WP: Yeah, a video for a local band. We were just experimenting and having fun together. That was actually my first trial attempt at animation. I didn't really know how to use a computer to draw, so I was using the video as practice.

TB: What was the name again?

WP: *Under the Lion Crotch* by No One Remains Virgin.

TB: It already had many elements you would use later. It had sex, a big penis being cut open…

WP: Yeah, another one of my fantasies.

TB: The title is a reference to Lion Rock, which is the mountain that rises above Hong Kong and is kind of the most important place for Hong Kongers. There's a well-known TV series called "Below the Lion Rock," which was about life in Hong Kong, but what's interesting about your video is that it's still on YouTube—even though it's quite sexual, it hasn't been censored yet.

WP: The Lion Rock has always been represented as the spirit of Hong Kong. In the 1970s, families that were poor and struggling used to live under the Lion Rock. It is a symbol of optimism in Hong Kong, kind of like the idea of the "American dream." It felt like exploitation when government tried to use the spirit of the Lion Rock as a political slogan in the context of the 2014 protests.

Unfortunately, last year, YouTube suspended my account suddenly. One day, I woke up, and all the weird videos I watch and my subscriptions from the last ten years were gone. I had one old work called *Slow Sex* (2013) on there, and they said it was violating community guidelines.

TB: Did they give you a warning?

WP: No. Also, it was a private video because I was putting more work on Vimeo at the time. The YouTube audience is different and I didn't really care about sharing my work there. I tried to argue with them and pleaded that it is only a cartoon, but they have weirder ideology than I do. We had a few email fights, but nothing happened, so I had to start a new account to watch strange stuff.

The standards for how social media companies censor things now is blurry, not only for sexual content but also for political content.

With YouTube, the world today is trapped in an algorithm. People used to say that TV brainwashed our minds, but I actually miss it. I would stumble upon different shows about wild animals, a random history channel, science documentaries, soap operas, wrestling matches, etc. That expanded my visual database as a child. Now, I watch thousands of cat videos every day, fed by an algorithmic system. What's terrible is I have the illusion that I have seen and know a lot about cats, but I don't. We are actually brainwashing ourselves.

TB: Let's talk more about the narratives in your videos. Many of them deal with conflict or violence between genders. Sometimes about conflict initiated by men toward women, like in *Jungle of Desire* (2015), but also by women toward men, like in *Who's the Daddy?* (2017). Can you talk about this gender conflict?

WP: When I write the stories, I don't start with a specific agenda of trying to address gender relations. The work is always inspired by a desire to address a perceived social norm or something about my own personal experience of society. I'm trying to understand the balance of a relationship. Since these observations come from life, they can happen from any side. Perhaps the male perspective often seems more prominent, but I don't start the scripts with that in mind.

Usually, there is a larger context to what happens in the film. For example, *Jungle of Desire* was a true story that I read in the newspaper. It deals with conflict between men and women, but it also comes directly from reading about this sex worker who chose to work out of her home and about police using their power to take advantage of sex workers. In the story, this expanded to the mental relationship between the couples and eventually to police revenge. The main character in the video enjoys her profession even if her personal living situation doesn't necessitate it. So it is always a bit complicated.

In *Who's the Daddy?*, I also didn't start out writing with the explicit theme of gender conflict in mind. I think the tendency toward revenge is quite a natural fantasy for everyone. Sometimes you despise someone when the relationship ends and just want to do something about it, but it is also a matter of wanting to punish yourself, right? There are different levels to these desires.

TB: It's more like a game of ping pong that kind of escalates.

WP: Yeah, but of course, when I translated my experience into an artwork, people would try to make it purely oppositional. I still wanted to push the limits of how I could describe my own situation without focusing so much on the issue of a generalized conflict. It's quite complicated because the main character in *Who's the Daddy?* also enjoyed what he was experiencing.

TB: Yes, but in many of your videos, the protagonist is a kind of powerless male character. Is that purely based on your relationships?

WP: Sometimes. I mean I'm just another powerless human being, but I believe everyone has similar feelings. It is just a matter of scale. It is interesting when people point out the powerless male characters, because it means that the stereotype of the powerful male role in relationships persists.

TB: When you started doing the works, was there already a wide public discussion of these kinds of issues?

WP: Yes, but not specifically related to issues in the works. *Who's the Daddy?* was from 2017, and after the opening, a critic from Hong Kong came up to me and told me he really hated it because he thought the part about abortion was wrong. He thought it should not be spoken about in public. I explained that the video is not encouraging abortion or even describing it in any detail, but I was finding a different angle to speak about it. I actually thought that his response was quite offensive. Like he was saying, "Women do this, and that's weird or wrong."

TB: But a lot of your work is about that. It's provoking or challenging, putting these unspeakable things that you cannot talk about, like abortion and incest, out there. You find a way to articulate them or at least find a nice way of bringing them into the discussion.

WP: I feel like when people don't like the work, they think I was careless when I wrote it, but really, I've been very careful about calibrating the line of what I think people might find acceptable. It does not mean I censor myself, but I also do not want to be misunderstood. I try to deal with these topics like a comedian, in the way they would take a different angle than what you would expect or to laugh at myself to show how ridiculous what we are doing nowadays really is. Animation also helps because people believe that I'm showing something that people would not or could not actually do. It helps me to push the boundaries of what I can talk about.

I started out making work after I would finish my day job and then I would upload it online, so the potential audience was not really on my mind then. I hope the audience now will see that it's a reflection of themselves or how funny our lives are. We have a laugh and then pause and think, "I do this every day. Why am I laughing?" Then the discussion can go on.

TB: Now that you are a celebrated artist, and people come up to you with their opinions, that must have changed the way you work.

WP: People confront me sometimes, but I would not say that it has changed the way I work. The only thing I changed is to make sure I have studied and thought through the issues I'm dealing with. The line shifts every single day. If I tried to match everyone else's desires for the work, it wouldn't be as interesting to me.

TB: I, and many others, really enjoy the contradictions in your work. On the one hand, it's deeply private because you talk about your inner feelings, fetishes, adventures, and so on, but then you make them public. You talk a lot about how guilty you feel in the work, but then you depict these things in a wonderfully innocent way, as if you don't feel guilty at all.

WP: I do, trust me. [*laughter*]

TB: Your voice in the videos is almost like a computer. The content is very emotional, but you present it like a documentary—very unemotional. These contradictions are part of your strategy, aren't they?

WP: I wouldn't call it a strategy because I've always used my voice, since the early works. It's really all by accident because I couldn't find anyone to help me, so I would just record myself through the phone, and then I'd do the voice-over. I tried to do a little bit of acting and it's terrible. My voice is terrible. Sadness, happiness—it doesn't matter which. I was so embarrassed that I decided to just read it straight. Now I read the script in the same speed and tone without cutting, then I draw something based on the voiceover—it's actually the other way around from what you would expect: I draw images for my voice. Sometime the lines are too fast for the viewer to catch but I tend not to fix them. Now that the works are mostly shown in non-Cantonese places, I have found that my voice turns into a background noise, more like a murmur.

People try to see me through my work, but of course, sometimes it's not me. When I say something really personal, people think that I'm making a joke, so it actually becomes safer to reveal uncomfortable things. One thing that's quite interesting is that when I showed my work to my parents, they actually began to talk more openly to me about sex and other topics.

Strangers speak to me differently now, too. They come up to me and say, "I thought you would be weirder. I thought you would be

funnier. Entertain me, entertain me." People say that they thought
I would be into weird sex. I was like, "Yeah, sometimes, but it's
not that extreme." [*laughter*] But most psychopaths usually act or
appear just like anyone else in public.

When I write about ridiculous situations, it's like a typical question
that we ask in Hong Kong: "Would you rather eat shit that tastes like
curry or a curry that tastes like shit?" The truth somehow can be
revealed or at least be better understood when things are put in an
extreme situation.

A conversation
between Wong Ping
and David Horvitz
with Chris Burden
and Nam Jun Paik,
facilitated by medium,
Shirley Lipner

Shirley Lipner: Here are five decks, but I think we should go with this one. This is a Visconti deck. It's Italian. That's my go-to deck. I'm going to shuffle them. So the artist that we are doing this for has questions that they want to ask Chris Burden, but I'm also going to give you my impressions of Chris Burden. The artist who we're doing this for, what's his name?

David Horvitz: Wong Ping.

SL: Wong Ping, okay. I want to get these names down. Oh, my hair— who is losing their hair?

DH: We all are?

SL: Somebody's losing their hair. I think it's Chris Burden. I feel like he's losing himself. He died of cancer, right?

DH: Yes.

SL: I felt a vortex when I went in that corner. I'm not saying it's bad. I think you've got great energy here, but I got a headache over there. It feels like it's an old energy, connected to the building, but definitely not to you. You're fabulous. You're a chameleon.

I see your energy as a tea diffuser, where you put all the herbs in and everything. You can absorb things, but you let things go pretty well. Are you a middle child or something, or baby in the family? Oldest?

DH: I'm the oldest.

SL: You have a lot of responsibility, but I see middle. Did your mom have one before you?

DH: Not that I know of.

SL: You should ask her. Like I said, you're a chameleon and a good soul, but I felt this grandpa energy around you that was so strong.

He was sitting, and I saw somebody that was wearing rolled-up jeans—very hip for the time that he was in. He was sitting off to the side, and I saw blue around him, and then I cried, it feels so emotional. Do you have kids?

DH: I have one daughter.

SL: Yes. So, maybe he was watching over. When I was putting on my makeup this morning, I started feeling like I was in Japan. You're Jewish, right? Your name is David Horvitz. I didn't know that you had a relationship to Japan, but I just felt like I was in Japan. Then I said to Chris, "tell me who you are," and he said, "I'm crazy; I'm a crazy motherfucker."

He chose art over therapy. He could have gone to a therapist, but he went to art, which was his therapy—working things out that he needed to work out. But I also felt that he was a marshmallow inside, very soft. This was a person that could be very nice.

You and I are both the conduits for this energy that's coming through. What I get about you is that things can go through you, but you don't hold onto them. They go through you, and you let it go. You have a great flow to you. With this Chris energy, I felt like things go in, and they stick. And he has to get it out. But it's sticking in him.

What I felt with Nam June Paik is that he is like a Tesla. This guy was electronics. I looked at my watch when I was talking to him. Even just now, when I look at my watch, a picture appears of a bamboo shoot, which takes me to green and growth. This Nam Jun Paik connects to everything that's growing. He's in another dimension— the fifth dimension. He's not grounded here. Chris came in somehow very grounded and stuck to things. That's what I feel. With Chris, I think I see somebody with anxiety. He creates from chaos, whereas Nam Jun Paik takes his stuff, and he creates, but it's not chaos to him. It's just so delicious. So go ahead. Start asking me questions and I'll pull cards to illustrate.

DH: Yes. My first question for Chris is that you wanted to keep a nice distance from the art world by moving to Topanga in your later career. Do you like the art world now from your side?

SL: This is him. This is a strength card. He wants to knock the shit out of it. What I get from him is he's angry. You have to explain the art world to me because I'm not in the art world. Are there a lot of institutions? He doesn't like the institution of art, the mainstream of it.

DH: That makes perfect sense.

SL: I feel like there's a lion on the ground, and the lion is the institution, and he just wants to kick the shit out of it.

DH: The card has a boy with a green stick, who is beating a lion down on the ground. It looks like it's an old renaissance painting or something.

SL: This guy Chris, when he gets an idea, he doesn't know where to chase it. He doesn't know where to go. He's a really interesting character. He's a little broken, and he's trying to find his way out. Anyway, go ahead, next question.

DH: Is humor a good way to throw stones against this world?

SL: Yes. I had just wrote: "sense of humor is key." This is the anxiety card that I said that was him before. I would say yes, it absolutely is; but this card is a falling tower. It represents anxiety, but it also represents breaking down society and then building something new in its place. I think that humor is key, but there's also a side that's a bit invested in what people think about him. Do you know what I mean?

DH: Interesting, yes.

SL: I don't want to go back and forth too much, but he's a sensitive guy and he also doesn't want to hurt people.

DH: You can tell him I'm thinking good things about him.

SL: Oh, by the way, when my watch goes off, we know I'm getting a text message, but it's also Nam Jun Paik and Chris Burden playing with us. We're all connected in the energy field. Some people call it a luminous light field. I call it a debris field, because it's mostly full of junk out there. But when my watch goes off, it means it's them talking. You heard it go off when you said, tell him that we like him. He knows that he's embraced.

DH: We're embracing you. Ask him how's it going?

SL: You're almost five years out now Chris. How's it going? The moon card. Was he married, this guy? Does he have a widow?

DH: Yes.

SL: He really loved his wife. I think he misses her. That's the moon, which is like a narrow road. He's working on himself. I think he's working on a project now, and he's going to give it to somebody. I feel like he's looking for the person who can do what he did. He might feel a little bit of sadness around the situation that he left. It's not a happy card. I don't know if he suffered from depression. Maybe he's worried about the world and other stuff going on.

DH: So what's going on with Nam Jun Paik?

SL: What's going on with him right now? Probably pure joy. That's how I see him. This is the empress—the mother card. I think this is intuition. I think this is a guy who's in his body, nothing grounded here, but doing things from intuition, from body and head. That's the number three. That's March and we're in March. He's very present, even though he's been gone a long time. He sprinkles fairy dust.

DH: He's got green hands.

SL: Green hands, like he's growing things. He's growing and planting. He's a seed planter. He plants ideas, and he's available 24/7. He doesn't sleep. I don't know if this guy slept.

DH: I think I heard that he never slept.

SL: I have a different feeling about Chris. I feel like Chris was searching for something and seemed to have a little bit more ego. He's a character.

Did one of them smoke?

DH: Paik did. Should we pour him some tea?

SL: He wants a smoke. We'll pour him a tea and just see what happens.

DH: Yes. Do two, for Paik and Chris.

SL: Okay, what would you like to ask next from Wong Ping?

DH: This is to Chris: "I always have uncertainty about the value of my works or even art. As a video maker, I put my thoughts into animation but hide myself behind it. They're only words, unlike your performances. You put your thoughts into action. You put your body into experiences. It is pure and powerful in contrast. I find myself a hypocrite, hiding behind the screen—like saying I love you to a person, but never acting on it. Am I a coward? Do you think virtual visual works are cowardly? Sadly, most of my thoughts are immoral and illegal."

SL: So Wong Ping is basically saying: "Chris, what do you think about me and my work?" Does he have father issues? He's asking him to be father to him, but I feel like he has a nice dad. Here is the death card which is very dramatic. This is clear to me. He loves what he's doing, and he says, go for it; and he says, keep chang- ing all the time. The death card, for me, is not physical death. It's more about change. Something new is around the corner. One idea leads to the next. Keep going for it. I also think he wants him to eat more. Is he thin or something, this guy? He wants him to take better care of his body and eat healthy food. Maybe Chris didn't in his life. He wants you to take care of your body so that you can be here for a long time, because you're going to get lots of ideas. Who likes music? Is that Wong Ping? Listen to soft music. Do you play guitar? I just noticed the guitar.

DH: I kind of play.

SL: Is that an old guitar that's been in your family for a long time?

DH: No, it came from a friend, who got it from a person who came from Brazil. There's a long story.

SL: There's a female behind that.

DH: Yes.

SL: Yes, I just noticed that. I got distracted while I was talking about Wong Ping. So Wong Ping needs to focus and not get distracted, and get out of that place of judging himself. You've got talent. Just do it.

DH: Okay, I'm going to keep reading from Wong Ping: "The thinking process is the best part of my practice. I enjoy it so much when I visualize the structure of the work in my head. However, I feel lost about the reason why I need to produce and make it. It seems to me the only the reason is to exhibit it to people, but why? I often get answers like: "It is to inspire people." But I don't really care if I inspire a stranger somewhere. Am I a selfish person?"

SL: No, he's not a selfish person. He has a nice mom, too. I just felt his mom. How old is he, in his 30s or so?

DH: I think so.

SL: This is a temperance card. No, he's not being selfish. He is doing it for himself and he's being his authentic self. He needs to take a step out there more, and then people will identify with it. I think he's going towards balance, but he's out of balance. Just keep doing the work, thinking about it, and let that thought go. Don't hold onto your thoughts for too long. Just let them go. Let them flow.

DH: How's Nam June Paik doing? Is he still here?

SL: Nam June Paik is traveling. He's always traveling. This is the chariot card. You have to remember that his energy lives in our memory. Paik's energy is saying that he is available, but he is also always on the go. Maybe a lot of people didn't understand that about him when he was here.

DH: We should ask him the same question we asked Chris about the art world.

SL: Nam June Paik, what do you want to do with the art world? Wheel of fortune card. I told you. This card is about letting go of ideas, keeping spinning. The world goes around. The wheel of fortune is different than smashing it. It's like, be at the center of it, but be grounded at the center of it, and let everybody do their crazy thing all around it.

DH: There's a guy on the card carrying the whole thing on this back.

SL: Right. The world is on your back, and you just keep moving. It may be slow. It may take a long time to move people to do things, but he's not going away. He's not trying to smash anything. He's trying to carry everybody on his back. He's saying: "Let's go, we've all got this."

DH: This is for Nam June Paik or Chris Burden: "What about aliens? Do they exist?"

SL: Do aliens exist? I think they do. I think I'm from another planet. This is the hierophant, who is a high priest. This is a very grounded card, but it's also a man. My answer, my Shirley answer, is, yes. It would be absurd and egocentric to say that there isn't life outside of our experience. What I see in this card is that we need structure.

I get blocked when you ask me that question about aliens. I'm getting a blockage from both of them, saying: "Well, you're talking to me right now. Isn't this alien?" It's almost like: "We can't talk about that." It's unusual. It's like: "I can try to teach you about this, but it's too foreign for some people to understand." So yes, they exist. But they're saying: "That's one of the ideas in your head that you should throw away, Ping. Let it go."

DH: Alright, here's a long one for Chris: "Since I'm working in the art world now, I sometimes feel shame or a lack of knowledge about art because I didn't go to art school. I have a beautiful fantasy of attending art class, but at the same time, I know I would hate it and myself for having this lame fantasy. You once said: 'To trust your intuition is exactly the opposite of any sort of formal education.' You were once a professor at UCLA. Was there any informal education you applied in your class?"

SL: That's a really good question. There's the devil card. Play with the devil, play with fire. That's what he would apply in his class. Go out in the dark. Go outside the body. He would say: "Go out there and take risks." And that would come from his own education for himself, do you know what I mean?

Really go risk it. Go play with the devil, play with fire like he did. Wong Ping shouldn't feel bad about not going to school. That's part of his journey. Because at school, don't they unteach us everything that we know intuitively?

Also, I don't know, honestly, why Chris was a professor, because he couldn't teach. All he could do was give an example of who he was. So I think he might have been brilliant in that way—an Avant-Garde kind of teacher. He would say: "This is who I am. Go for it. Put your feet into the fire."

I wonder if he had a dog. Who has a dog? I just saw a dog.

DH: I'm pretty sure he did.

SL: I just saw a beautiful dog.

DH: Ask Chris about the coyotes.

SL: The coyotes in Topanga?

DH: Yes. There were coyotes. He talked about them.

SL: Maybe it's a coyote that I saw.

DH: It could be, yes.

SL: I saw something with fur. Was he friends with coyotes or something?

DH: Well, he had this story that a coyote stole his wallet.

SL: Oh wow, coyotes are weird. I've got coyotes out in Palm Springs now, and I have to watch out, because I have a little dog. What do you want to tell us about coyotes and your dog? You said they took his wallet, where he had his money?

DH: Yes.

SL: He didn't care that much about money, did he?

DH: I don't think he did.

SL: He made money in his life as an artist, didn't he?

DH: I think, by the end.

SL: Yes. That's a thinking card. You asked about the coyotes, and then I pulled up the emperor. He's the father of the coyotes. They're his pack. He's the coyote whisperer, or the dog whisperer. That would be a good animal symbol for him. That's a funny story about a coyote taking a wallet. Is that real? I see him being friendly, like "Dances with Wolves." I wonder if his dog is still here or passed away.

DH: I don't know. We could find out.

SL: Find out, because that dog is very important to him and his wife. I just saw the dog connected to him.

DH: I'll look into it. Here's another question: "Is leaving flowers on graves another capitalist scam like Valentine's Day? Let me and your family know, since you are the user on the other side. By the way, there are 32 e-flowers left on your grave."

SL: Wow. Where is he buried?

DH: I don't know. But there's a memorial website where people can leave fake flowers.

SL: Okay Chris, what do you say to that? Sunshine. This is the sun card, and it's new energy. I think that it's not a scam. In a way it's a scam, but it makes people feel good. They're bringing some brightness to him. It makes him feel good.

It makes the energy of spirit feel good that they're being thought of, because somebody is thinking about them, and that's what immortality is. See, you just heard my watch. When it goes off, he's saying yes, yes, yes.

What I'm saying is that, when you leave a flower for somebody, you're saying: "I'm thinking about you today and what you did in your life that inspires me to become an artist or do something that is memorializing you and making you immortal. It's not a Valentine's Day thing. Valentine's Day is automatic. It's an "I'm thinking of you, Chris, and you affected me." He loves it.

DH: Cool, another question: "You have been gone since 2015. It might be a sequel to your early work about disappearing. Are we interrupting or just continuing your work right now?"

SL: Continuing. This is the lovers card. "You're not an interruption to me. This is a collaboration. It's never an interruption." Then I just saw somebody again. I saw a very long scarf, a man wearing a scarf. It feels like maybe the other guy, Paik, but I don't know if Chris wore a scarf. But I see this flamboyant, long scarf.

Is something happening in June with Wong Ping? Does he have something coming up in June, an exhibition or something like that?

DH: Well, this is for his exhibition at the New Museum.

SL: Is he going to be showing in June? This is the number six, which makes me think of the month of June. Chris loves being thought of, but he's tormented. When I saw the moon card, I saw that he's working on something in himself that he's trying to express. He's always seeking something. He's a little manic but his work calms him down. It's his therapy. He chose art over therapy, but he did that on purpose.

DH: Yes. Alright, I've got another question for Chris Burden: Chris, you made the streetlights that are in front of LACMA, and it's become a super iconic and famous piece. Everyone goes there takes their picture with your work in the background. They love it, but many of these people don't know who you are. They are having this nice, romantic moment taking pictures with your work, but they don't know that you're this crazy motherfucker. And I always want to tell them: "That guy shot himself. That guy locked himself in a locker. Do you know who this guy is?"

SL: So the question is, what does he think about these people taking photos of themselves with his stuff?

DH: Yes. They're not waking up.

SL: This is what he thinks. This card is the number eight in this deck. It's a justice card. There's a horse there, and the guy's holding a sword, and it's saying: "This is your immortality—these lamps." And he's going: "No, I want something else to be it." But I don't think he thinks about it that much. I think he's trying to disconnect himself from that a little bit. The curious person will go figure it out. They're going to look into his work more and the lamps are the seed. I don't think he minds it, but I think it's a little bit of a pain in the ass to him, and he wishes it wasn't his legacy, but it is. It's about illuminating. It just came out of him for people. But he overthinks things. He overthinks it.

He needs to practice letting go more, and that's maybe what Wong Ping is identifying with. There may be a similarity with their two energies that they just can't let it go. We have anal-retentive people. You didn't get something when you were a baby, and then you can't just let go of something. It's very intelligent people we're talking about here and being so smart can really fuck you up. It's like being an alien from another planet.

DH: Is there a work he wished he had made or that he wants to be made?

SL: Do you mean, does he want Wong Ping to make a work on his behalf?

DH: Yes, or anyone, or what work does he regret not making?

SL: Chris, do you regret not doing something? So this is the world card. This would be something that would come out in 2021. I don't know why I just got that, because it's a number 21 card. When I look at this, I see two men, and I see a collaboration. Did he ever collaborate? Was he going to collaborate with somebody? I think he's sorry that he didn't get to do a collaboration.

Now, he could do a collaboration with Wong Ping in energy, because we see two men here. Yes, he would love to do a collaboration with you. It looks like it would be somewhere that's an island. Perhaps Hawaii or something? This is the world, and these two guys are holding the world. And Wong Ping has the ability, being here in this world, to actually bring something down. That's what artists do. That's what I do, it's a form of art. I'm downloading, I'm listening, and I notice. I feel ambidextrous. Who's ambidextrous? Can one of these guys use both hands?

I'm taking one person who's here and one person who's not here and creating a channel between the two of them. If you study Akashic records, it says our soul comes in with a purpose. His purpose is to create; and he continues to create through other artists. I think that he will send him an idea. I see pink, which is a really nice energy, but I also an idea about using his body for something. When you ask about what piece he regrets not making, it looks like somebody who would put themselves in one of those glass bottles with the ships inside. The word that I'm hearing, actually, is miniaturization. I wish that I could shrink myself or do something to make myself look like I'm in there. A hologram. He'd like you to make a hologram of him. I don't know if Wong Ping could do that, but take his recordings and do a hologram of him doing performance art. That's it. Boom. Thank you. See why you needed to be here?

DH: Yes.

SL: Like when Natalie Cole did a hologram of her dad and sang with him. He would do a hologram, and that may have also come from Nam Jun Paik, but I think it came from Chris.

DH: Maybe they're collaborating right now.

SL: Put the two of them together in a hologram. Hologram performance art—boom.

DH: What's the piece?

SL: Wong Ping has to go away to an island and figure it out. He has to take a couple of weeks and put himself in a nice prison.

DH: Well, Chris Burden has this old piece where he sails to an island, and he disappears for a week or a couple of weeks.

SL: See, I didn't even know that. It's everything I'm talking about, right? He just goes, but then appears in a hologram in different places. Where in the world is Chris Burden?

DH: Is there anything urgent that either of them want to say?

SL: Do they have an urgent message to say? Chris is the hermit card. The hermit card for me suggests to go inside and keep digging. His whole life, to me, was about digging. It was like he was on an archeological dig for himself, excavating things inside himself that weren't just belonging to him in this life. His message is just go inside and trust, and don't second guess.

Whereas this Nam Jun Paik is more aligned with your energy in a sense. I don't know you, but remember before I said that you have this very chameleon-like energy where you experience things, but don't hold onto stuff. You're just totally Zen. Everything flows through you. That's what I think Paik is like too. Chris has residue of stuff he's holding on to, and Wong Ping might be doing that too.

But you are who you are. You can only work on yourself if you want to change things. What other questions do you have?

DH: Do they miss the rain?

SL: No. This is the high priestess. They're like: "That's another crazy question." They can feel rain when they want to, or not. That's a very spiritual card. That's an angel card. The rain is like angel tears. I wonder if one of them was susceptible to colds and got sick from colds.

DH: All right, here's a long one: "Have relationships, breakups, and marriage affected and changed you? You spoke about it in interviews and made a confession video or two. Putting the private parts of yourself in works like fetishes or sexual experiences, can be risky. Blues musician Son House said, 'love hides all fault and makes you do things you don't want to do. Sometimes that kind of blues will make you even kill one another or do anything that kind of low.'"

Have you ever thought about using art to be a tool for revenge?

SL: Let's see what he says with this card. Surrender. This is the hangman.

DH: Guilty.

SL: Yes. I think that it's inevitable that art could be a revenge tool, but when I look at him, I think he would not openly do that. The surrender is: "I've got no control over what comes out of me in my art." It's not revenge, it's more: "I have no control. I feel like he had ego in other areas of his life, but not in this one. He could have been a real asshole, but he's not showing that side to me. Things like revenge are human, and he's not in that form anymore. He's in an energy form, and he's like: "This is what was going on at the time. It's how I expressed myself at the time. I'm working through everything."

DH: Okay. I am going to read one more: "Just so you know, the expense of your TV advertisement work *Full Financial Disclosure* (1976) was about $6000. Today, in 2020, it can buy 1.2 seconds of airtime from a Hong Kong broadcast station."

SL: What does he think about inflation, right?

DH: How does it feel to not have a bank account or a mortgage?

SL: This is the star card. The star is his greatest wish. This is the best question. He's like: "I'm free." He's very happy. He might come back and reincarnate. Is Wong Ping married?

DH: I don't know.

SL: You should ask him to come back as Wong Ping's child. That would be crazy. That's performance art.

DH: What should the child be named? Chris? Or something else?

SL: Oh, it would be a girl.

DH: Christina?

SL: Let me ask him: What would you like your name to be? It would be really funny if he said a name like Christina. No, that's not it. Does Chris have any connection to England?

DH: I don't know.

SL: I just heard a name like Paisley or Presley. It wasn't Christina.

DH: So Wong Ping needs to have a daughter that is Chris reincarnated, to be named Paisley. Hong Kong was British.

SL: I have the last card here and I have a question: Chris, what message would you like to give Wong Ping, and why did you go into Wong Ping's consciousness when we had Paik planned originally?

This card is very interesting, because it's the first card in the major arcana. It's the fool. Now, I'm going to pick up another card because it makes total sense to me that we're coming full circle. When we asked the first question, the first card to be picked was the strength card.

The fool card to me is: "You can do anything you want, Wong Ping. You just go out into the world and wait for when that moment comes."

Then I just see the color blue all around Wong Ping that makes me think of storm clouds, and it makes me think of all the angst that Wong might feel when he's starting to get inspired to create something, which is something that Chris might have also gone through. Then I think: Just wait for it, and you're going to bring something beautiful into the world. It's also about the body of work and not just one specific piece, which goes back to what Chris said about the lights outside the museum.

As an artist, David, what are you leaving behind? What's your legacy? That connects to the question about the flowers. That's what people are leaving behind for Chris as a tribute to you. That's that.

DH: Thank you.

SL: You're welcome.

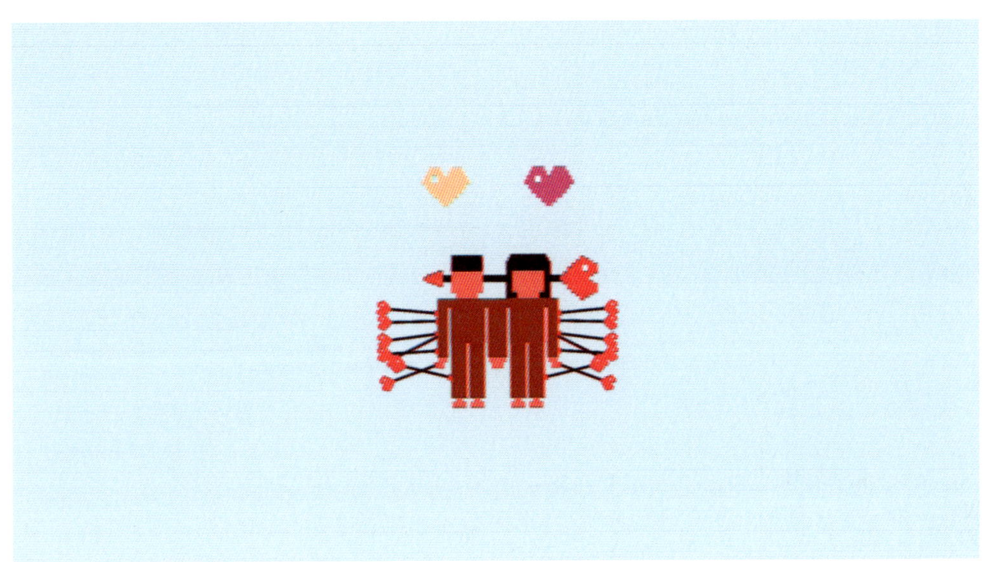

FRUITPUNCH – *We Want More*, 2010

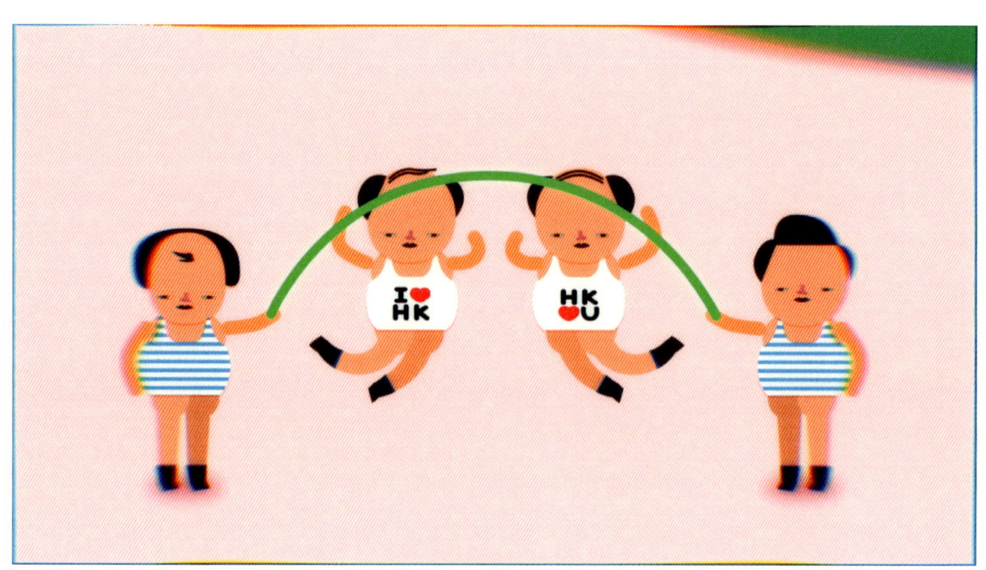

Under the Lion Crotch, 2011

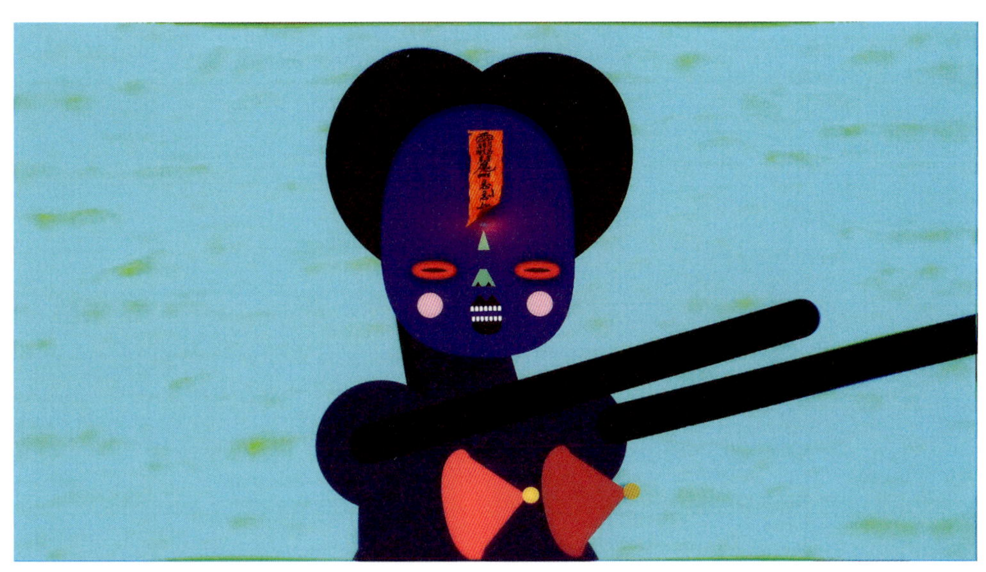

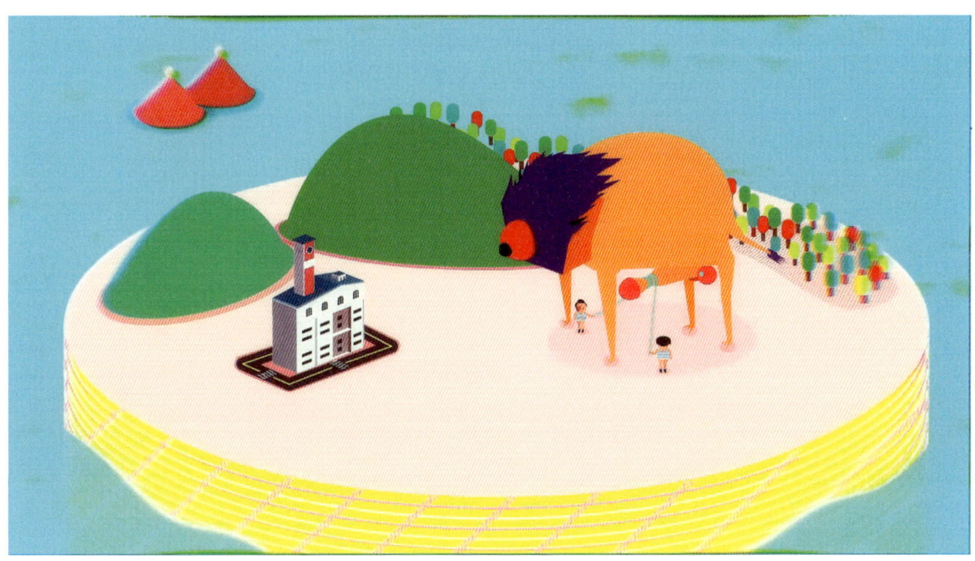

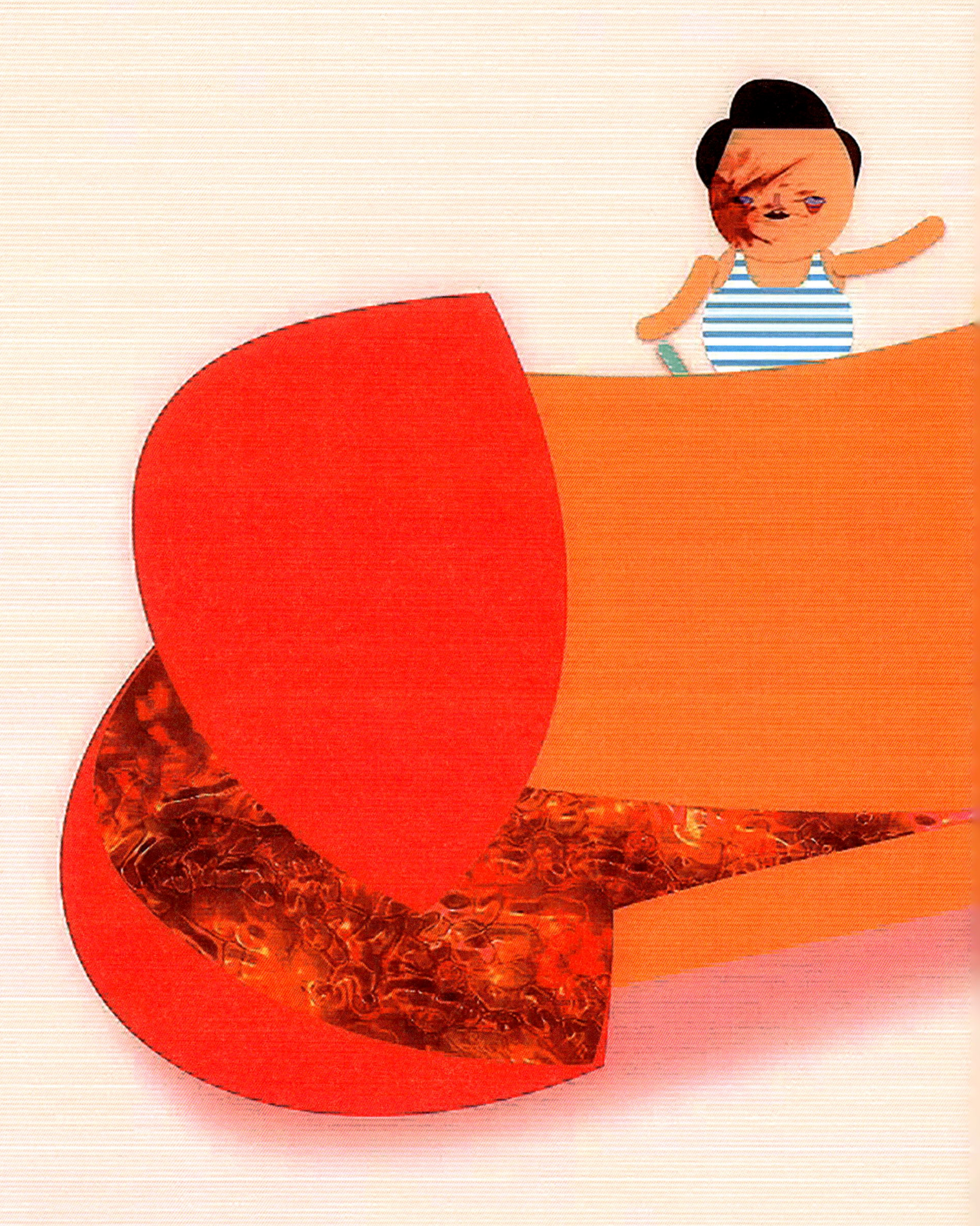

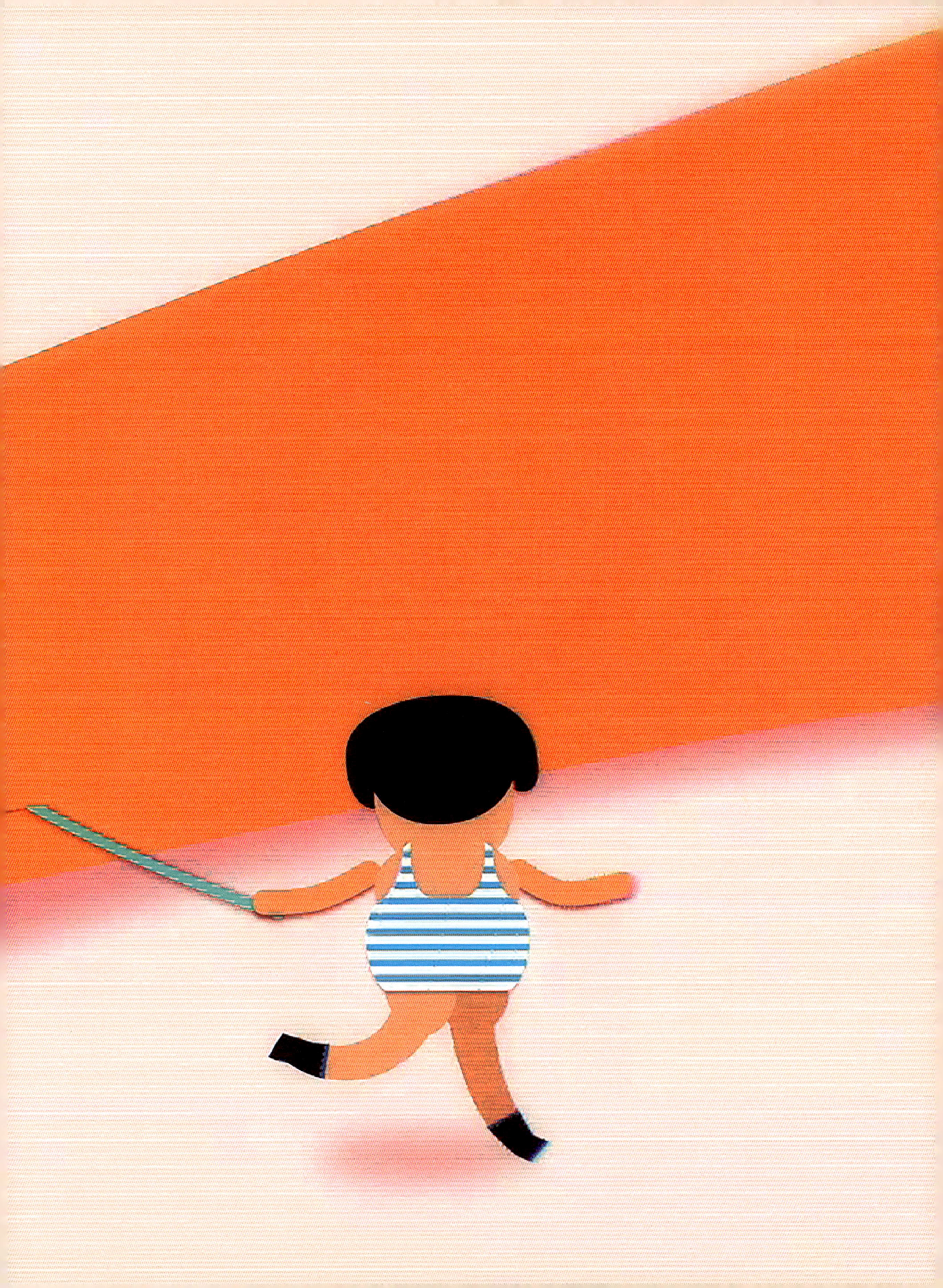

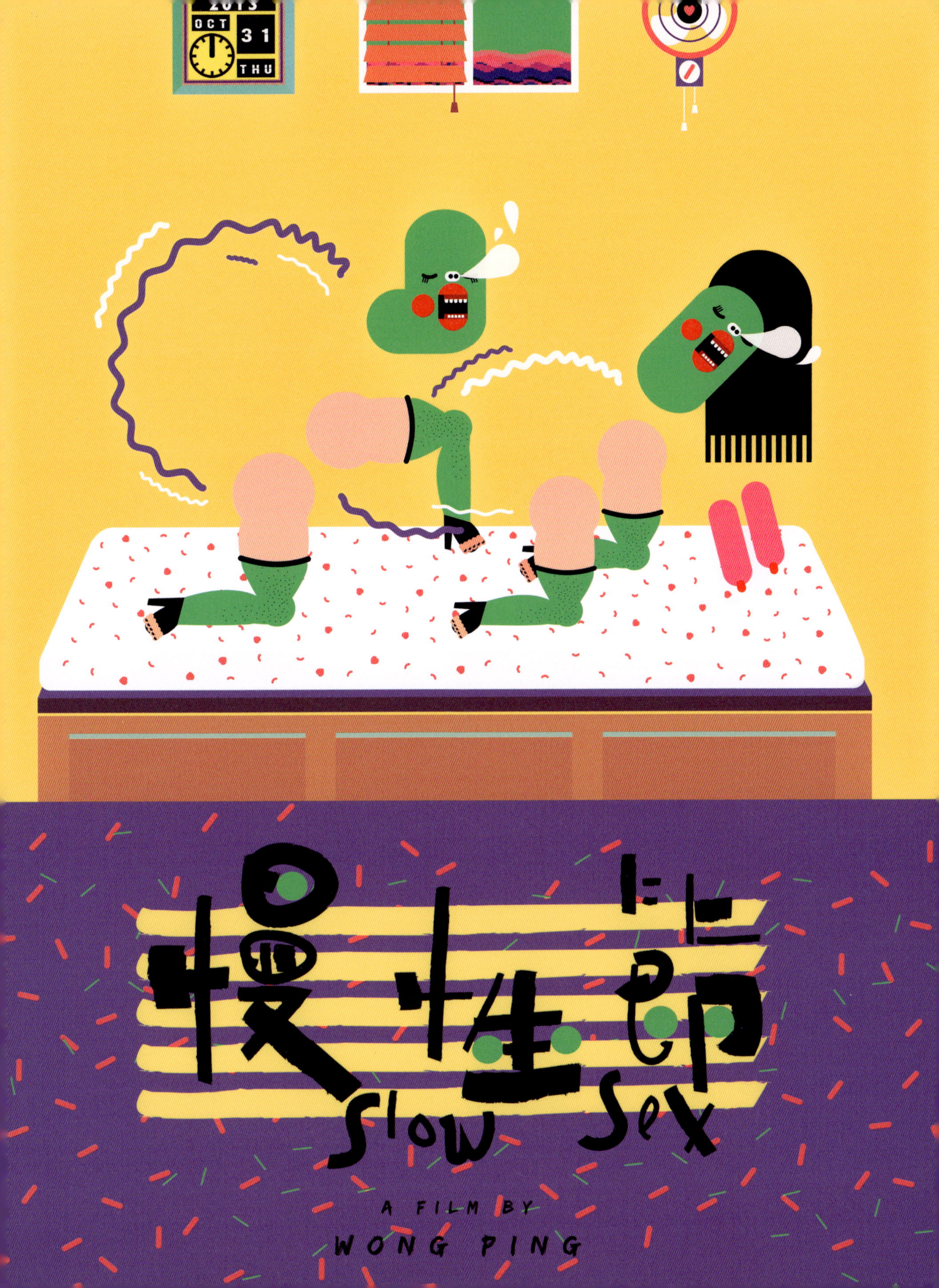

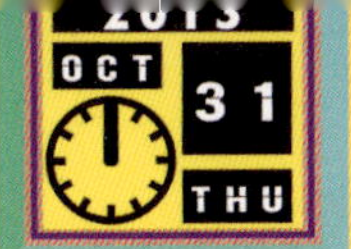
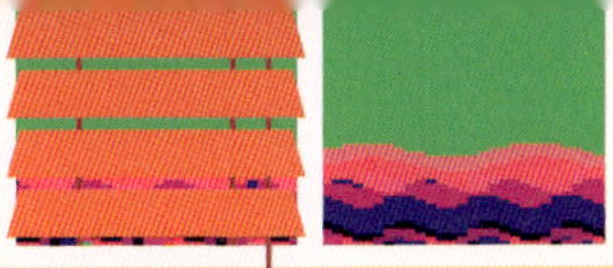
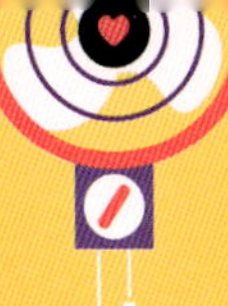

慢性節
SLOW SEX

A FILM BY
WONG PING

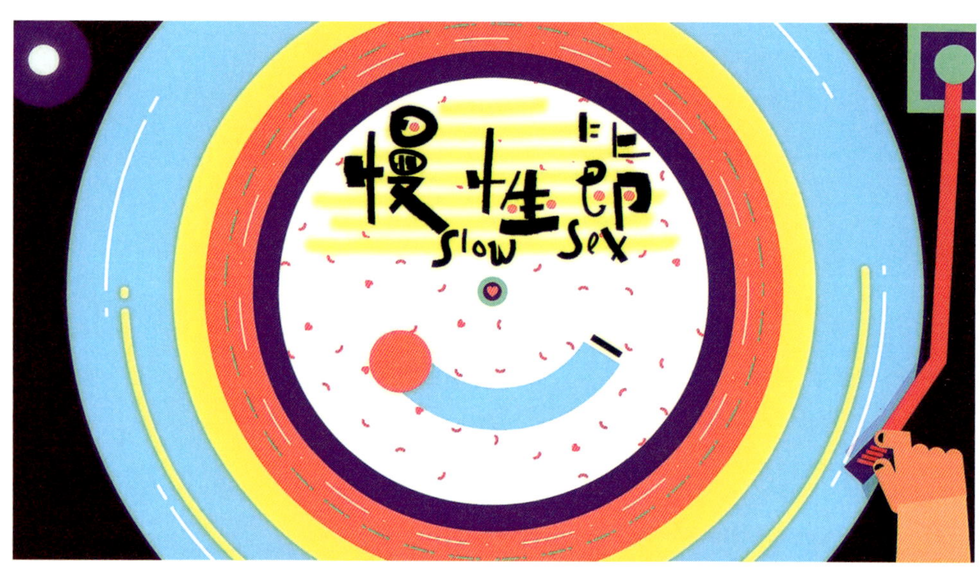

慢性節
ニニ
slow sex

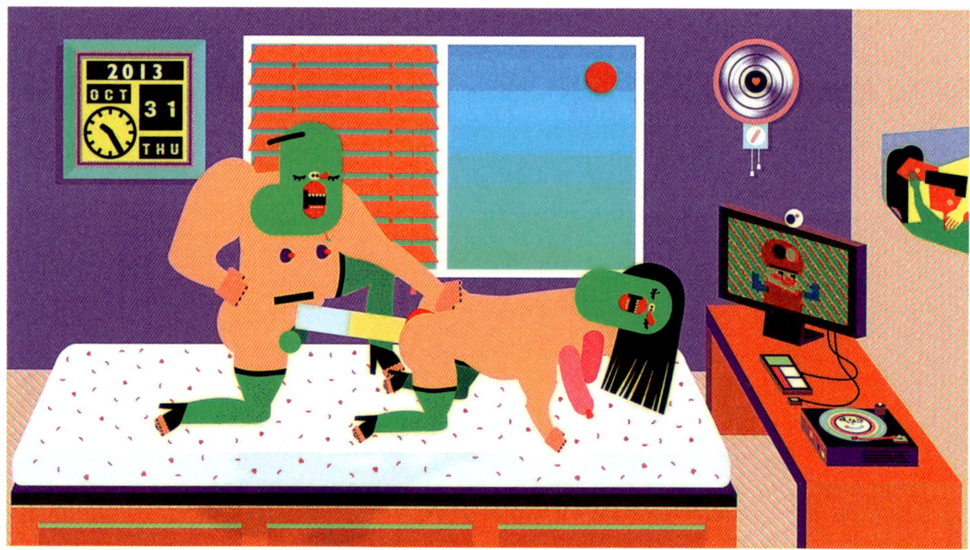

2013
OCT
31
THU

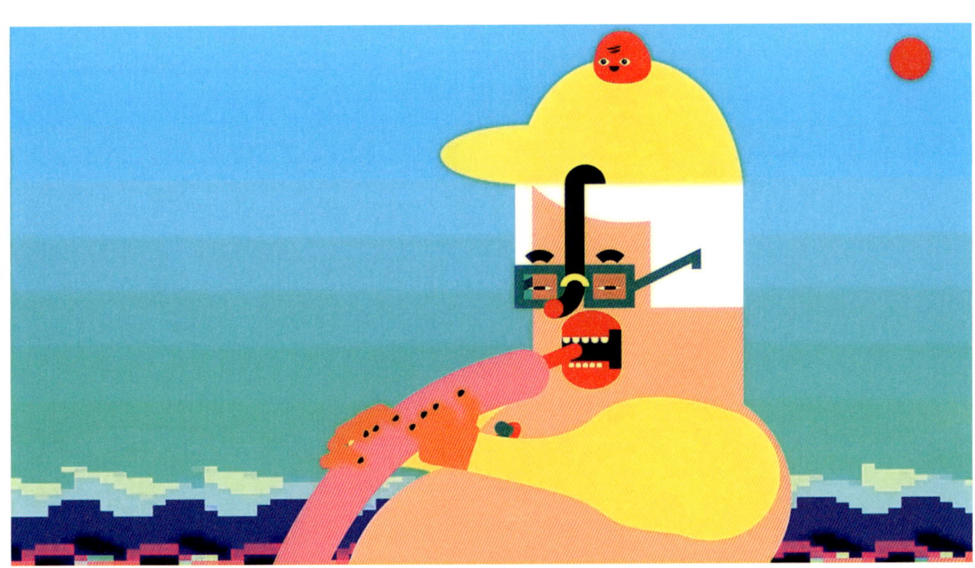

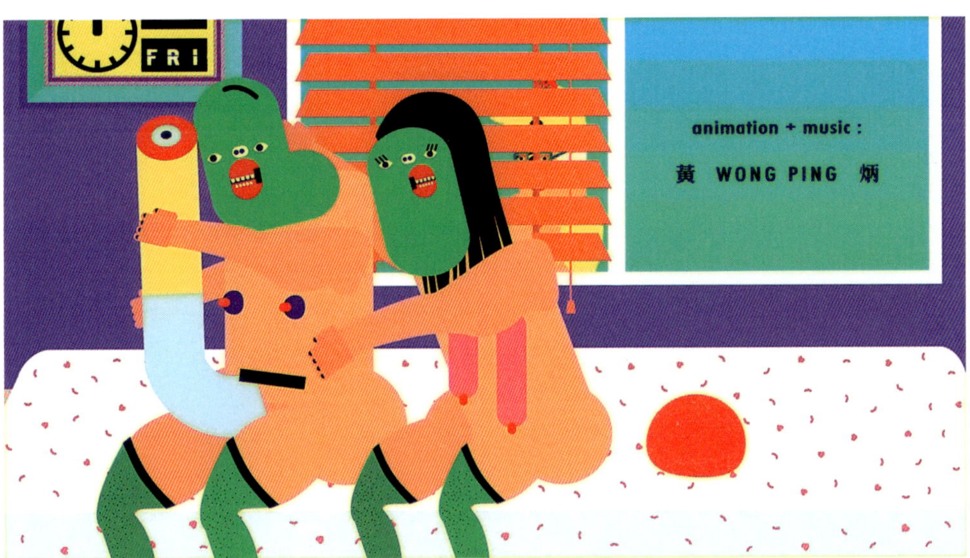
FRI
animation + music :
黃　WONG PING　炳

A FILM BY
WONG PING

STOP PEEPING

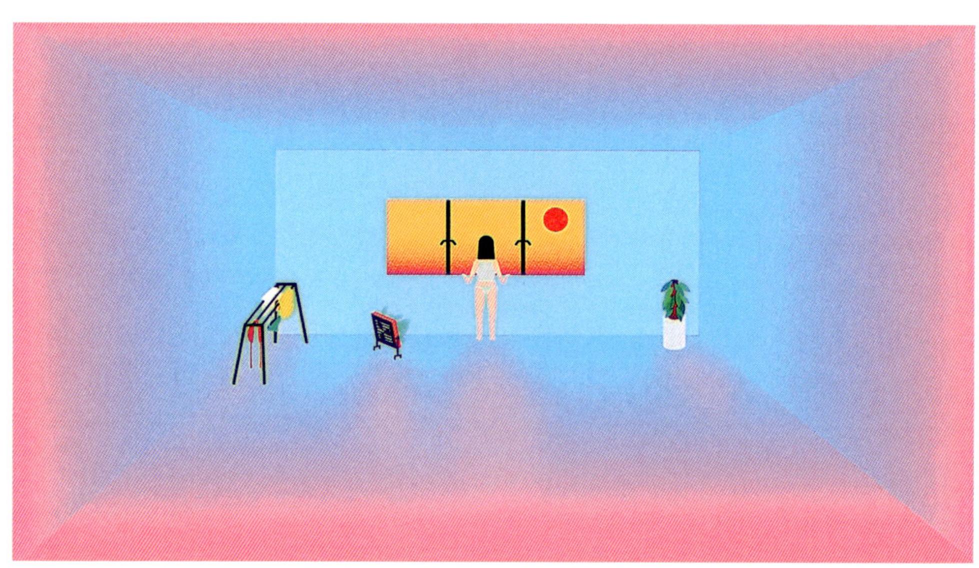

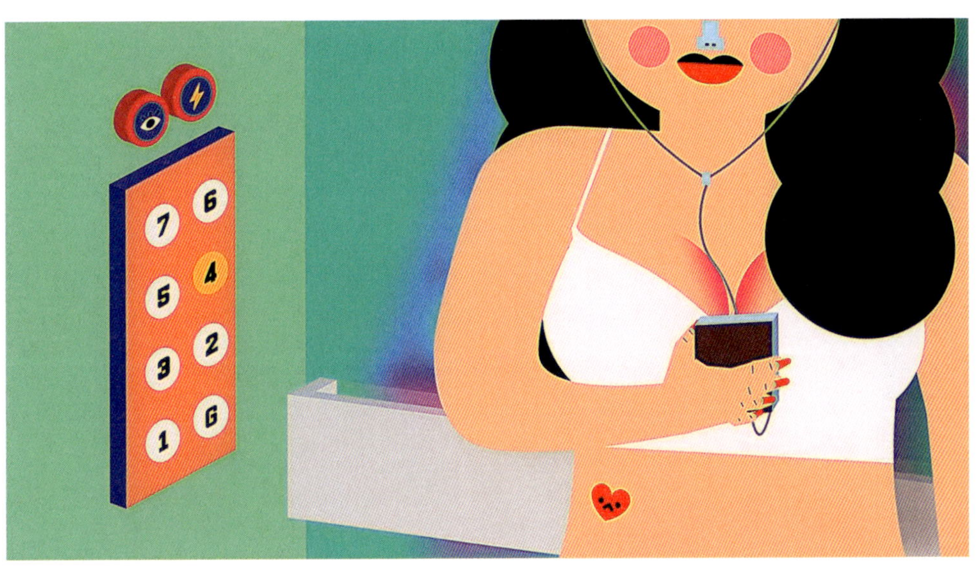

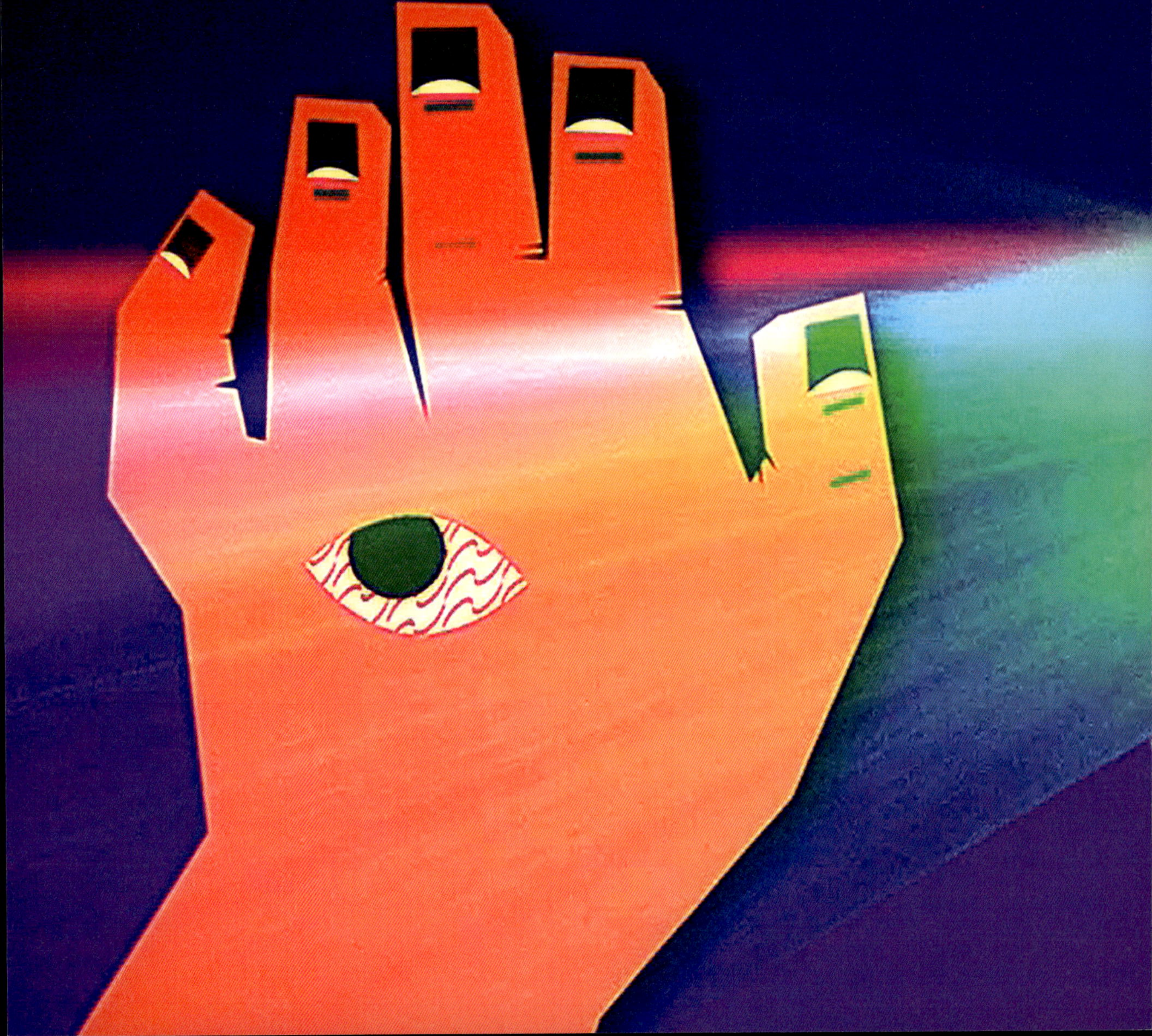

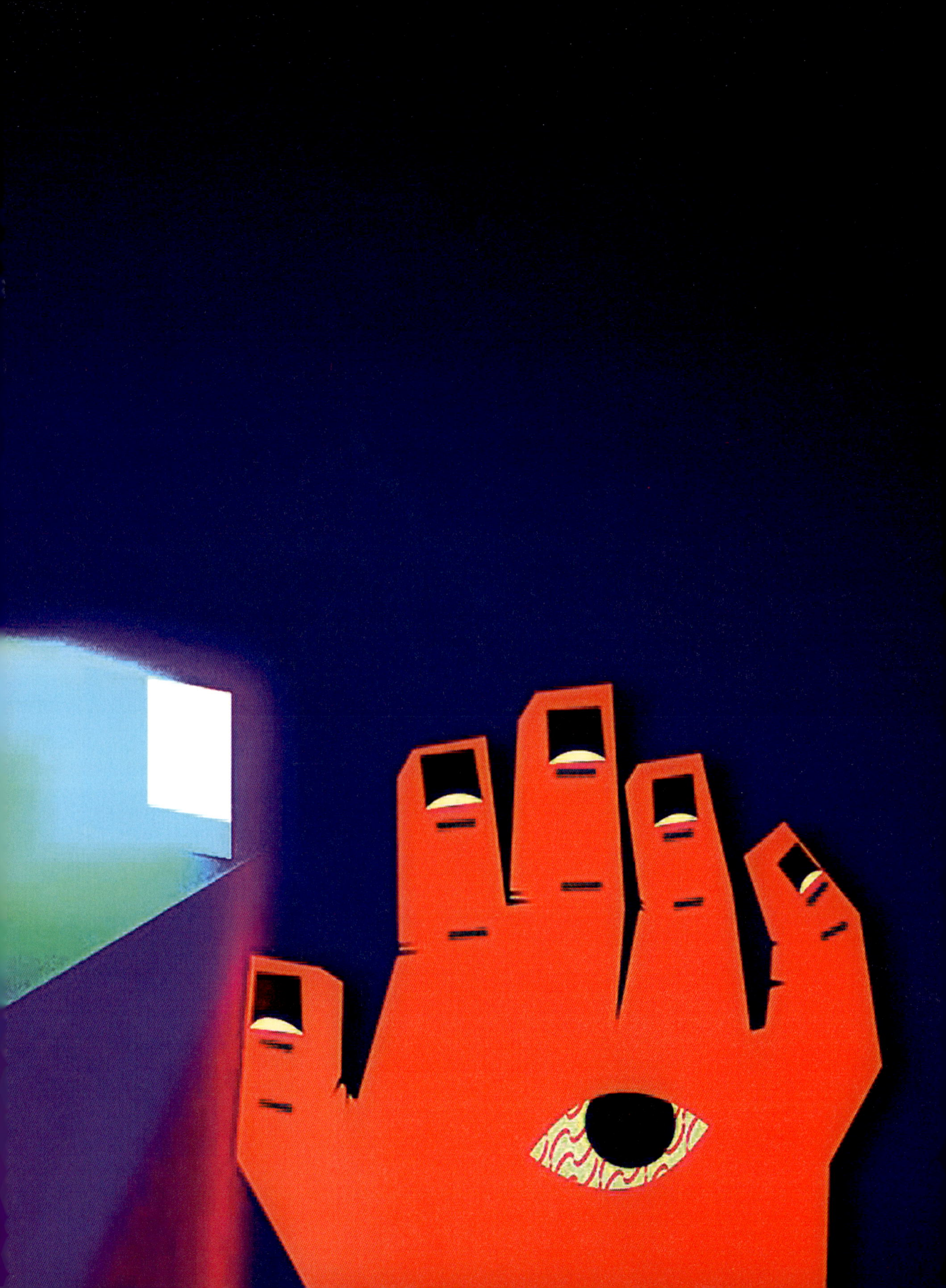

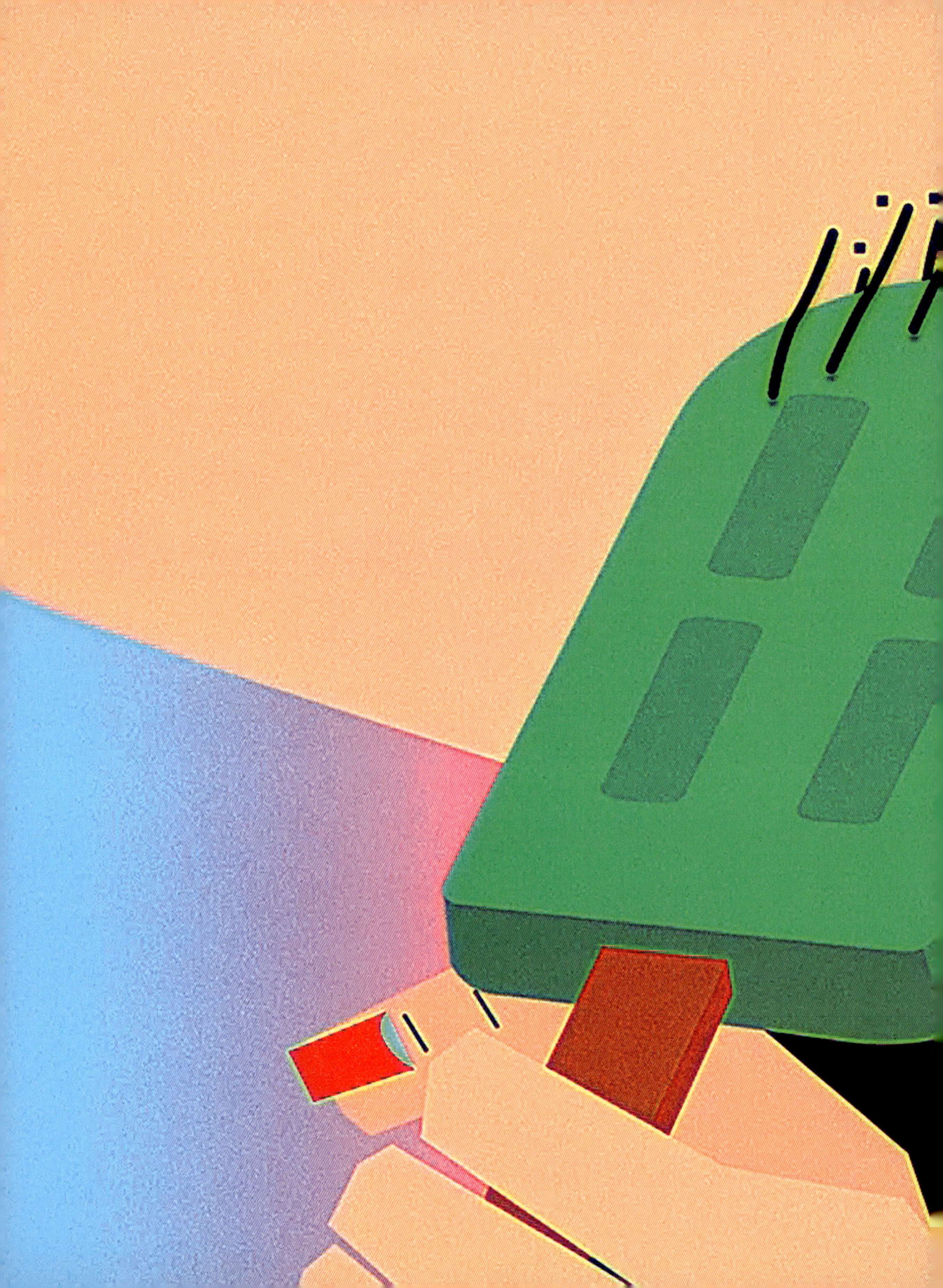

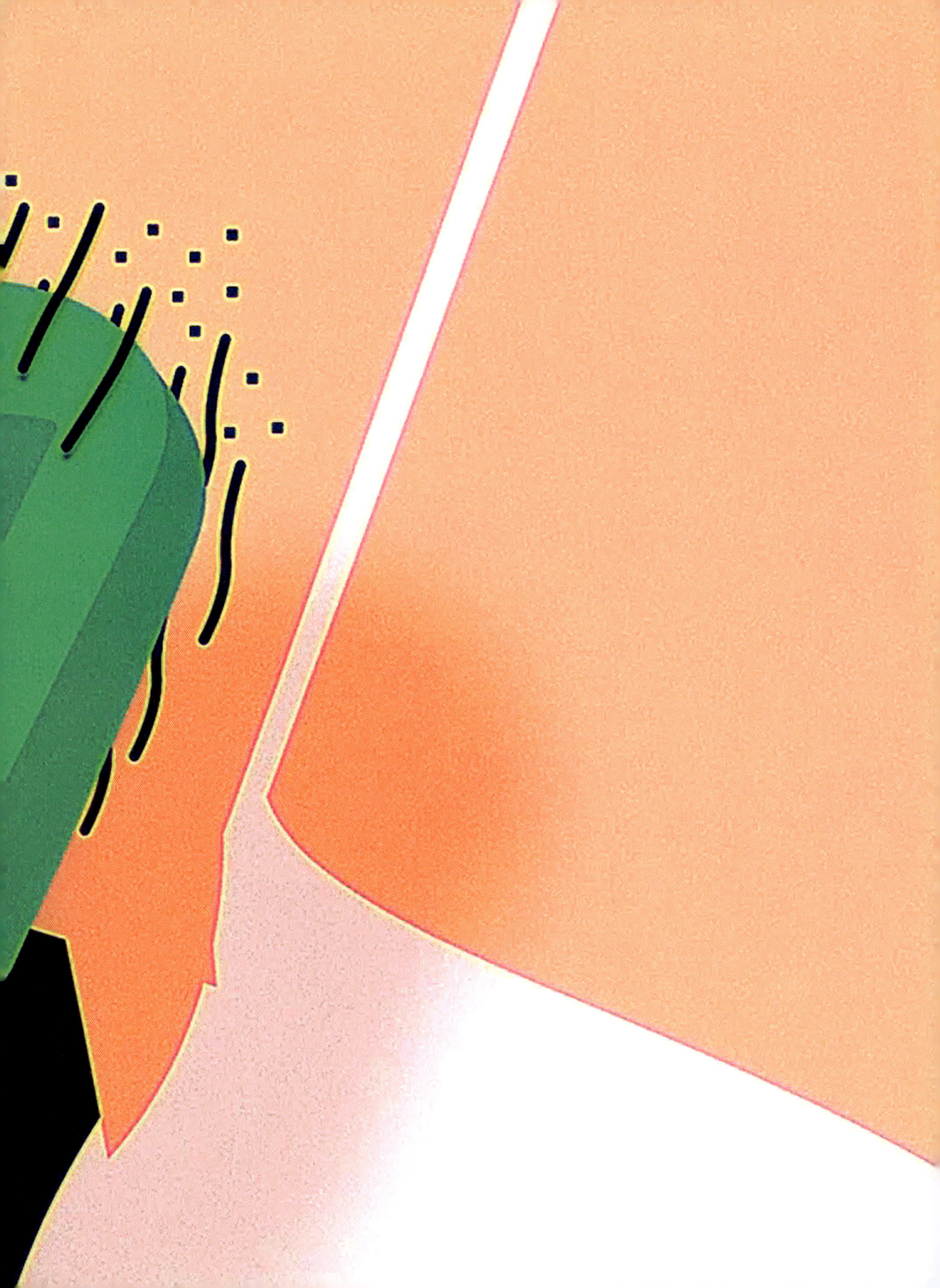

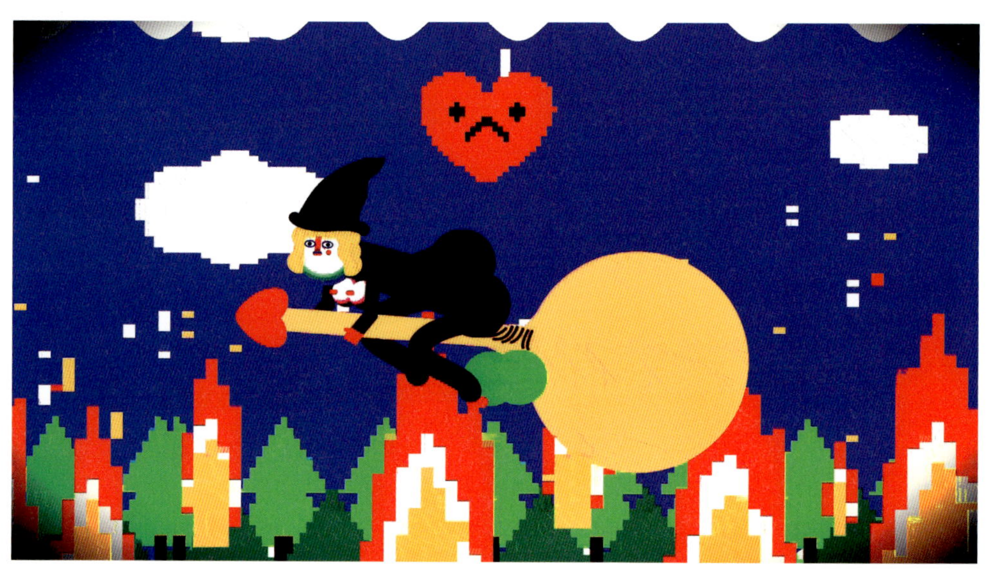

Witch, 2015

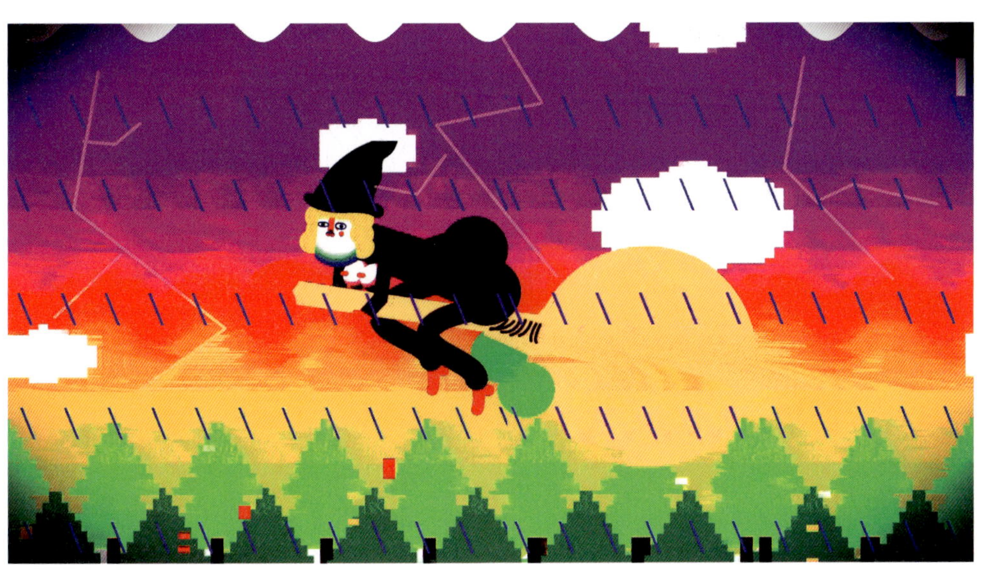

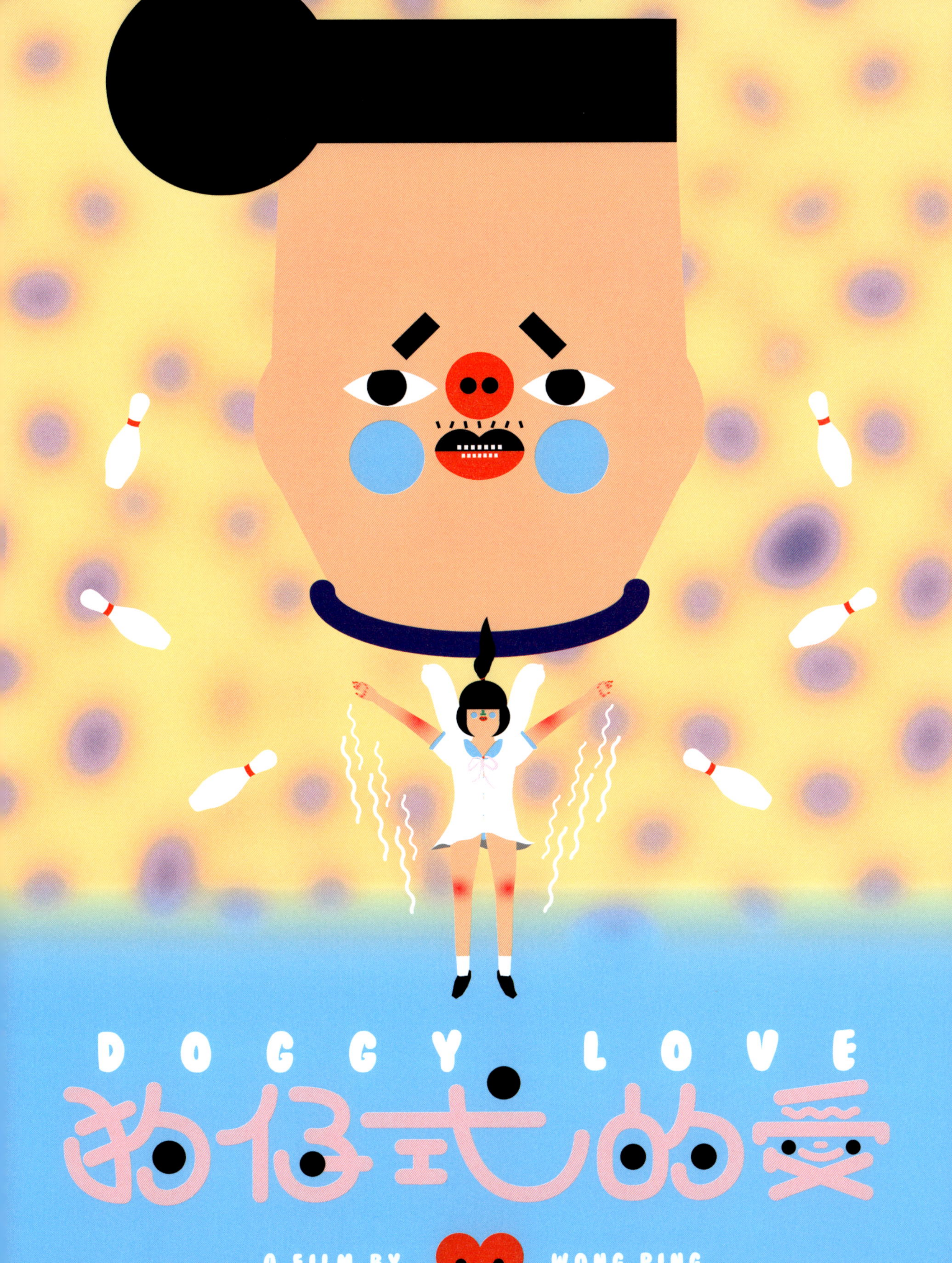

DOGGY LOVE
狗仔式的愛
A FILM BY WONG PING

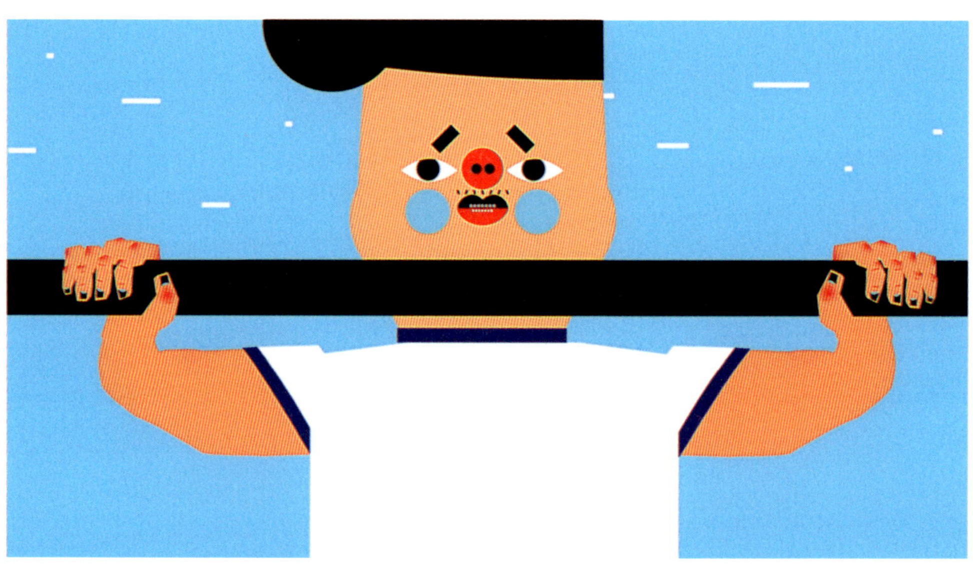

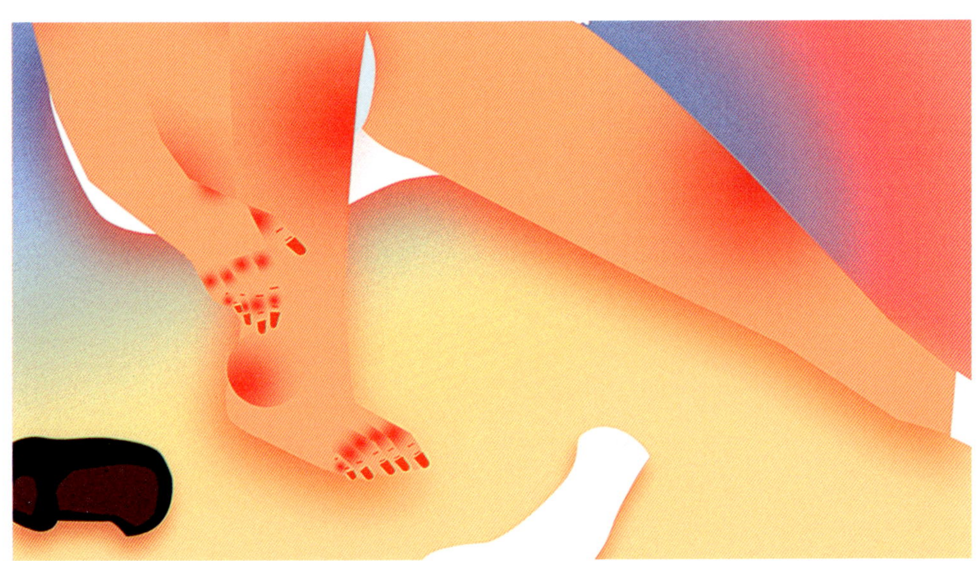

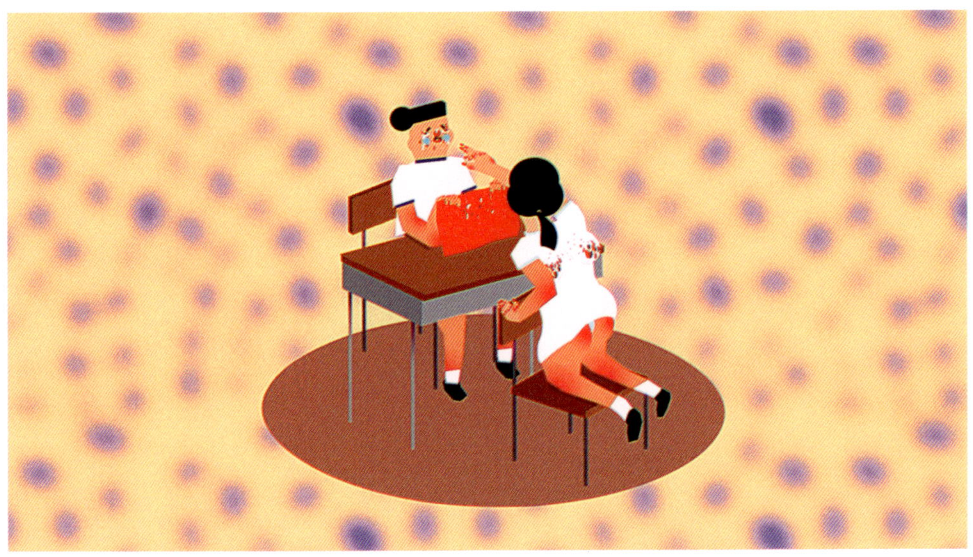

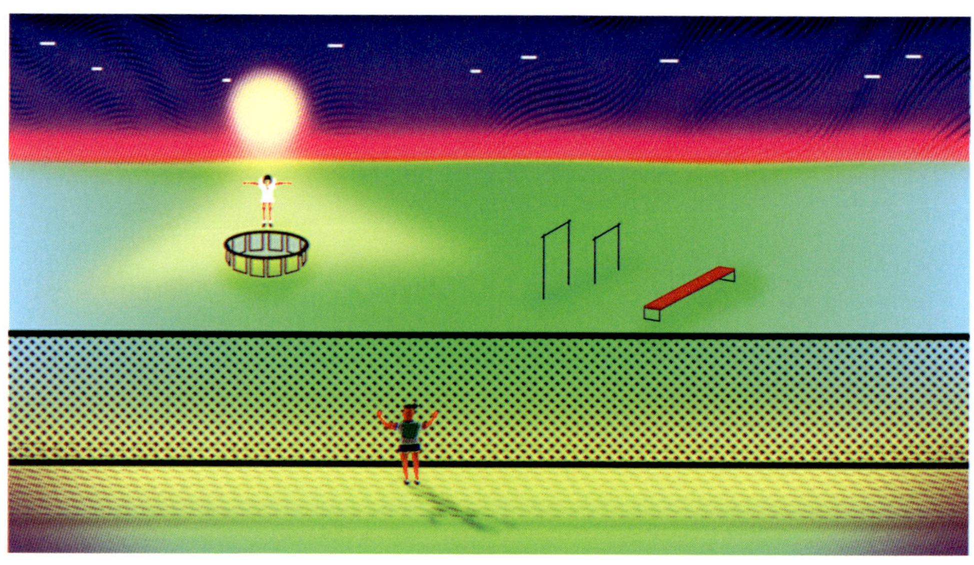

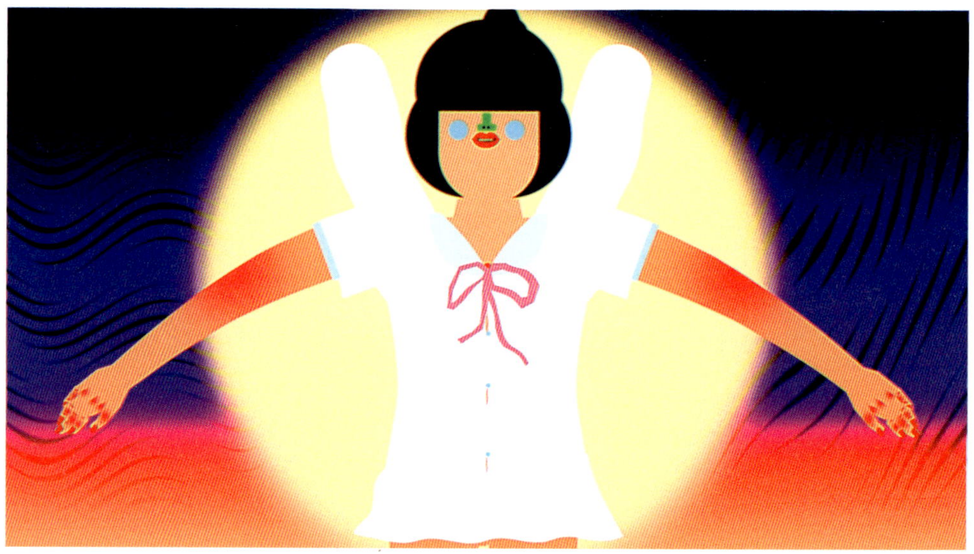

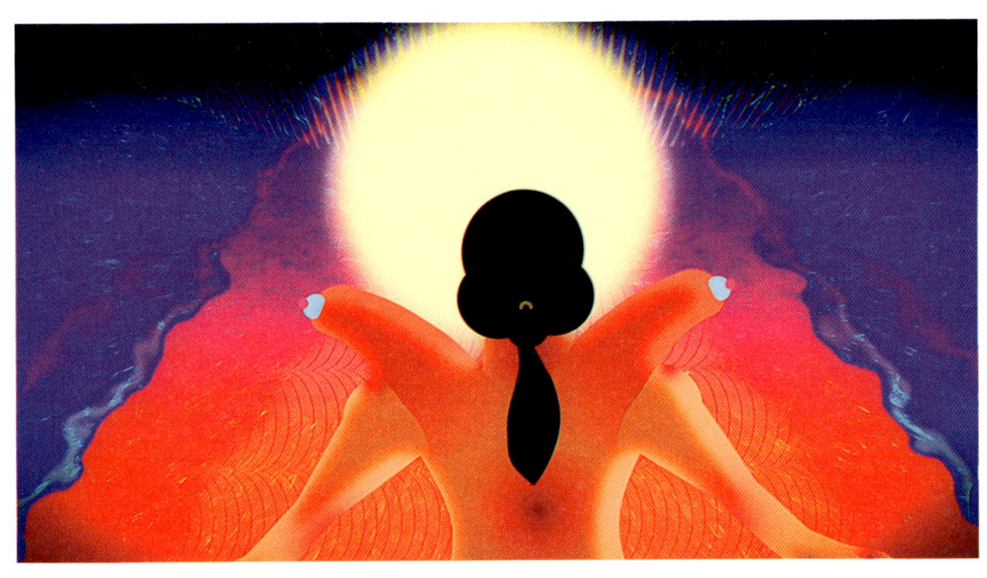

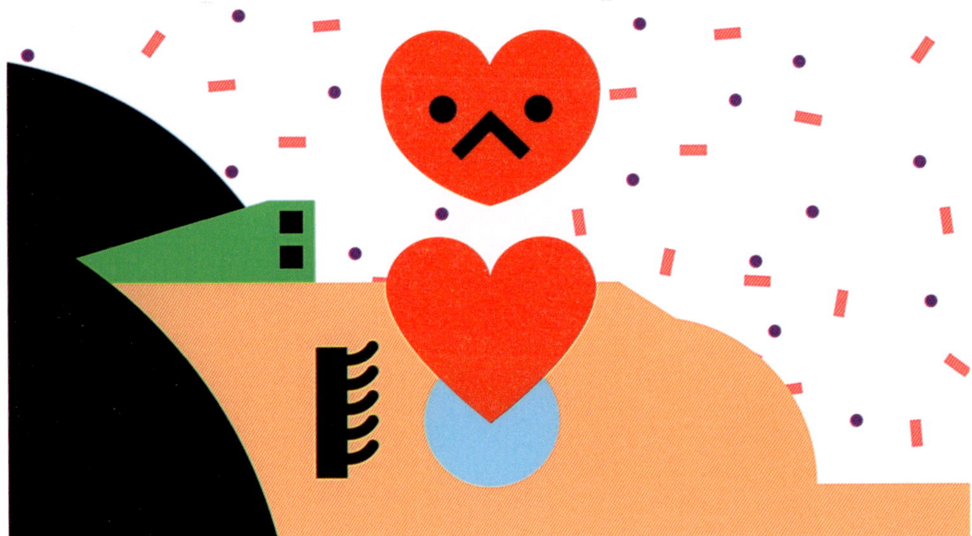

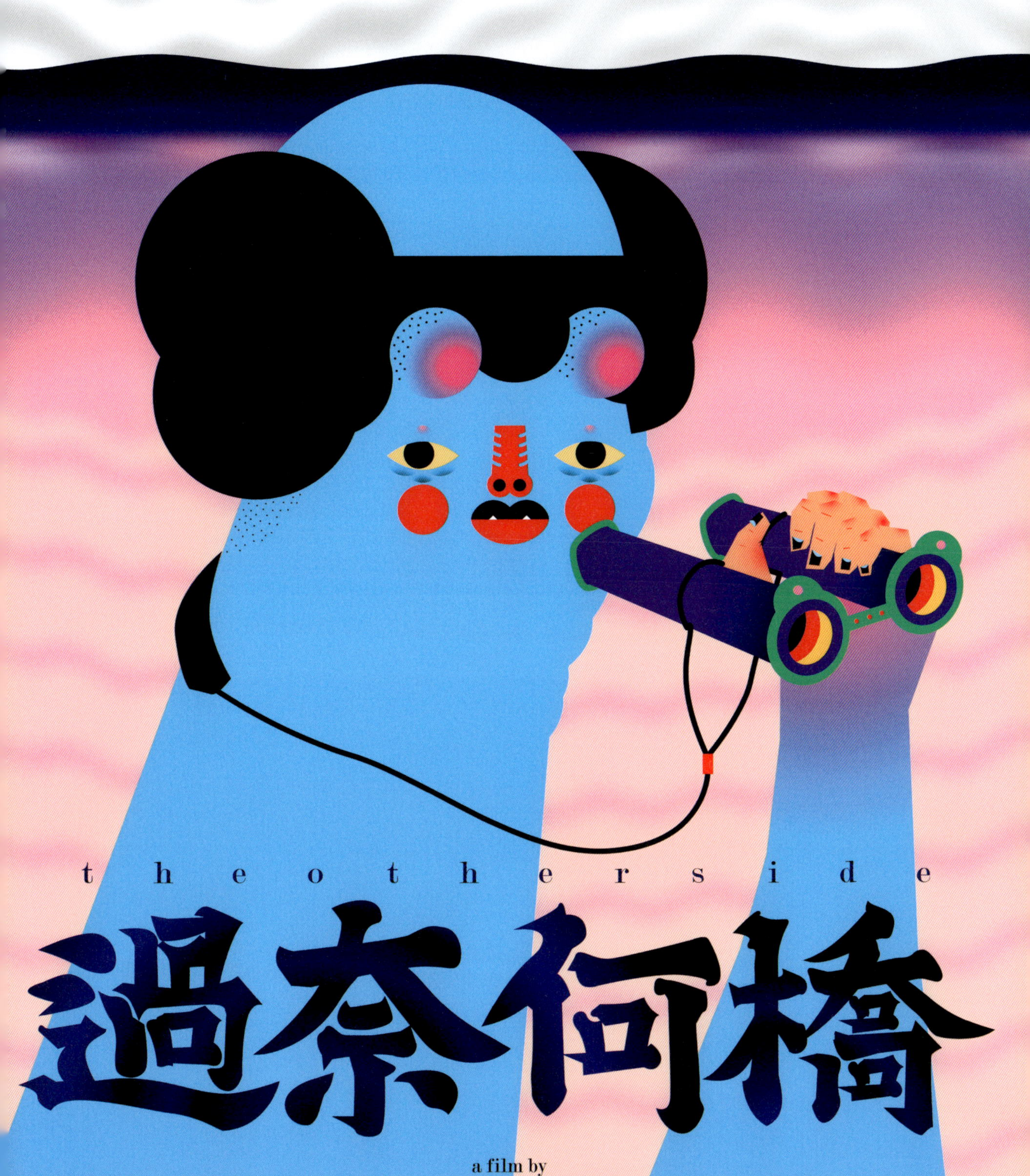

t h e o t h e r s i d e
過奈何橋
a film by
Wong Ping

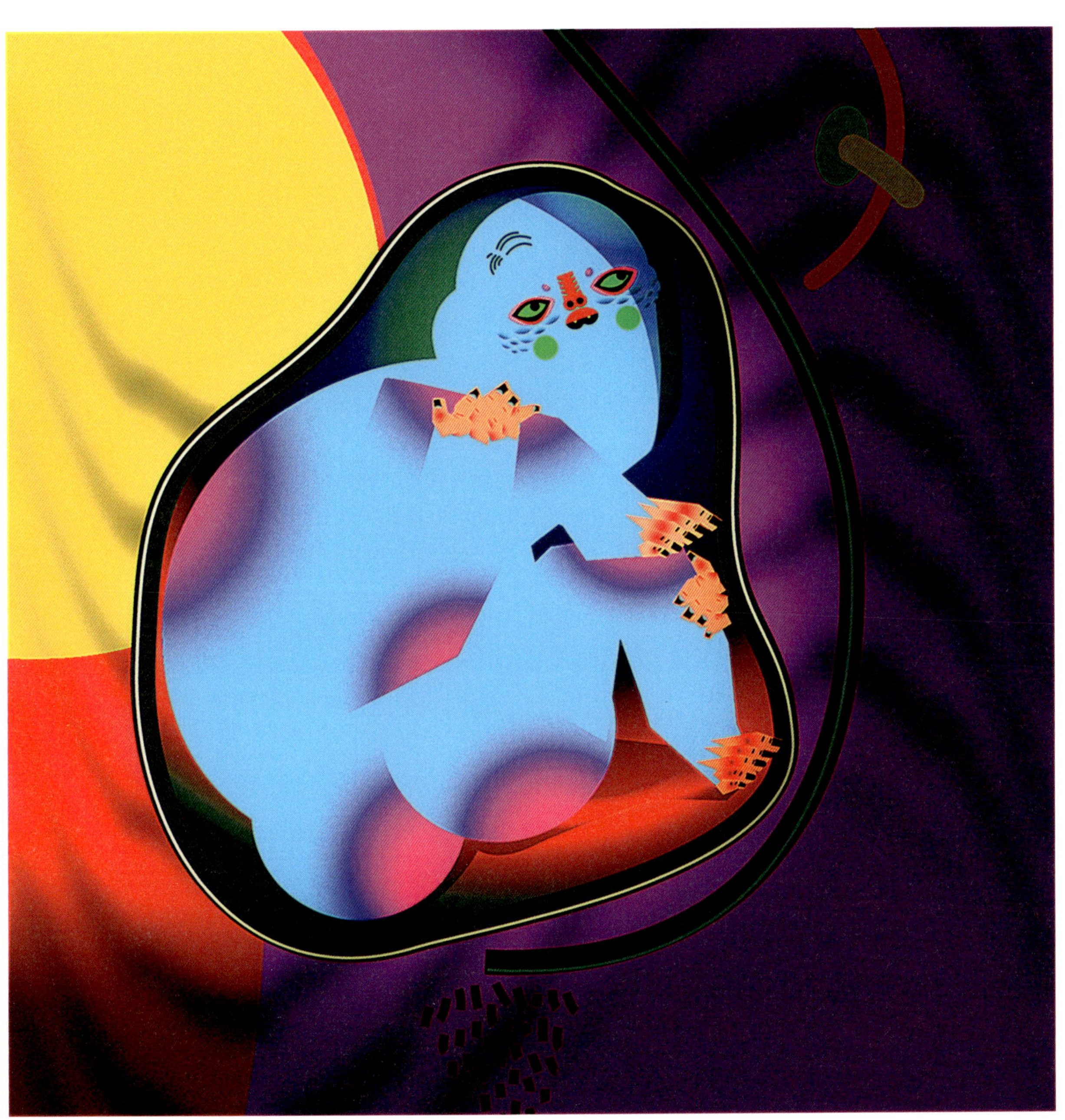

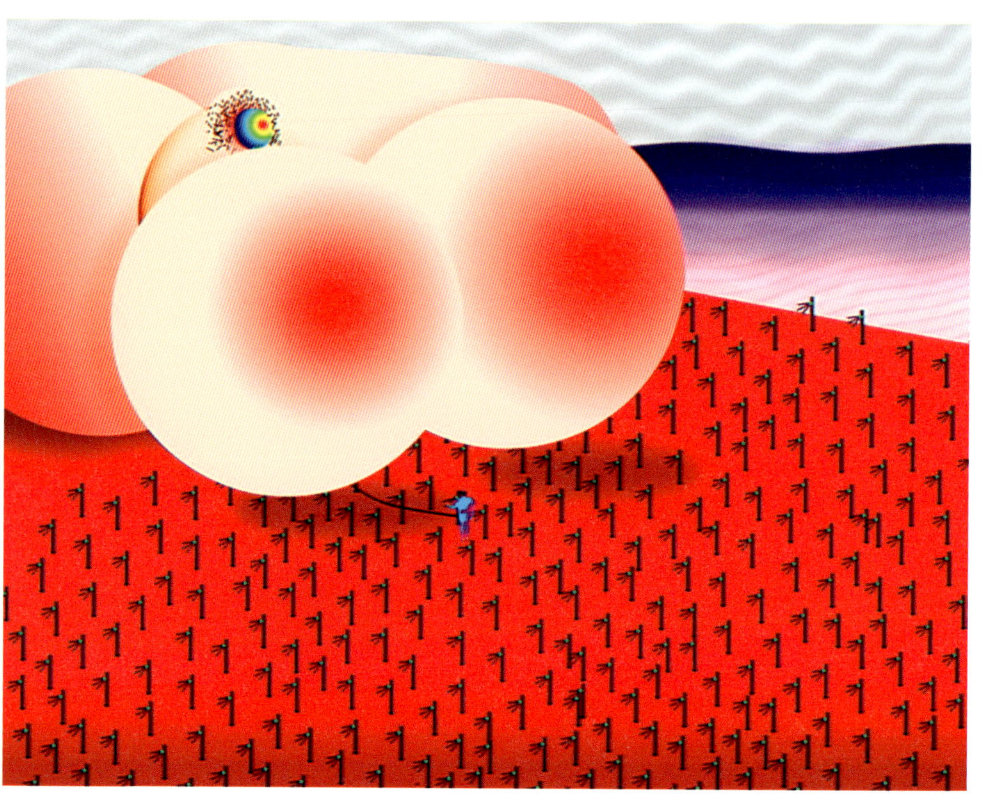

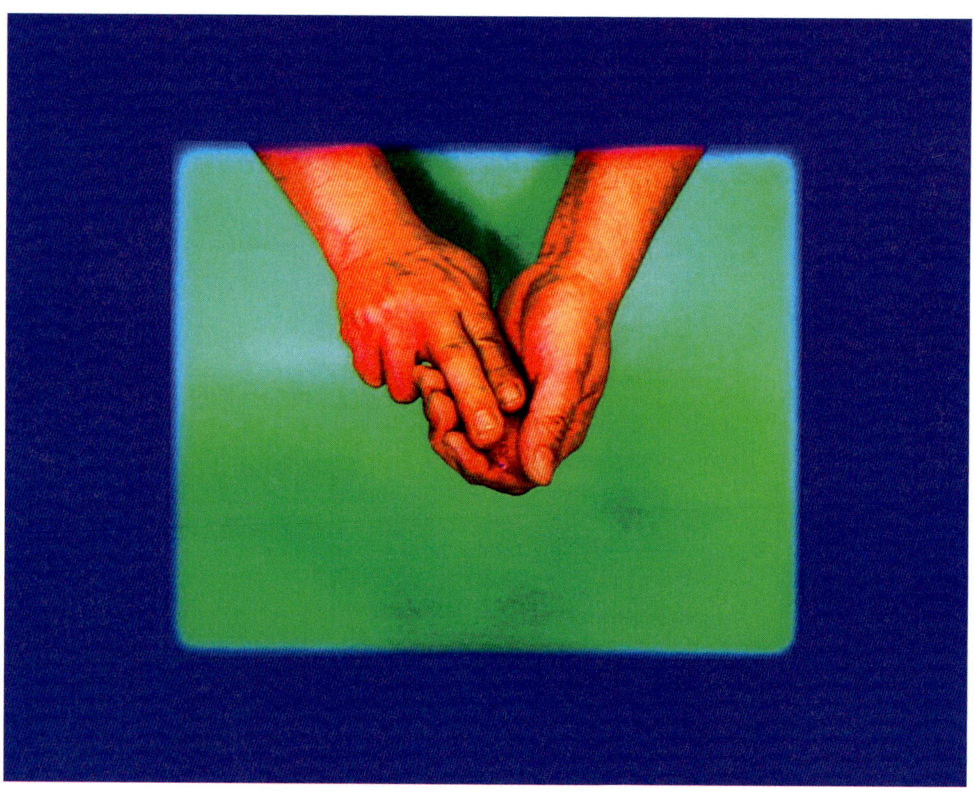

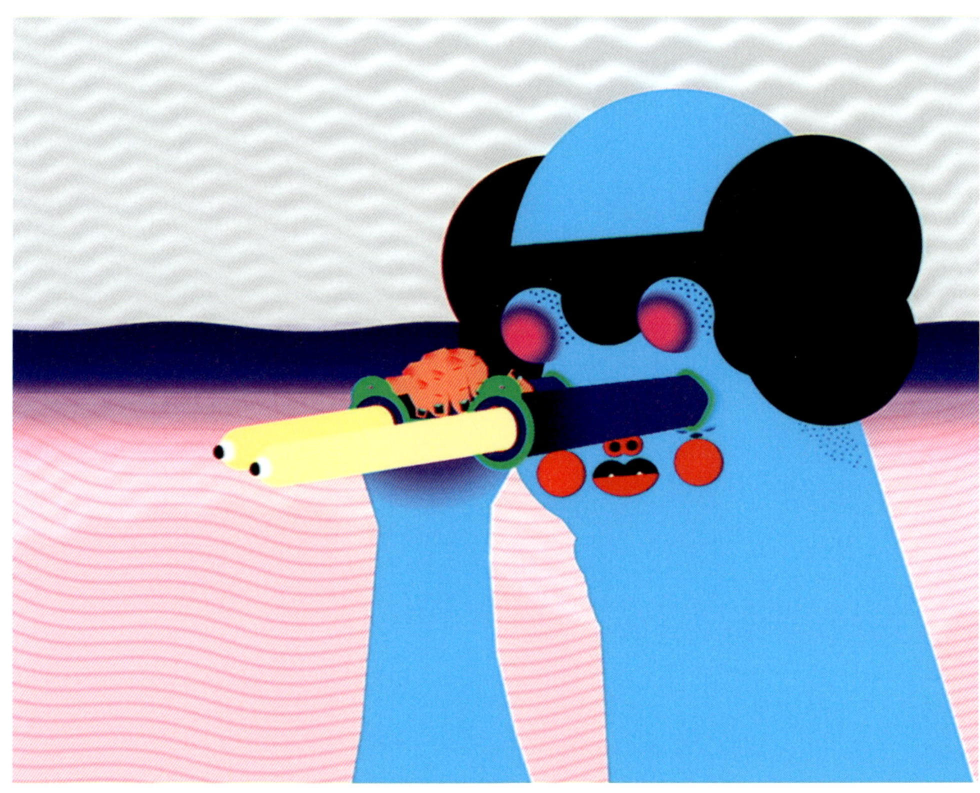

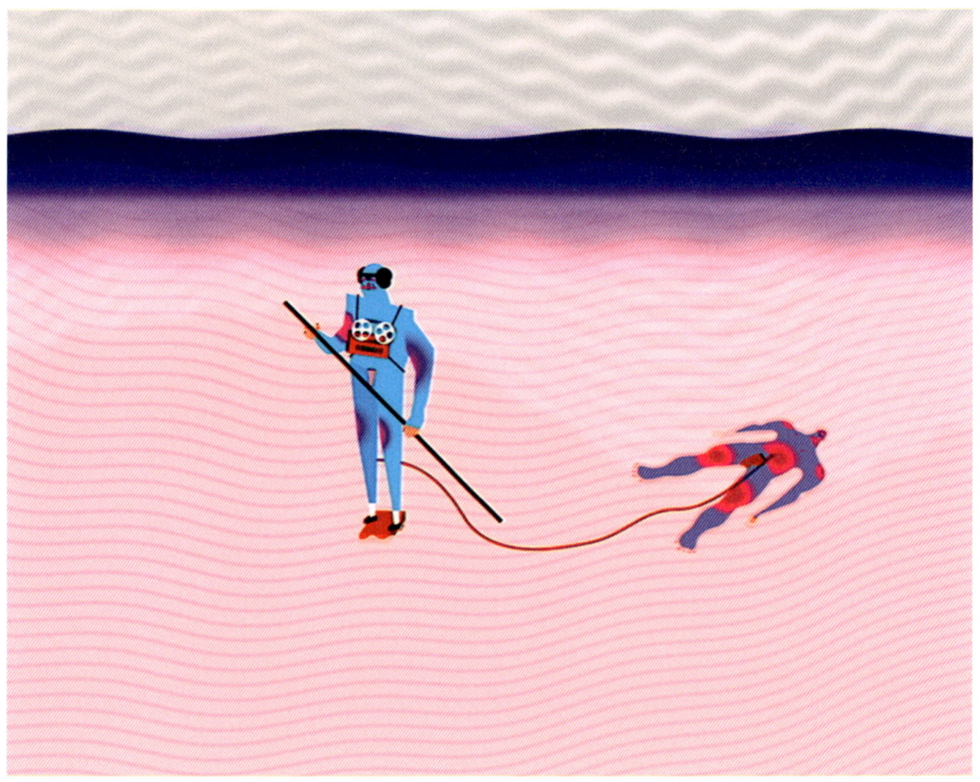

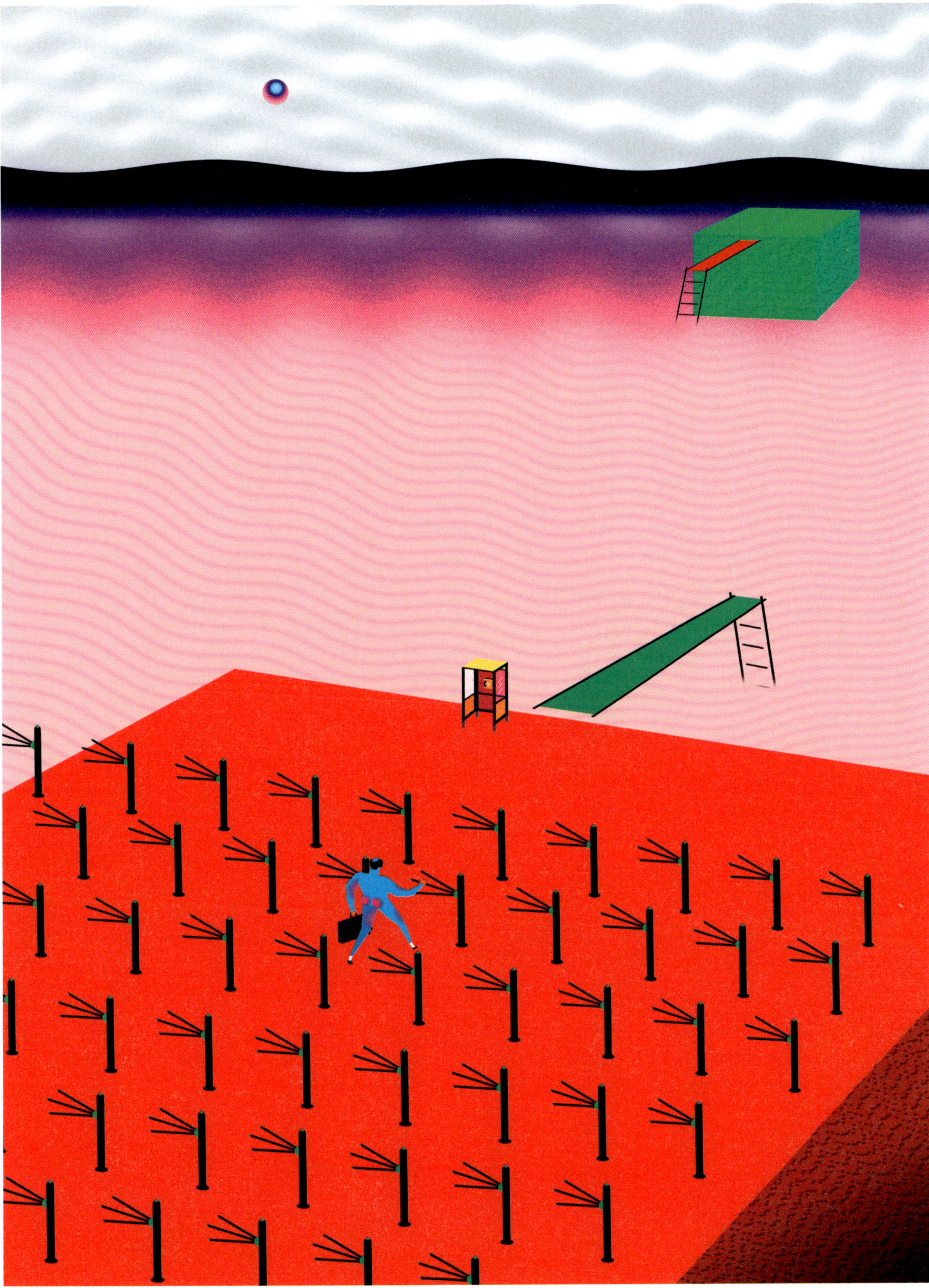

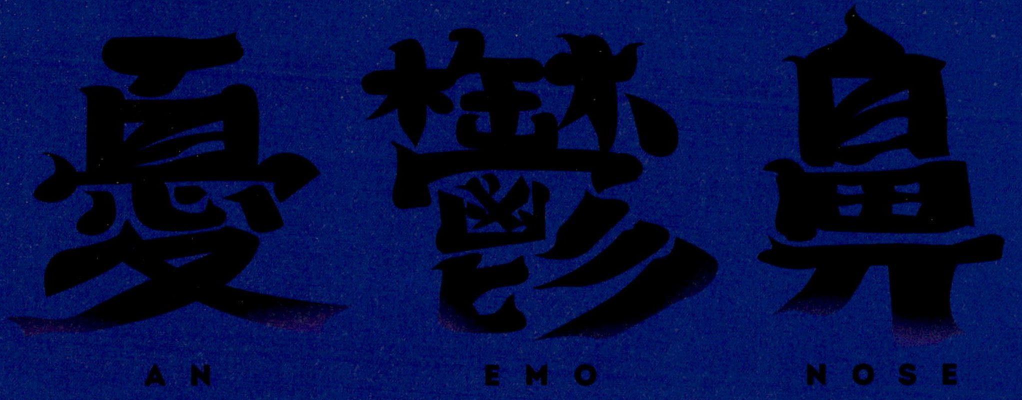

憂鬱鼻
AN EMO NOSE 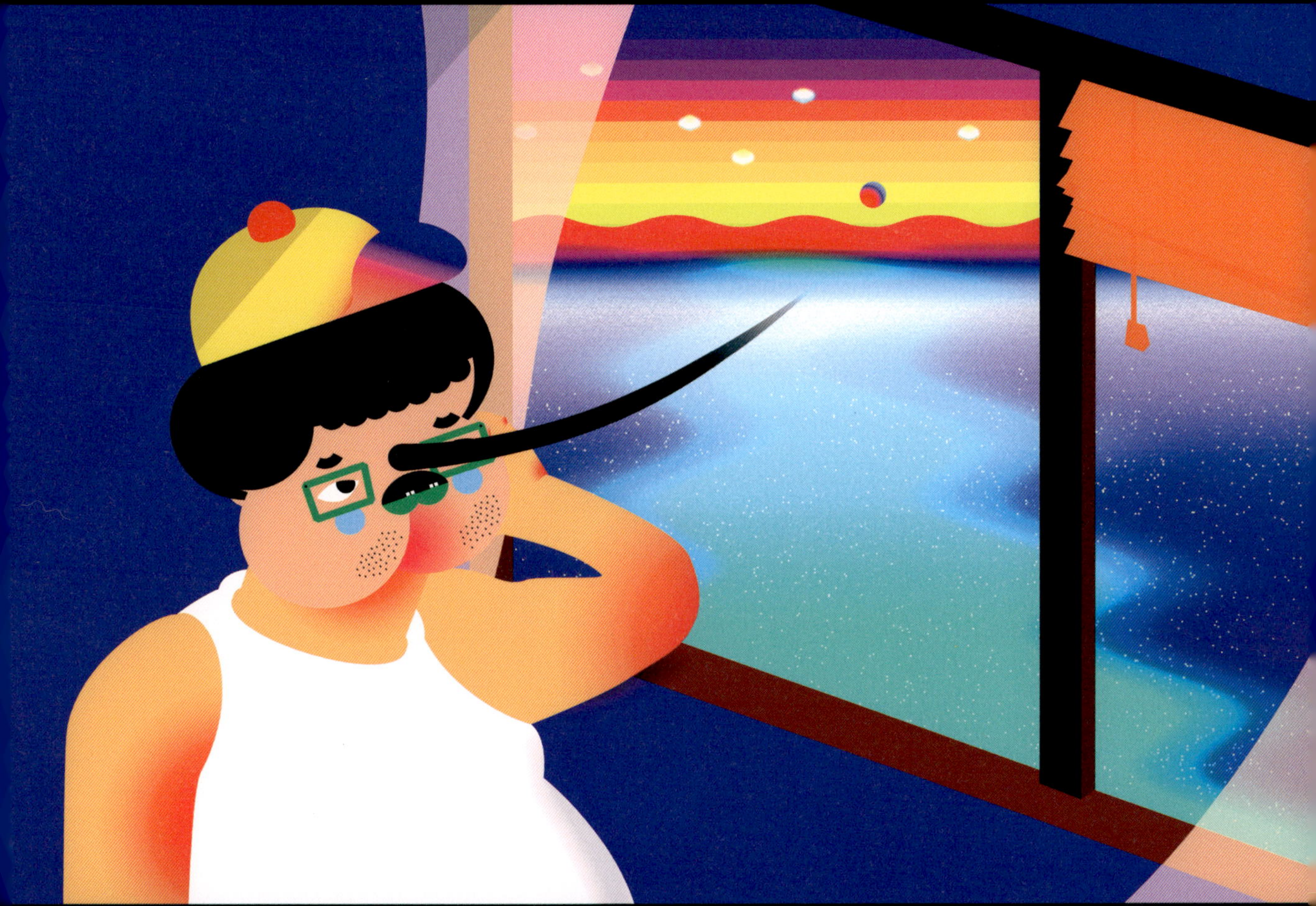
A FILM BY
WONG PING

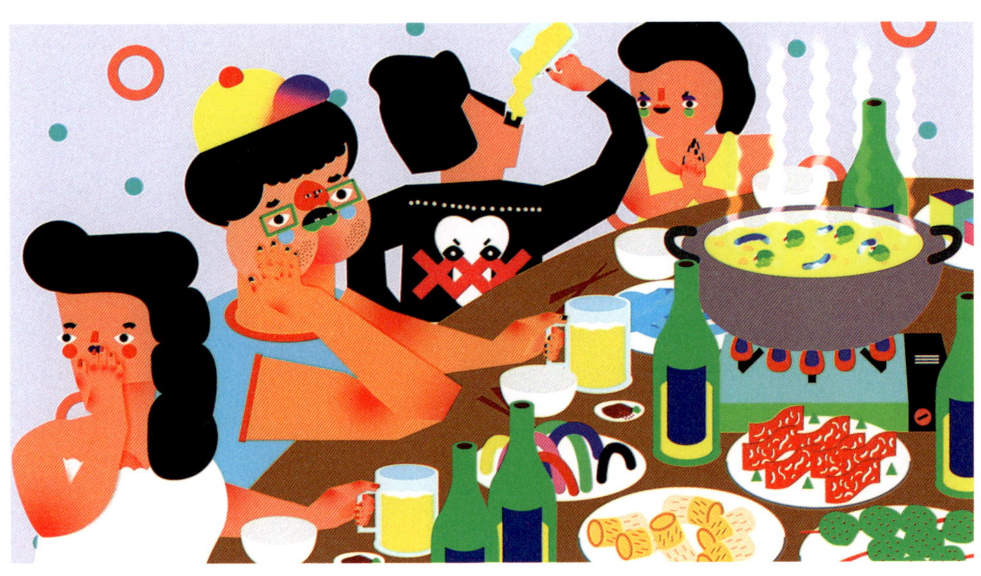

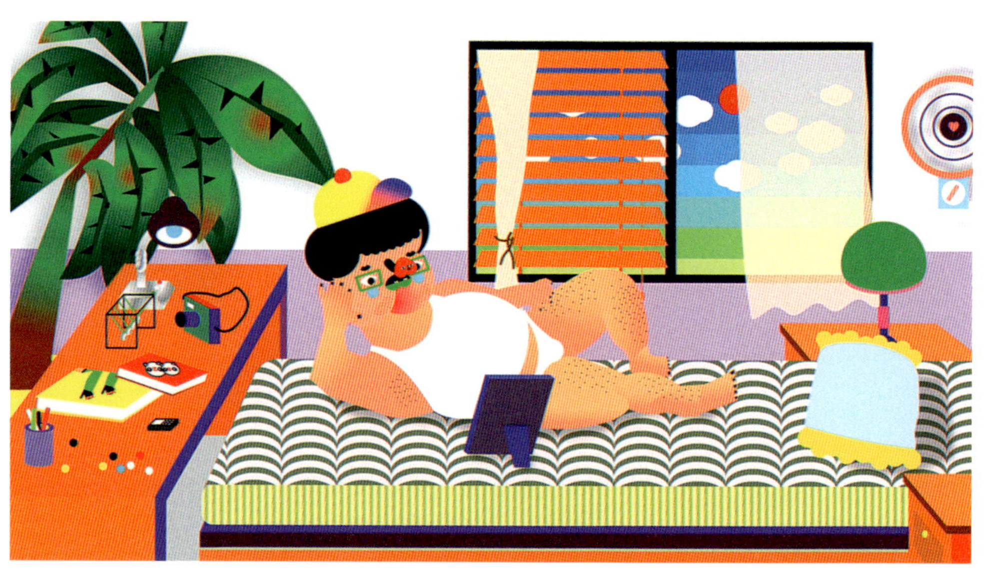
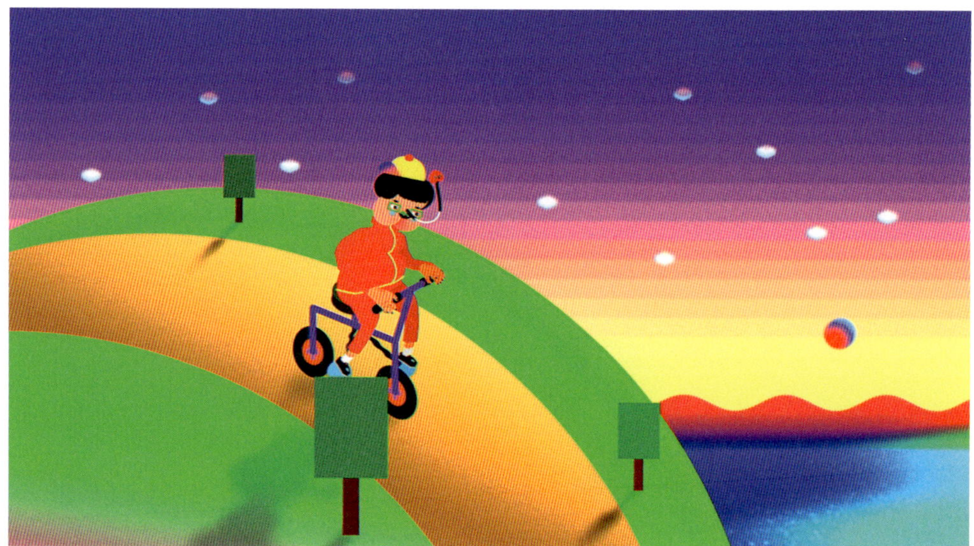

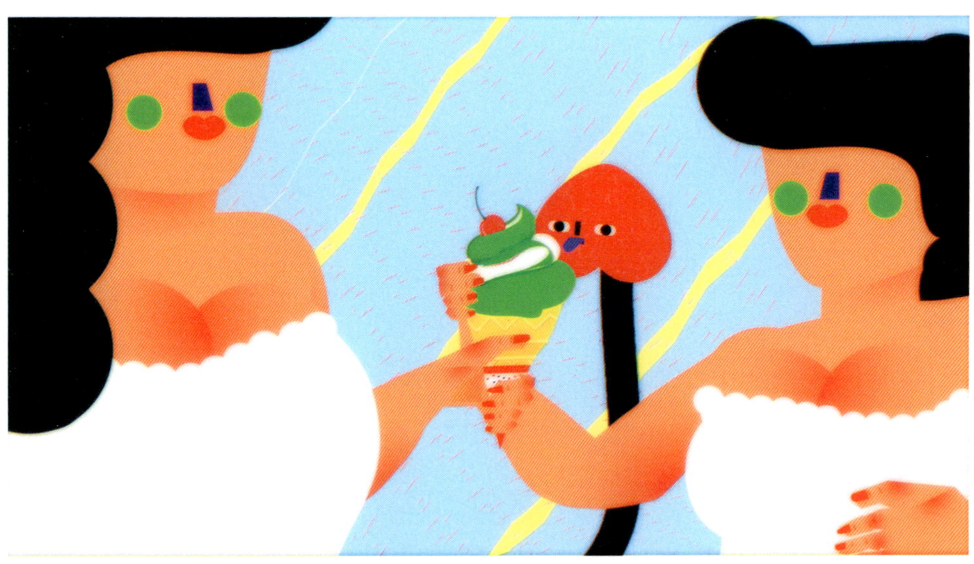

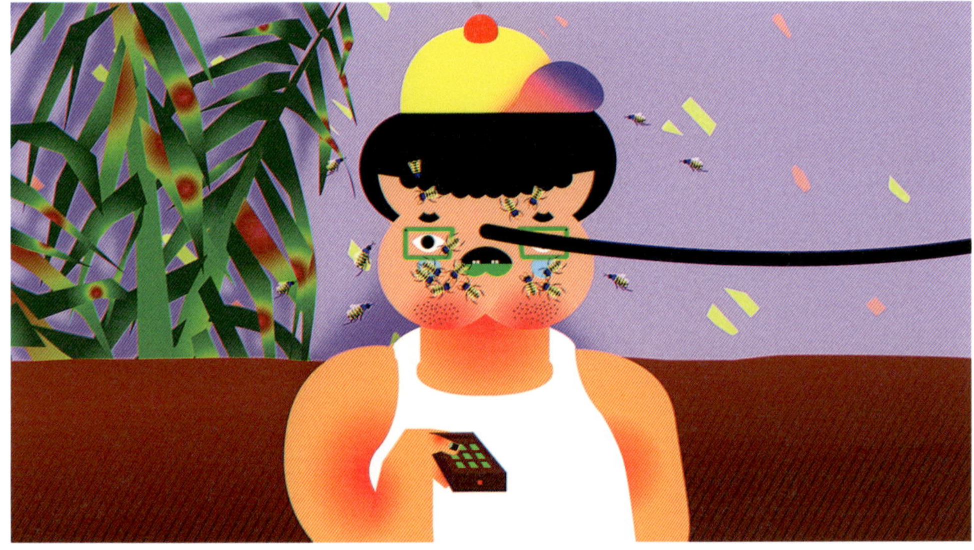

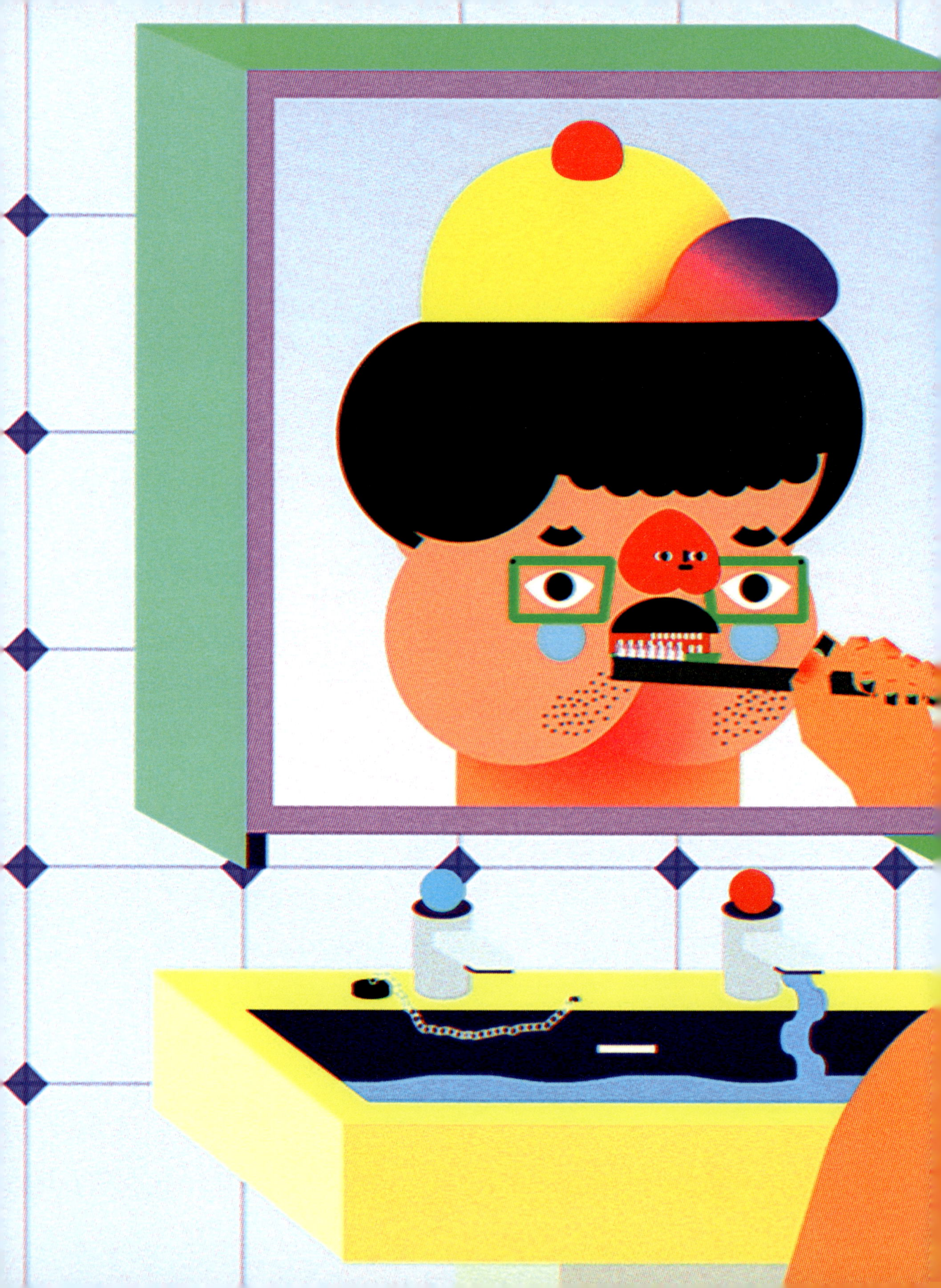

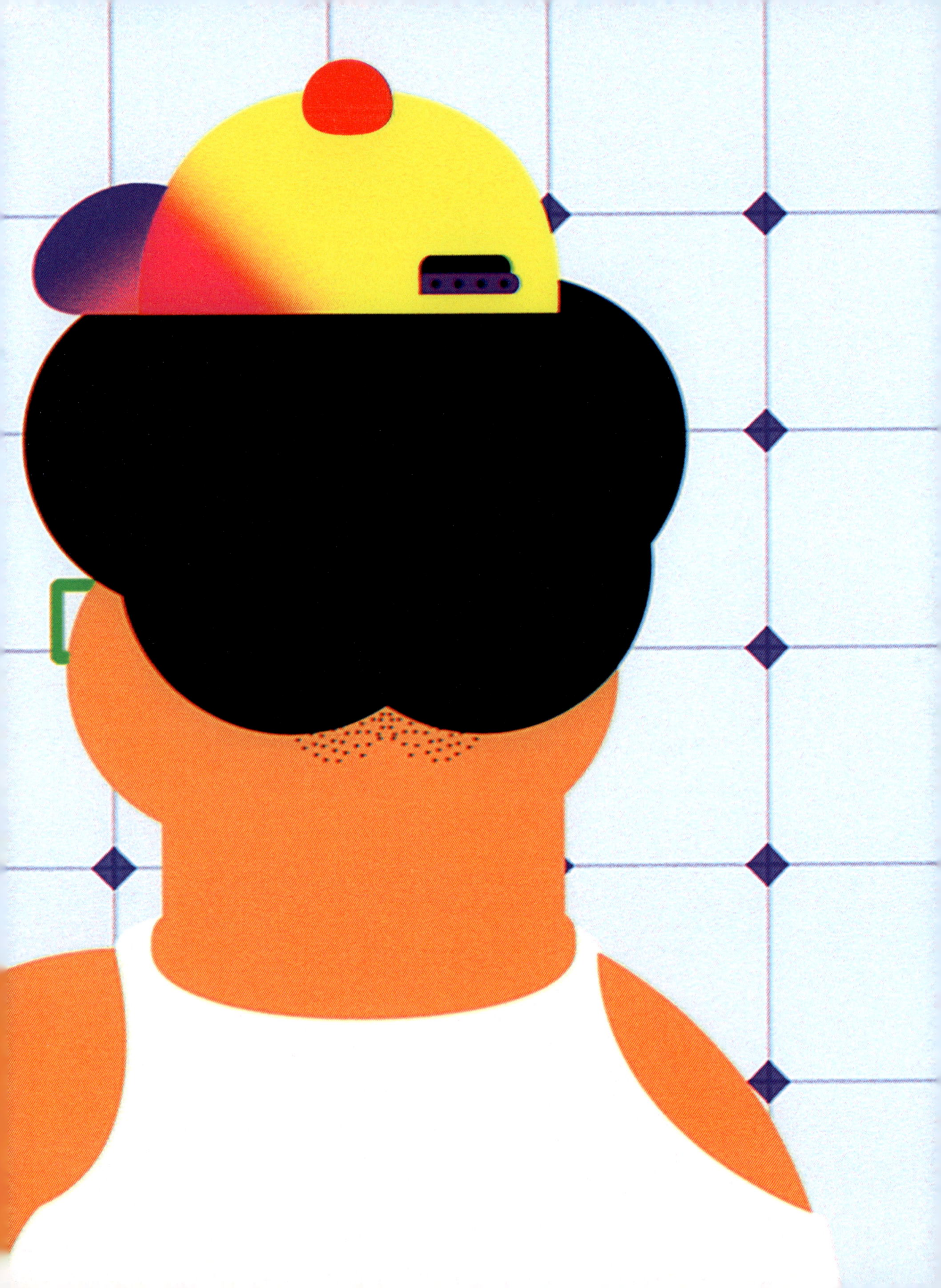

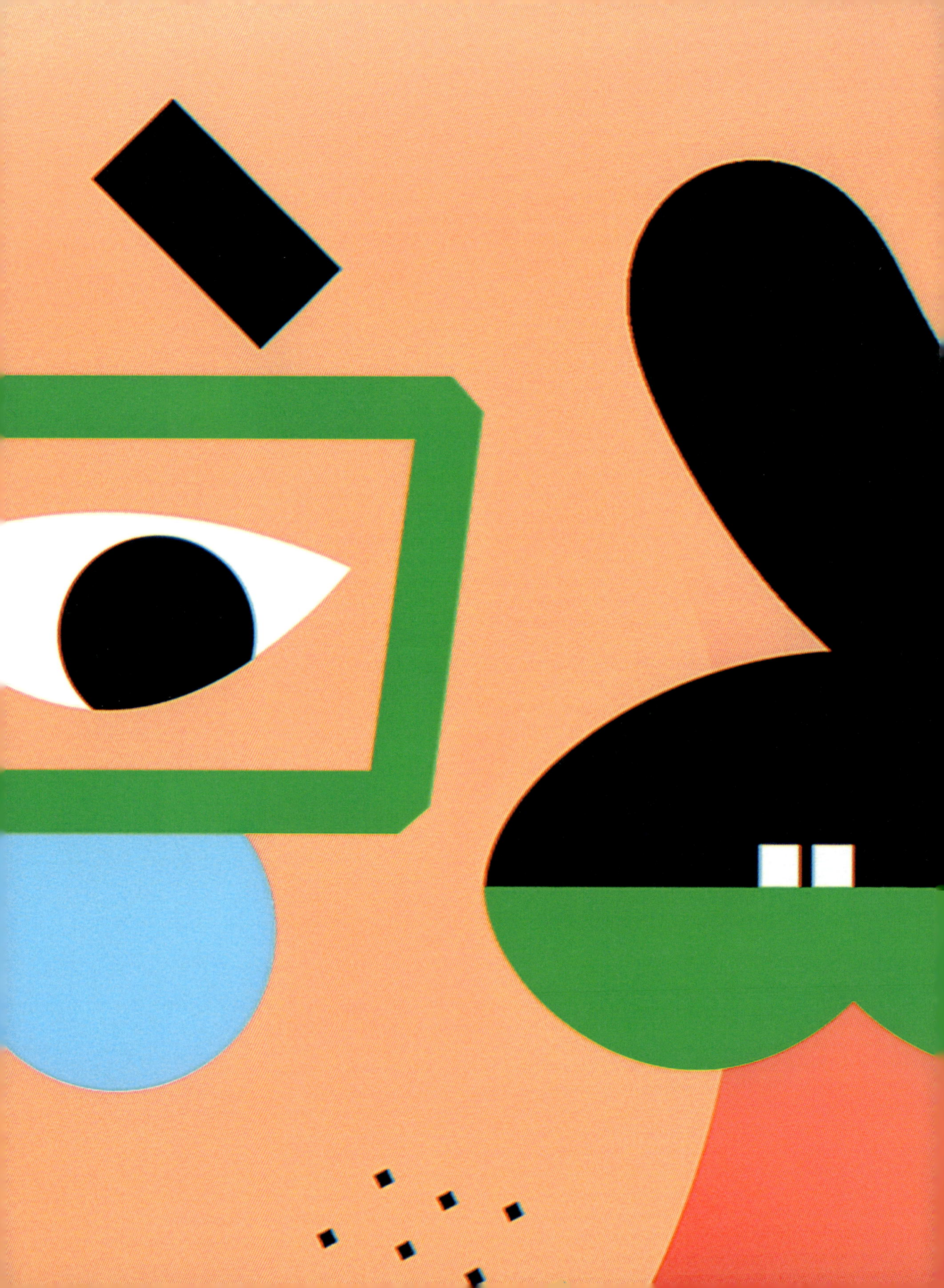

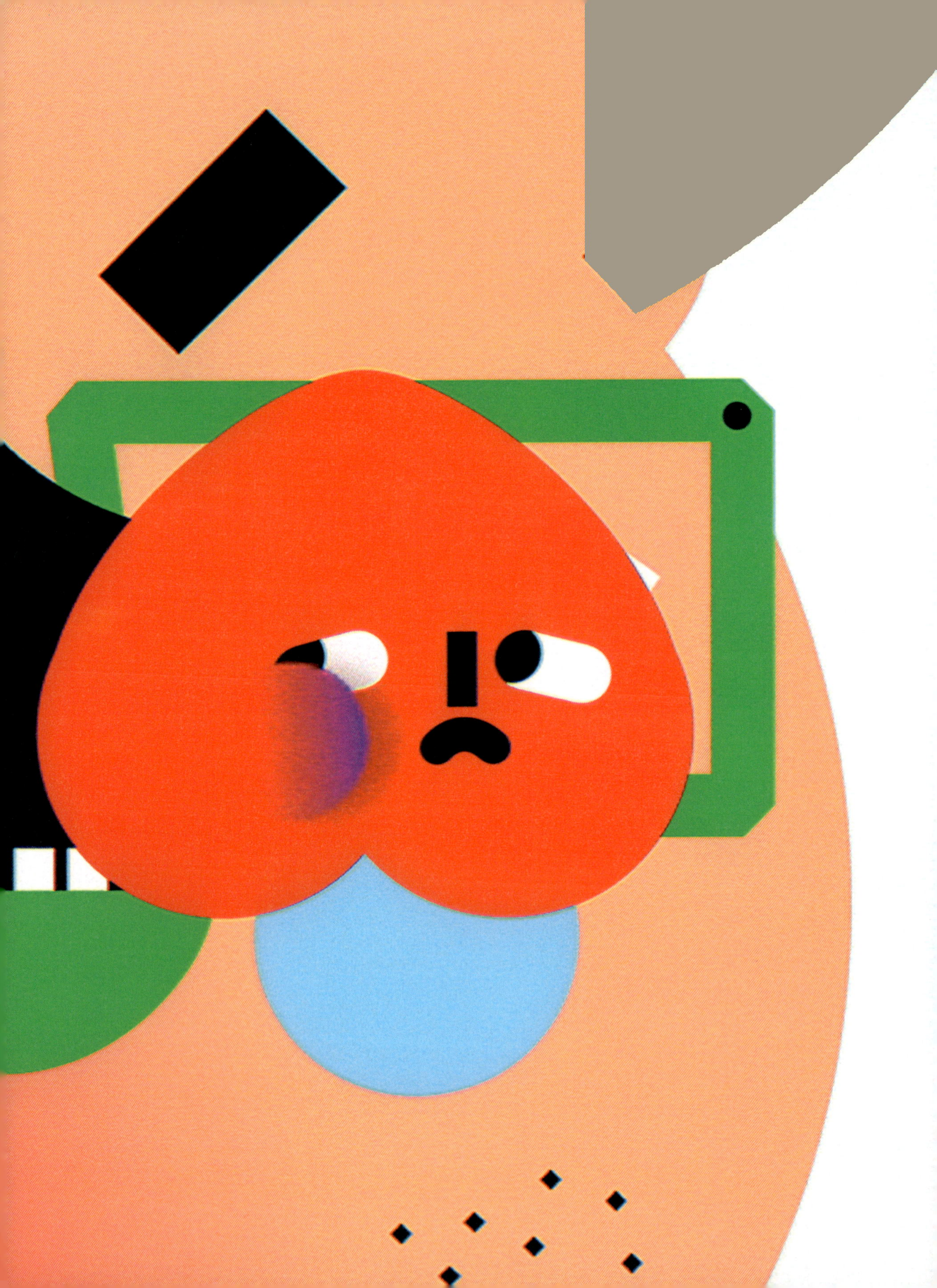

JUNGLE OF DESIRE

A FILM BY
WONG PING

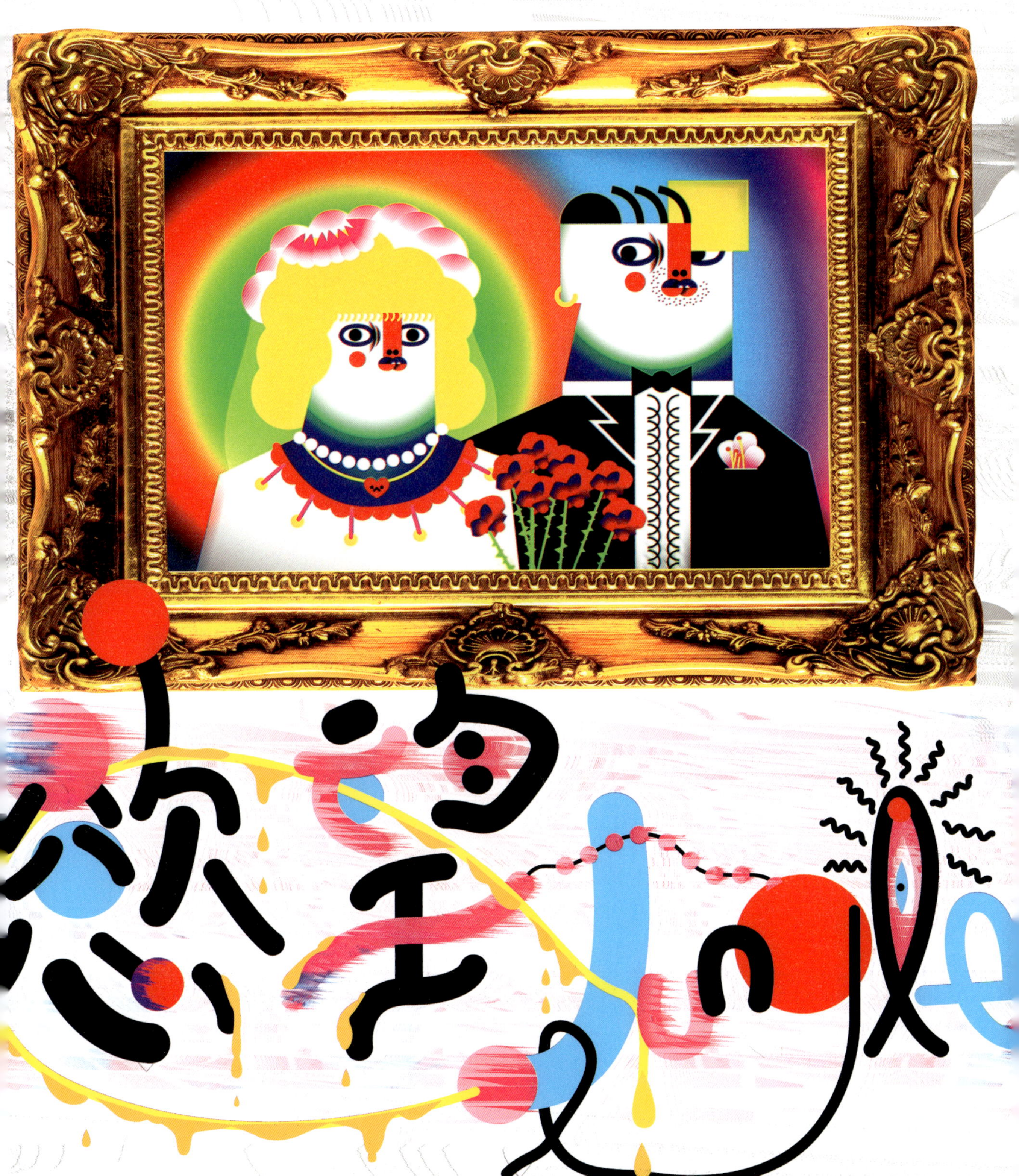

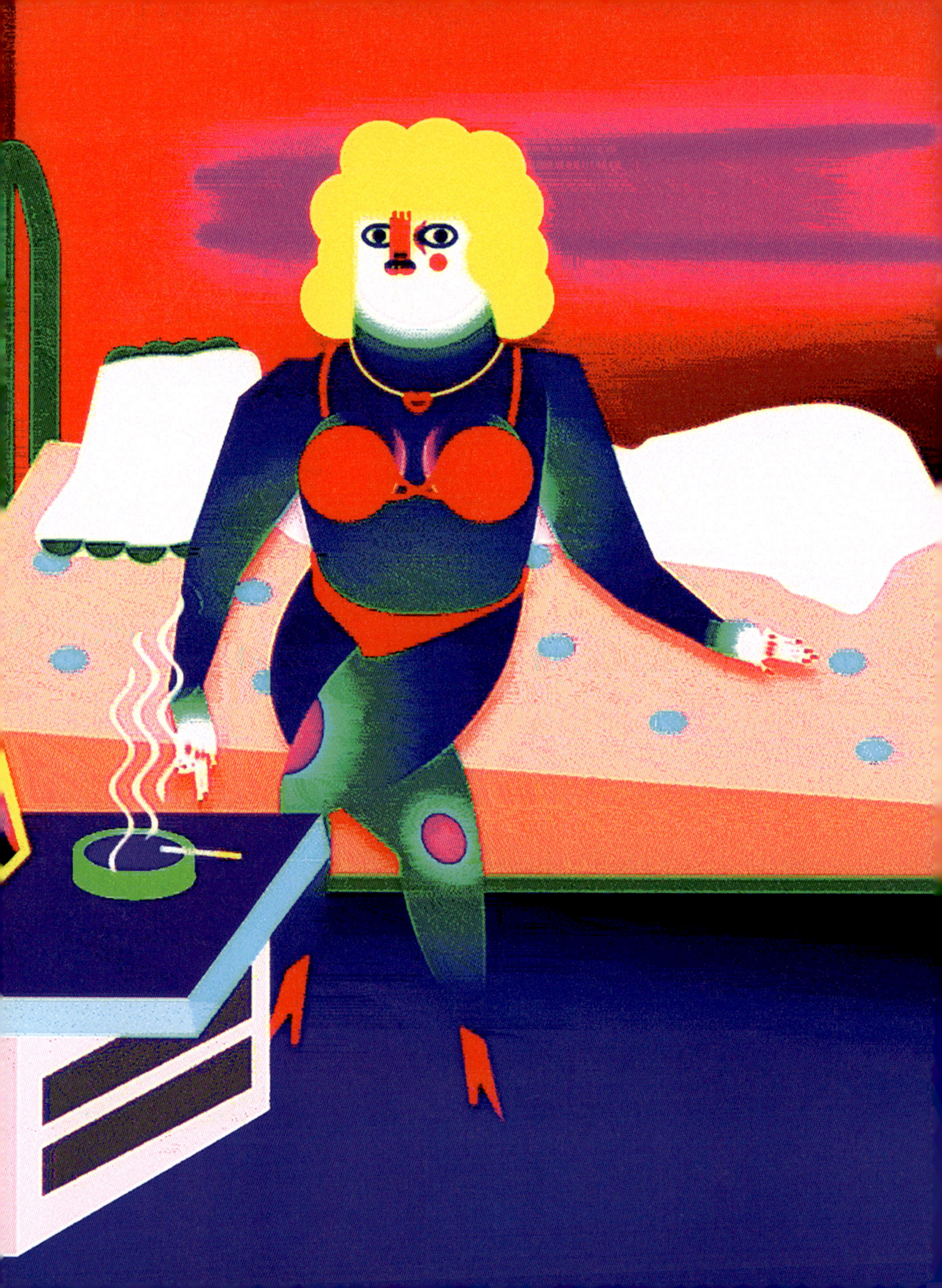

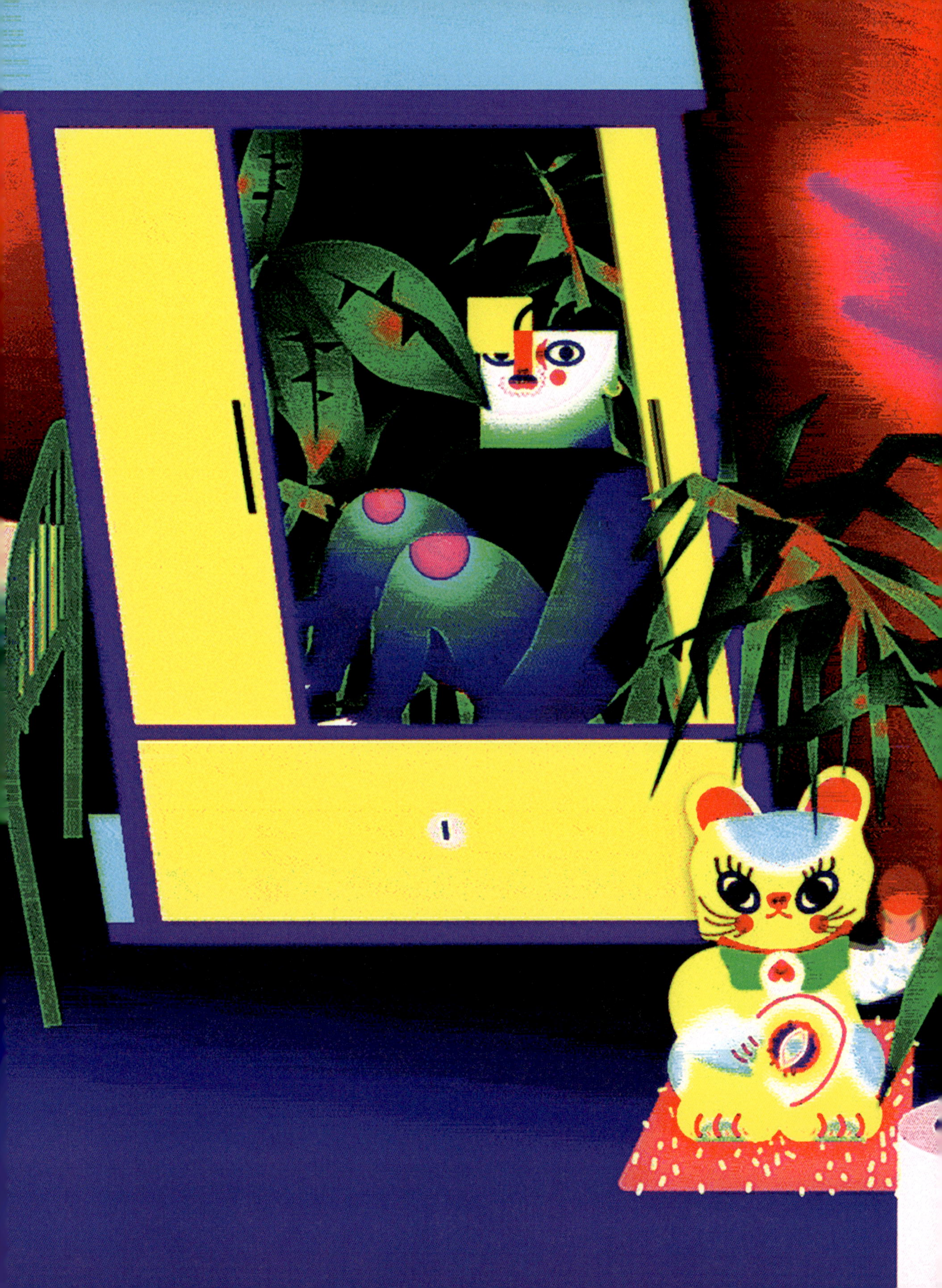

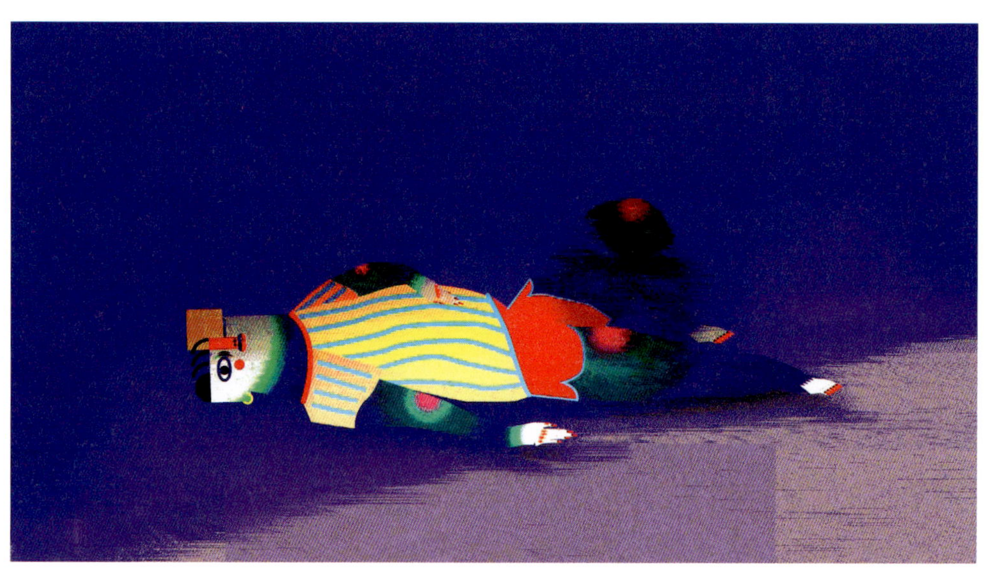

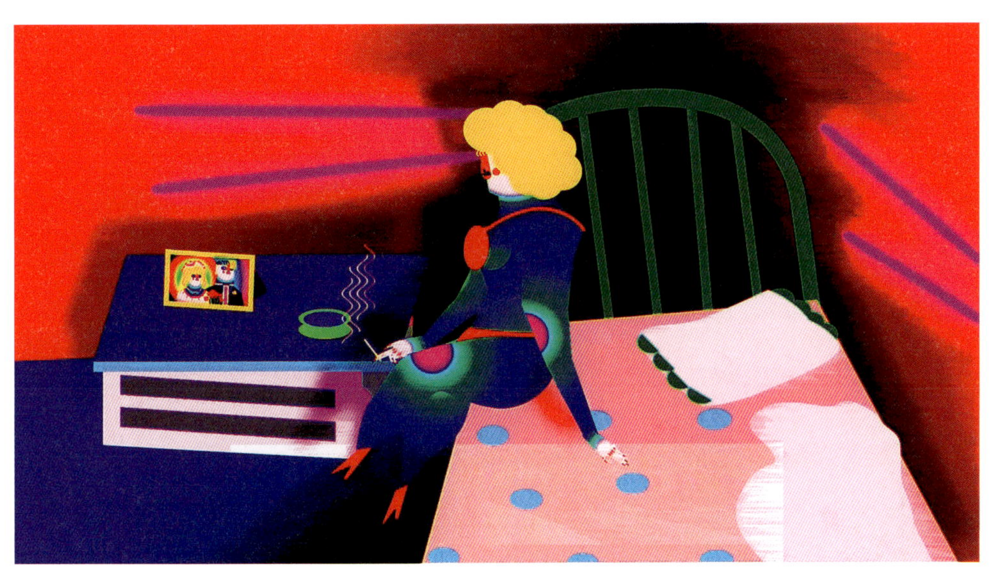

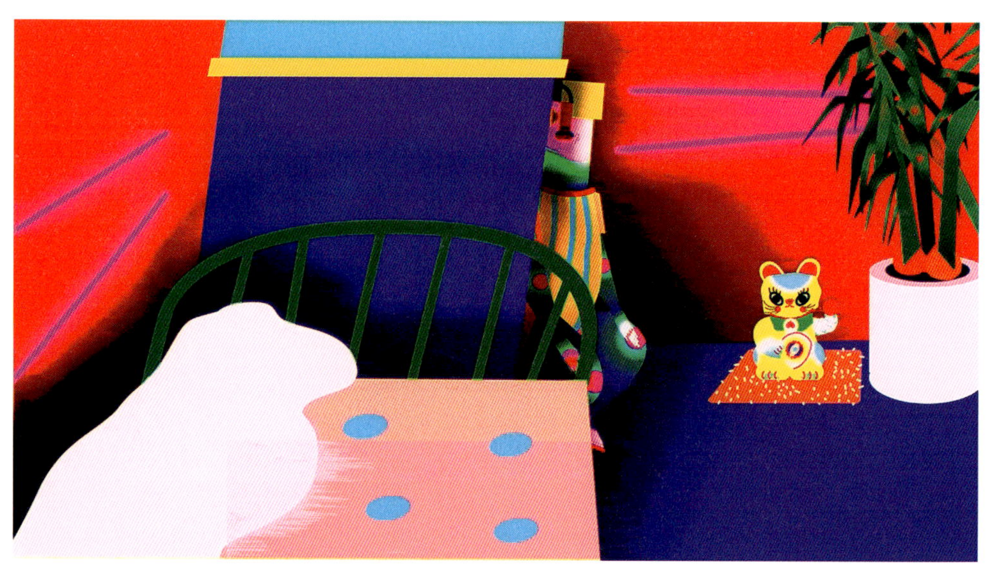

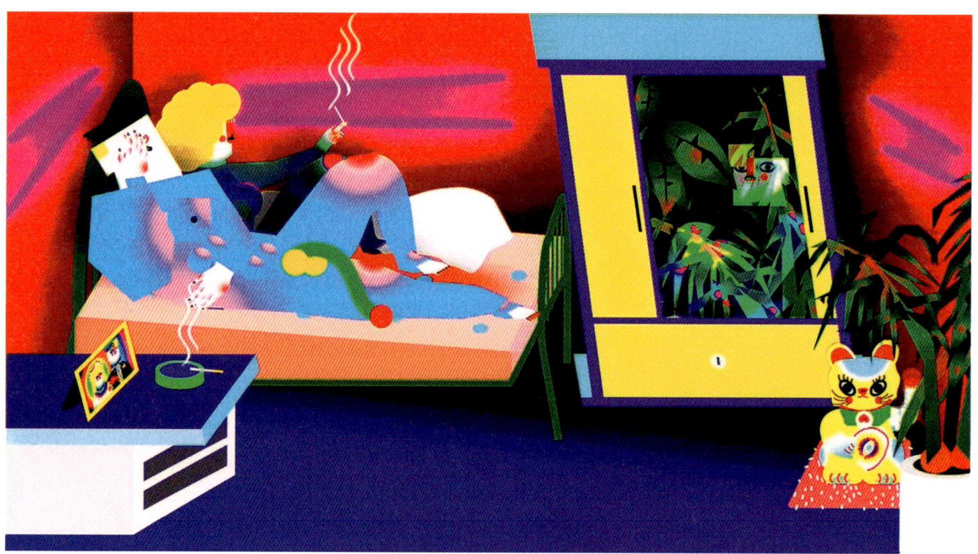

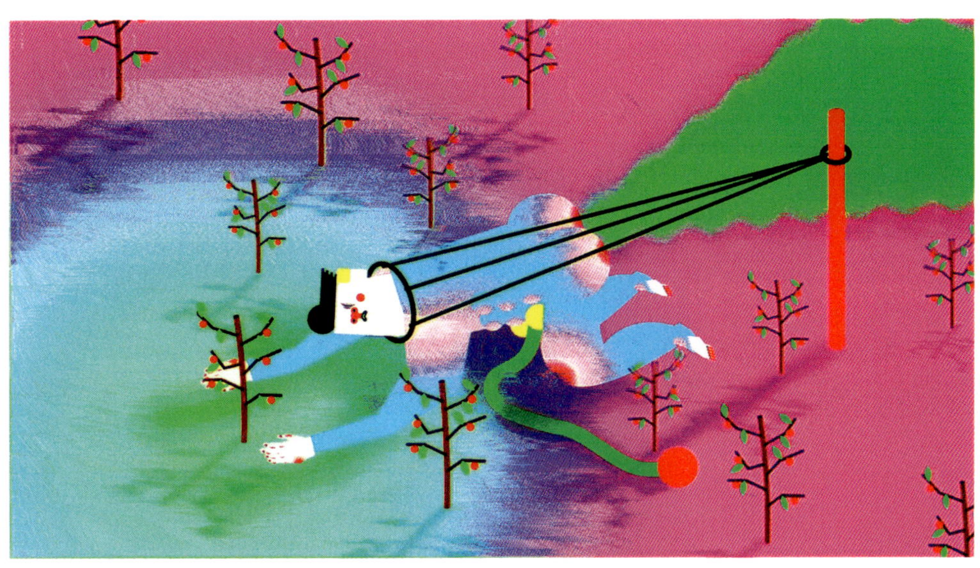

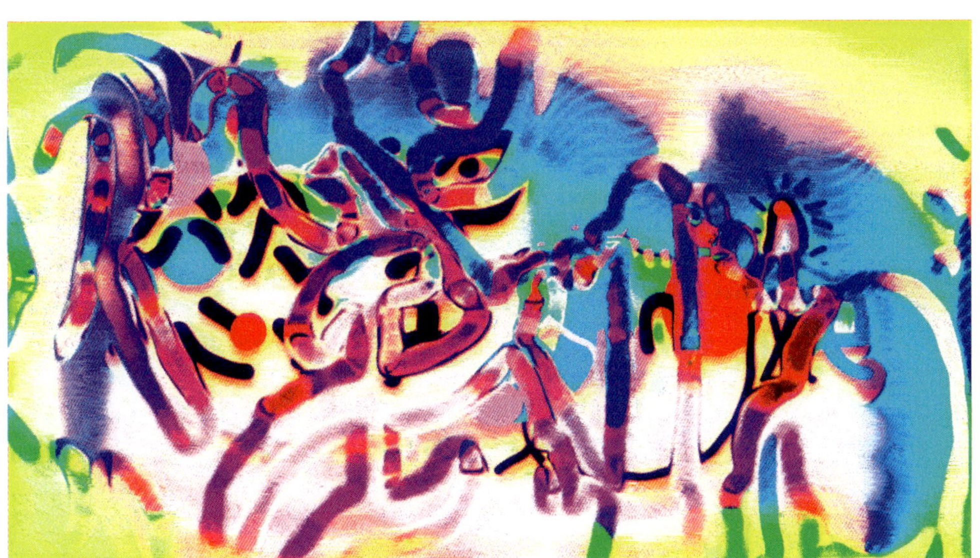

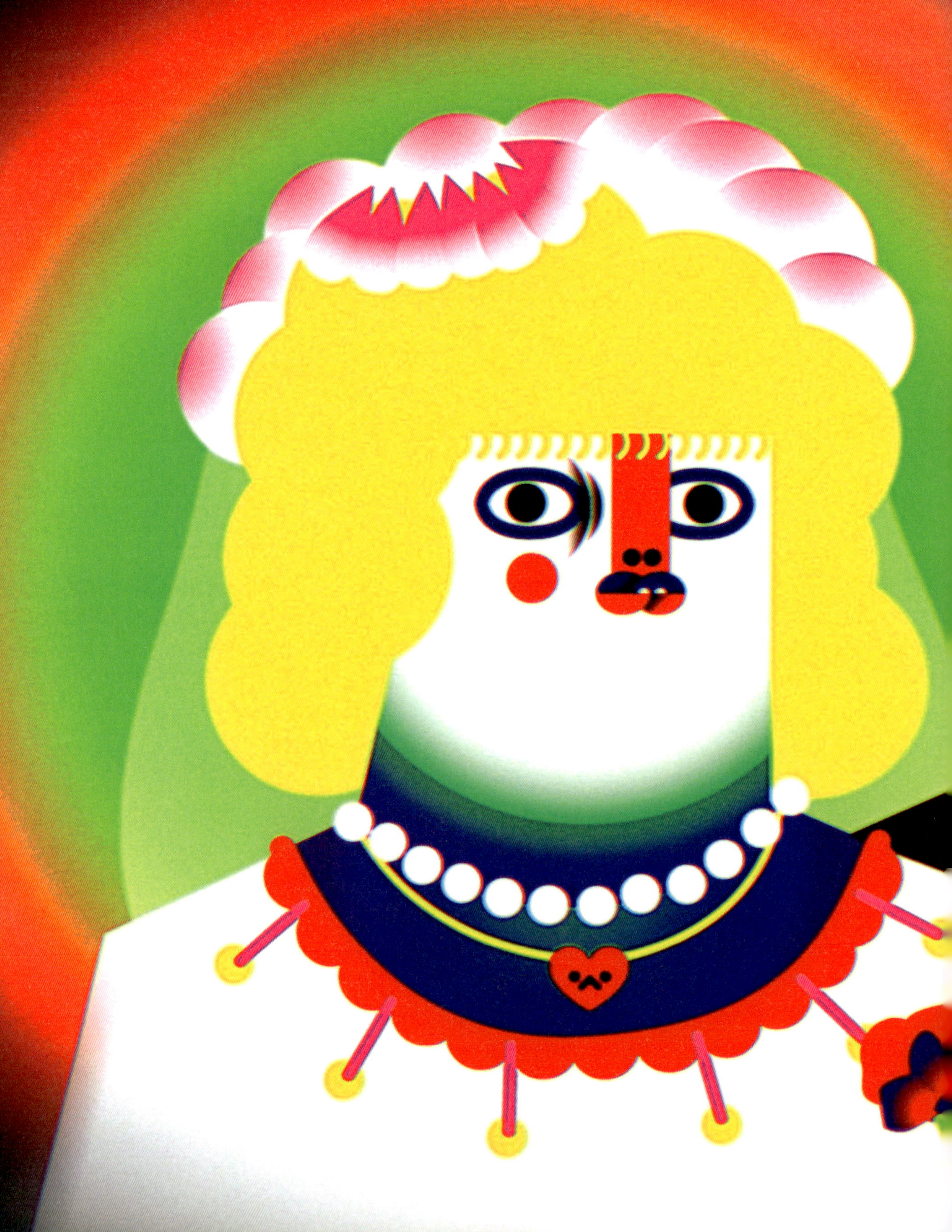

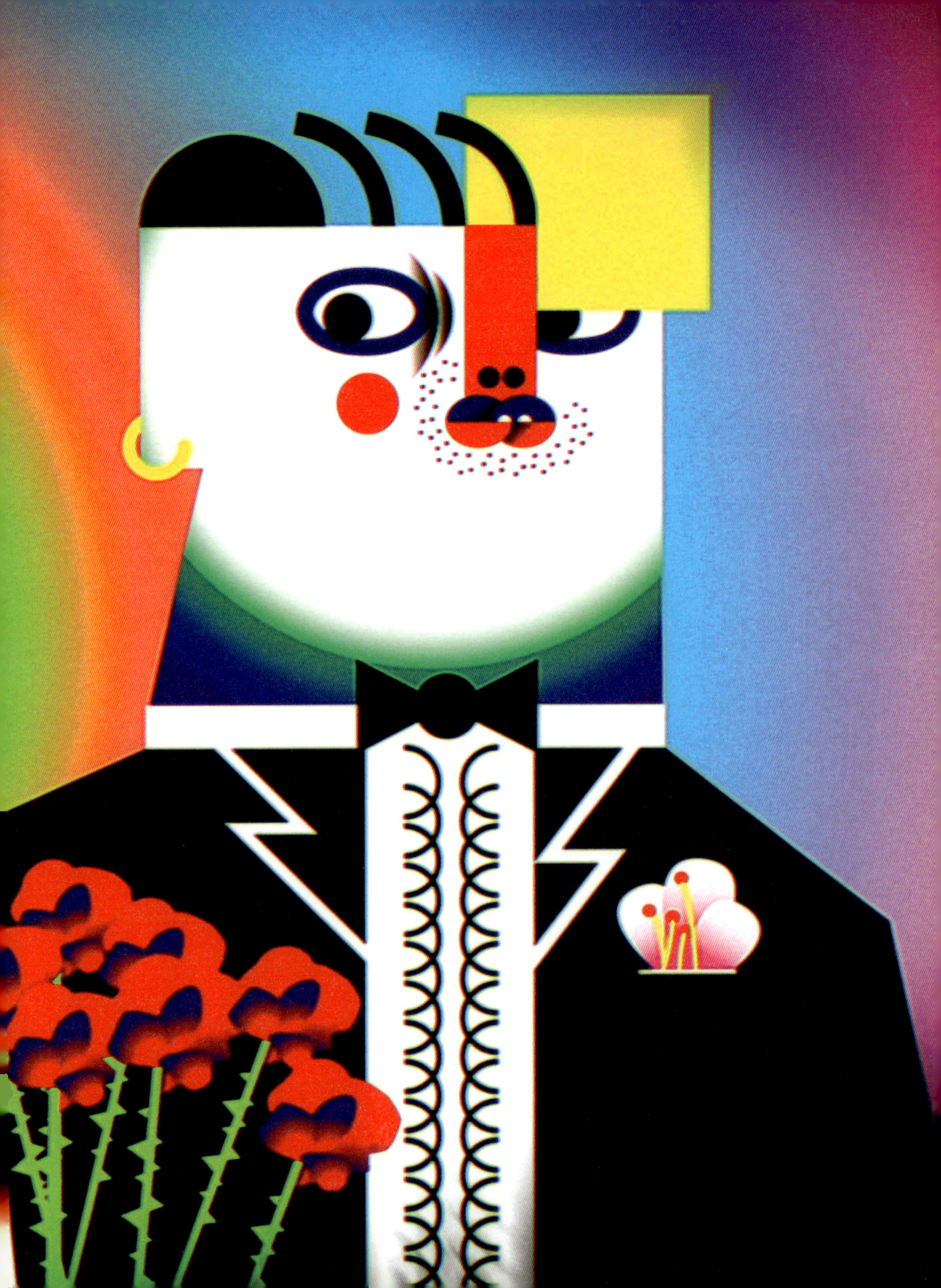

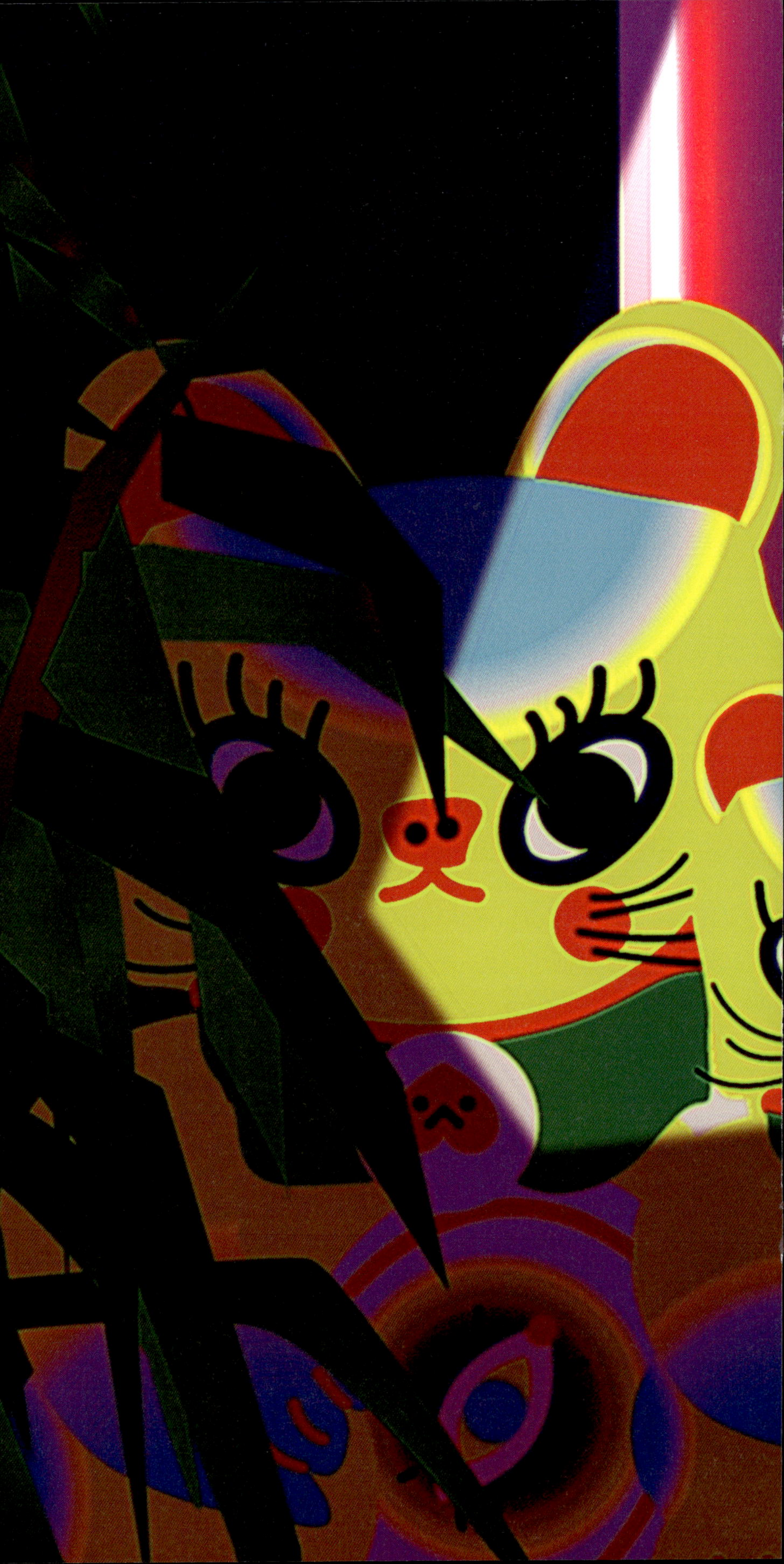

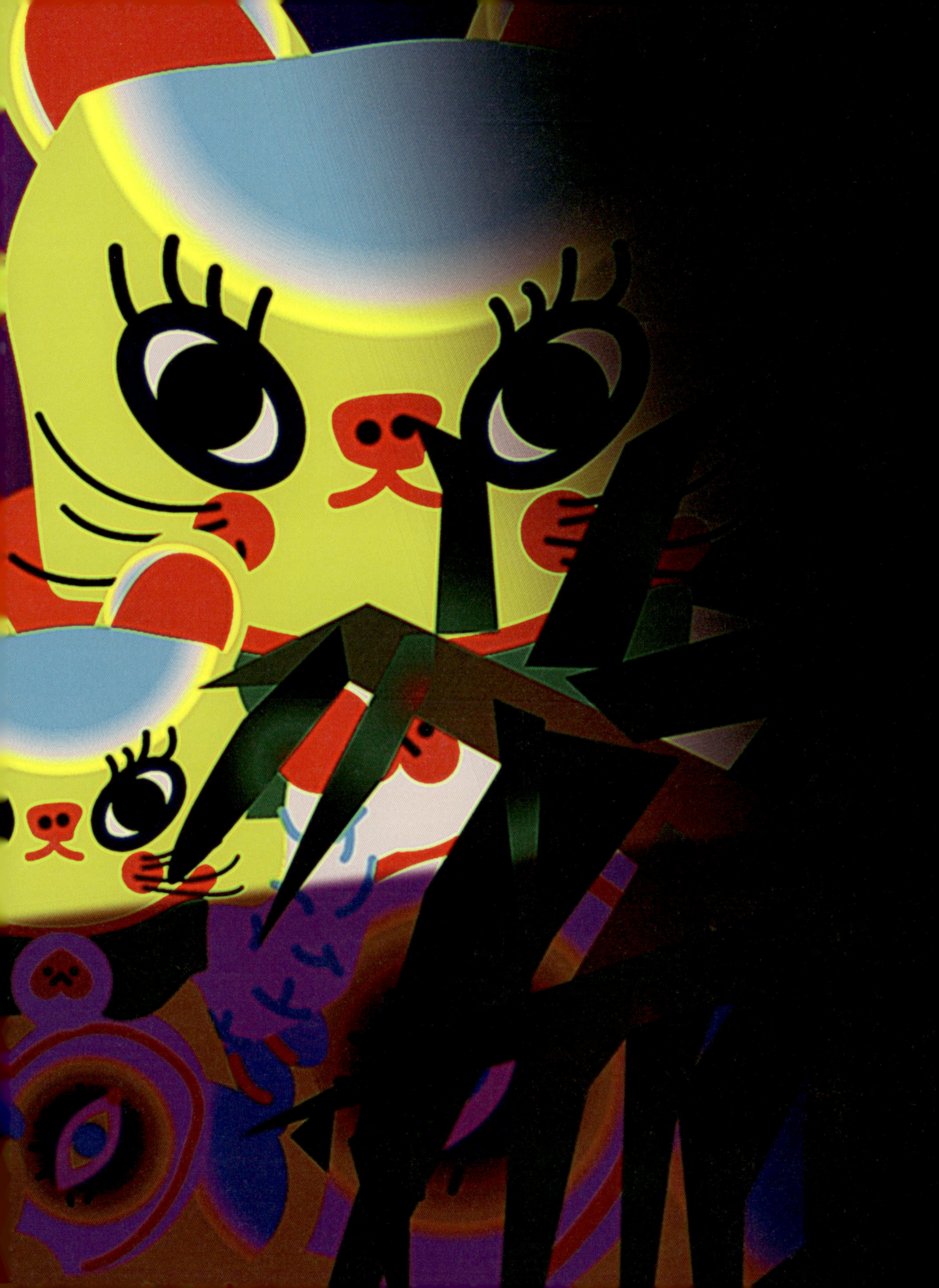

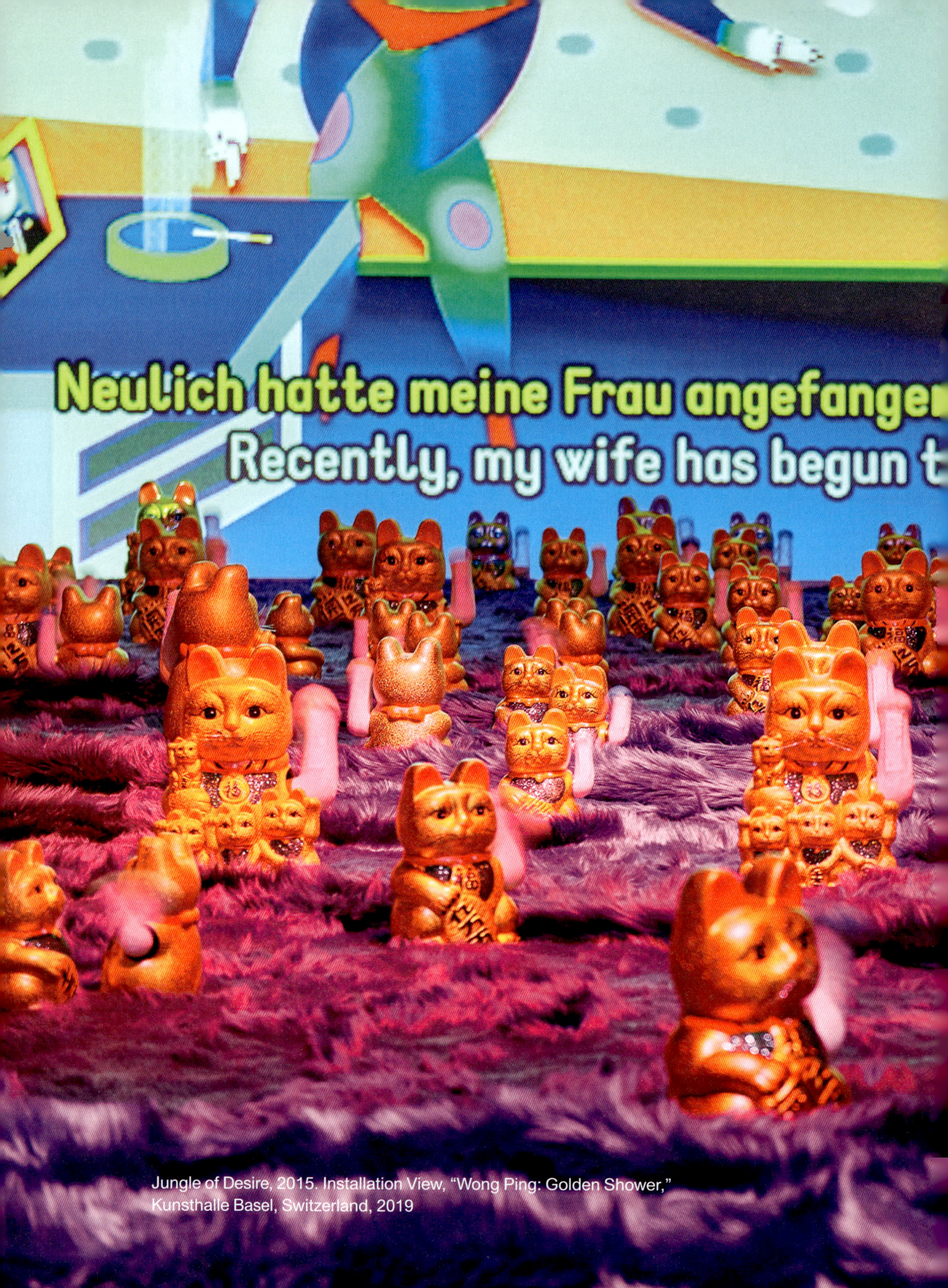

Jungle of Desire, 2015. Installation View, "Wong Ping: Golden Shower,"
Kunsthalle Basel, Switzerland, 2019

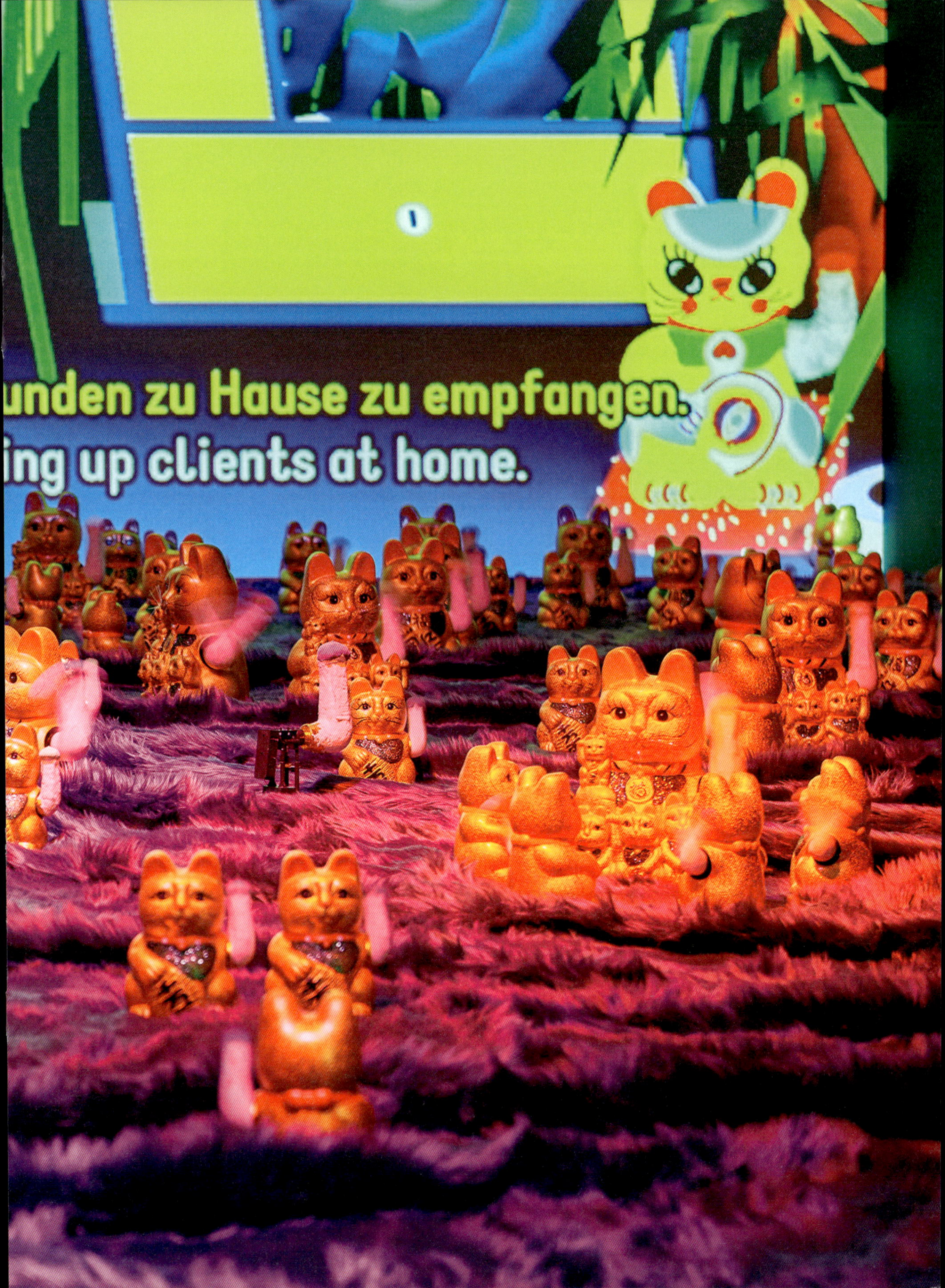
unden zu Hause zu empfangen.
ing up clients at home.

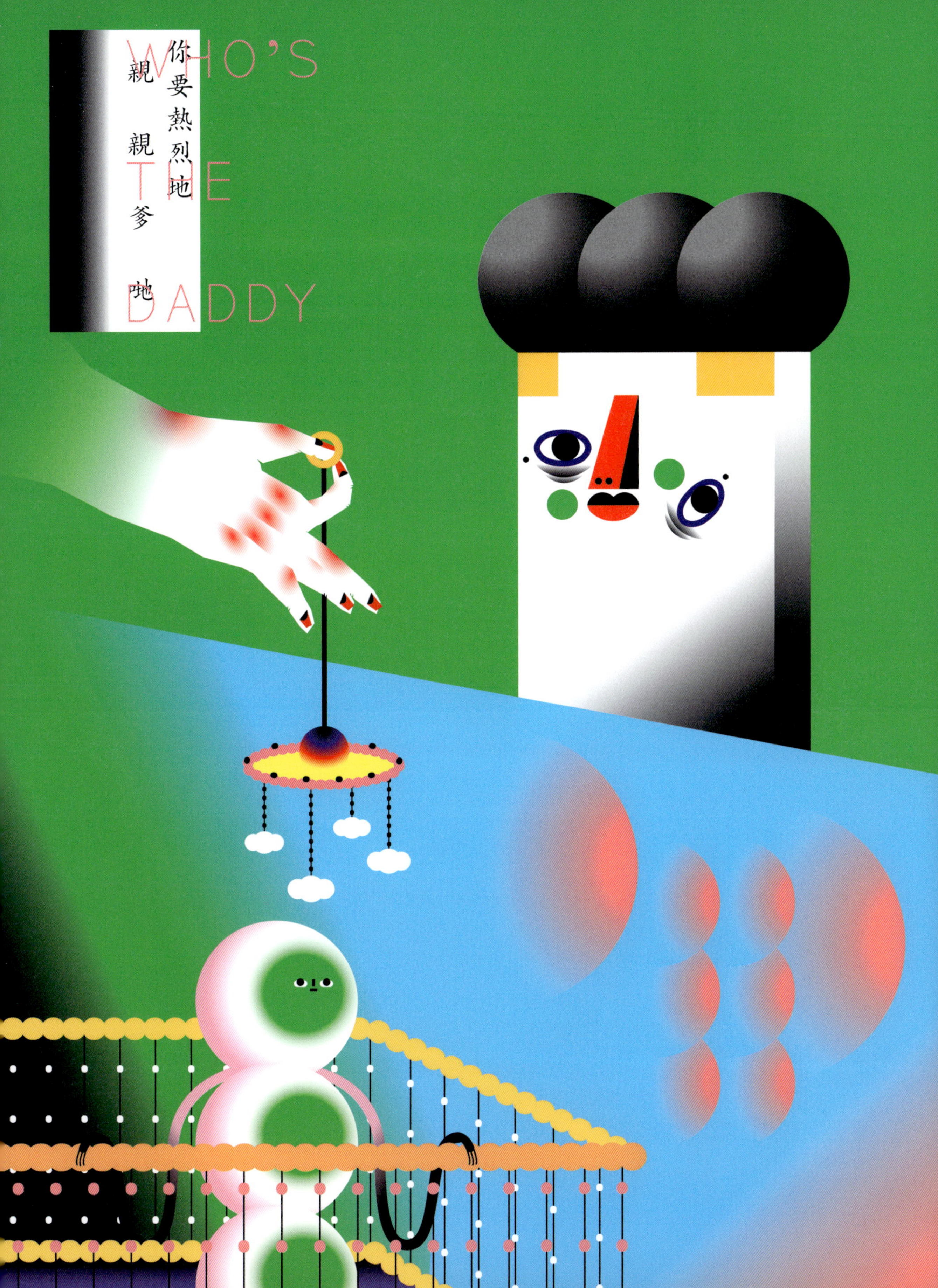

WHO'S THE DADDY
親親地
親 爹
你要熱烈地
啦

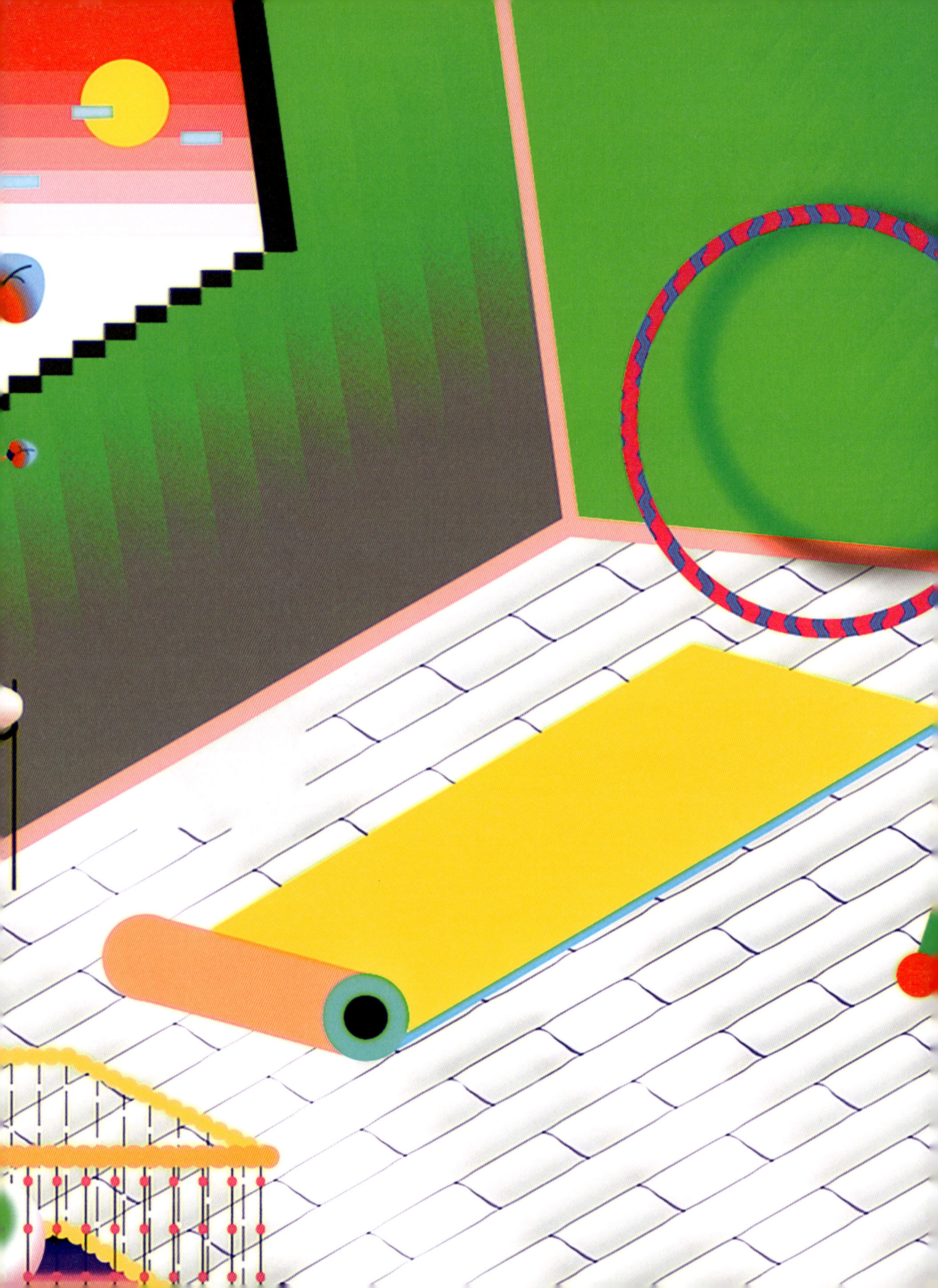

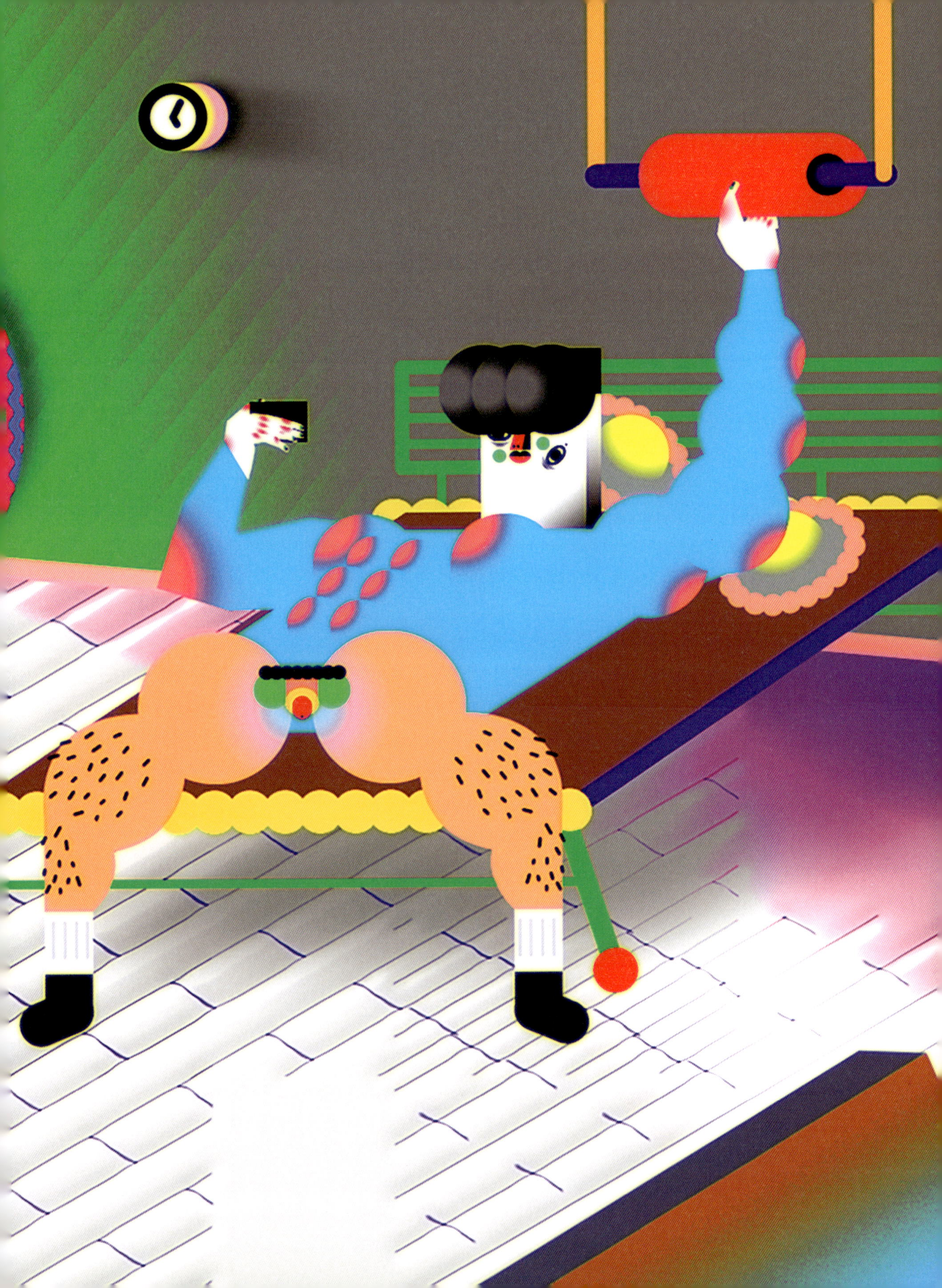

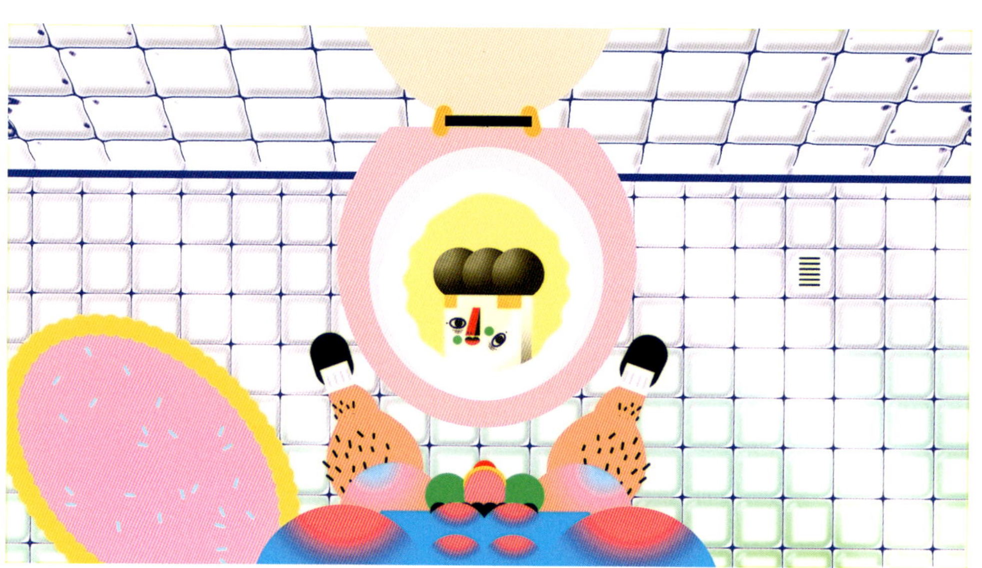

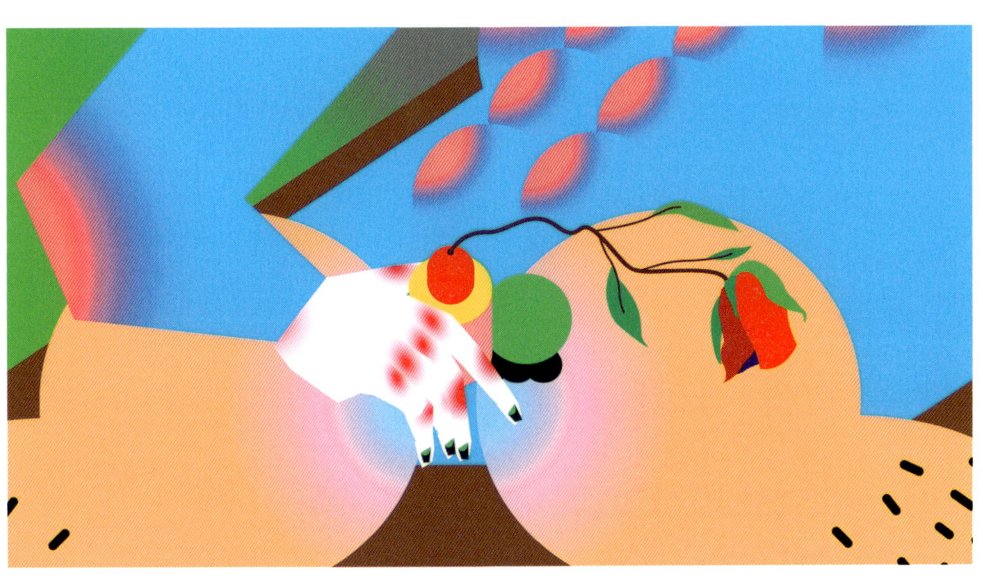

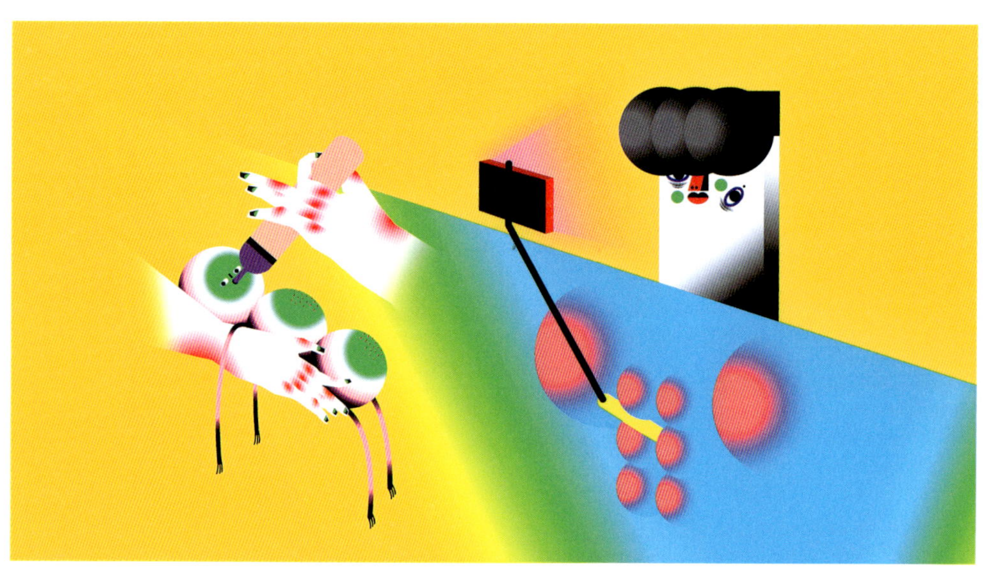

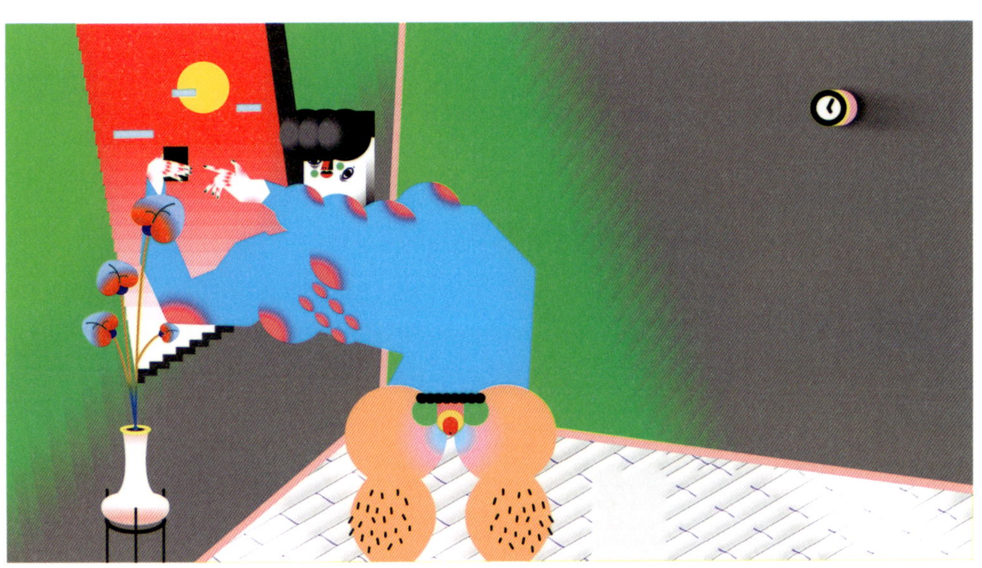

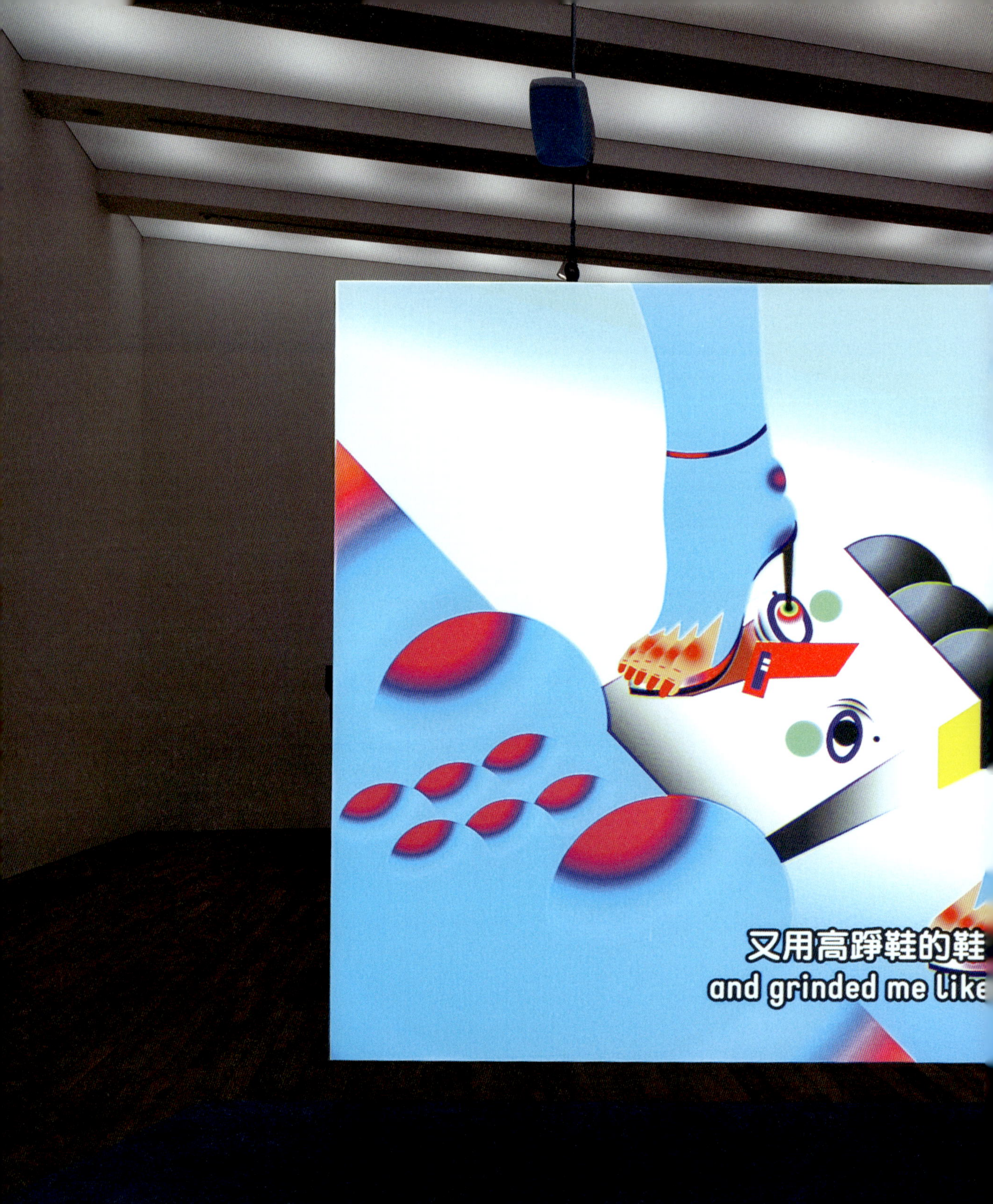

Who's the Daddy?, 2017. Installation view, "Performing Society: The Violence of Gender,"
Tai Kwun Contemporary, Hong Kong, 2019

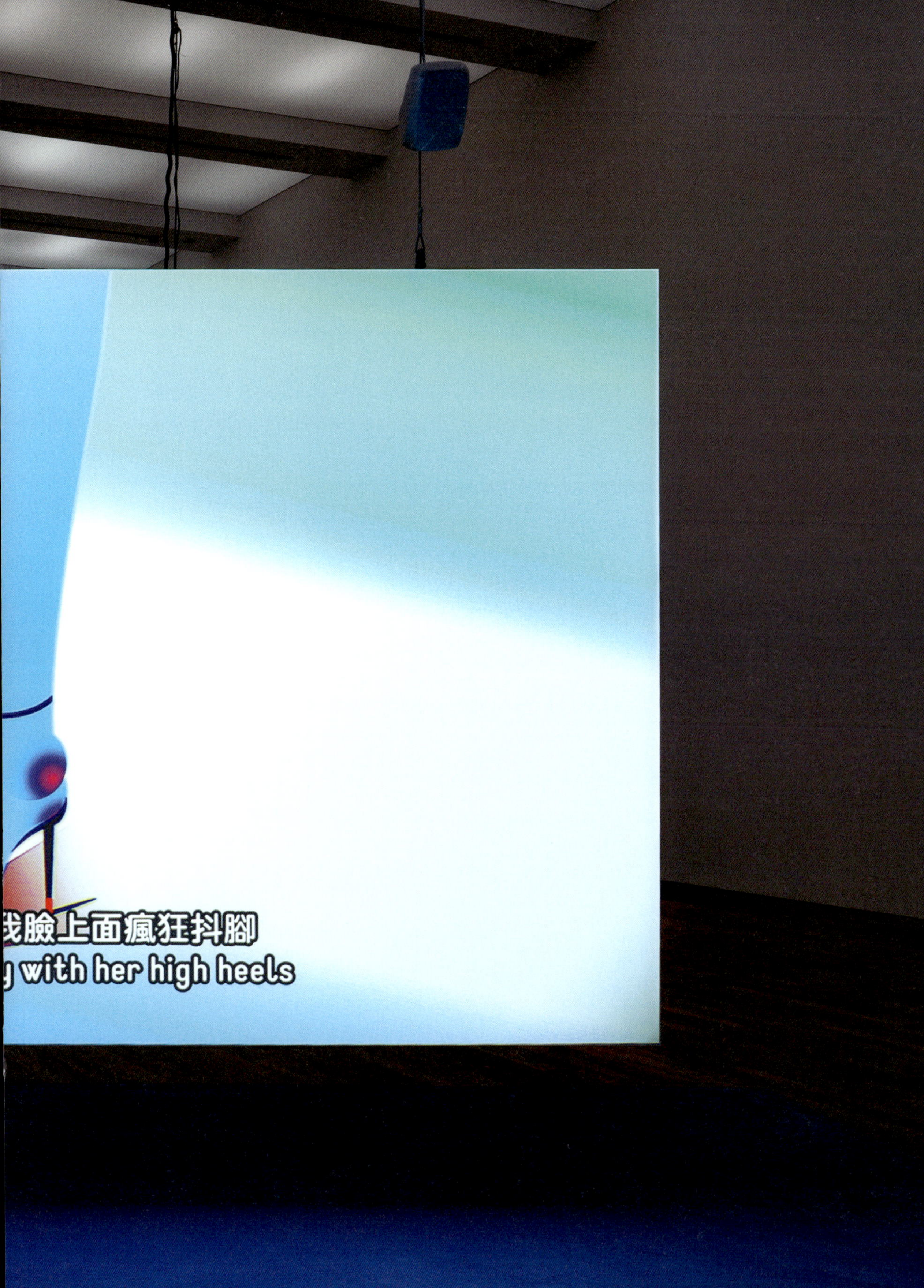

我臉上面瘋狂抖腳
g with her high heels

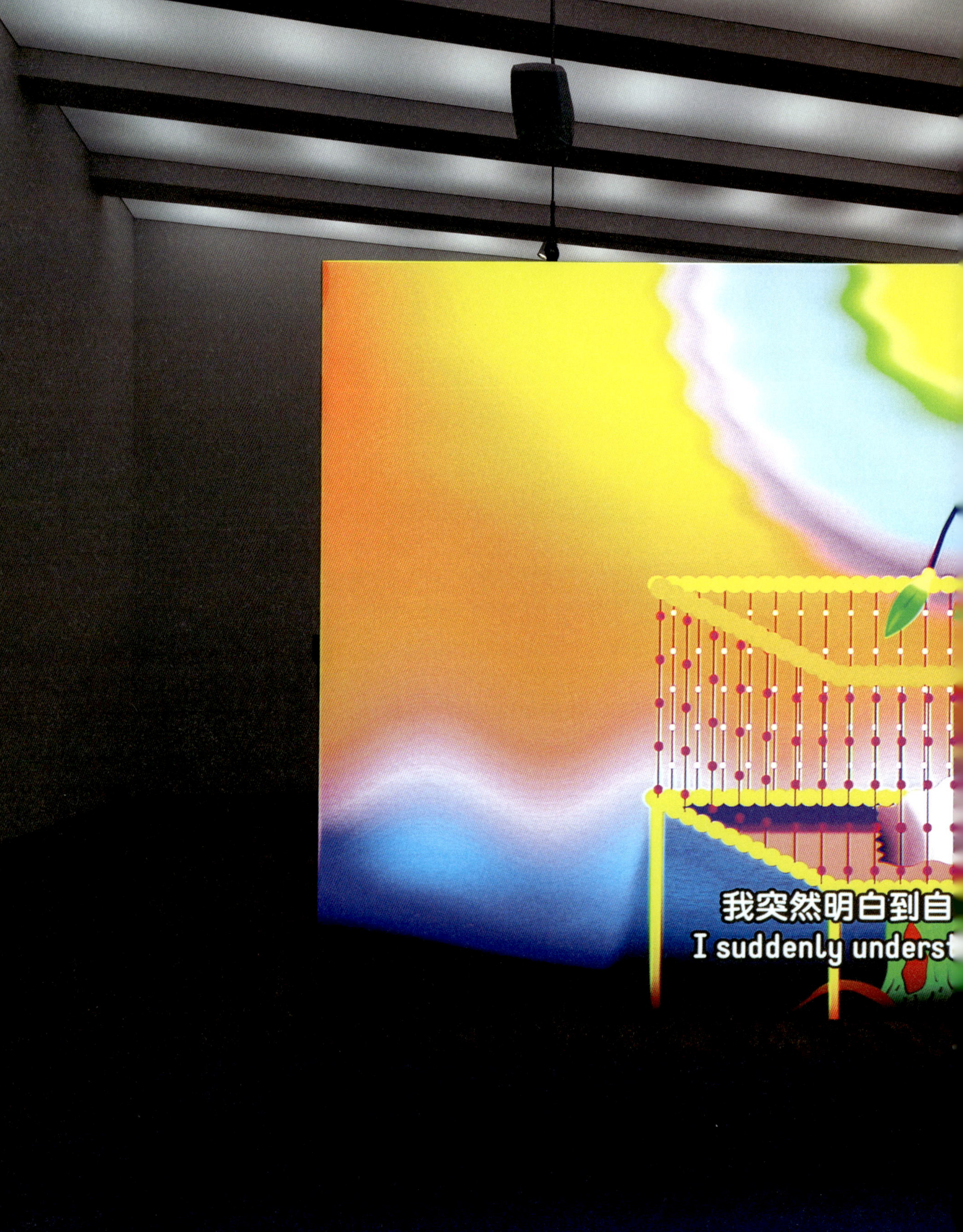

我突然明白到自
I suddenly underst

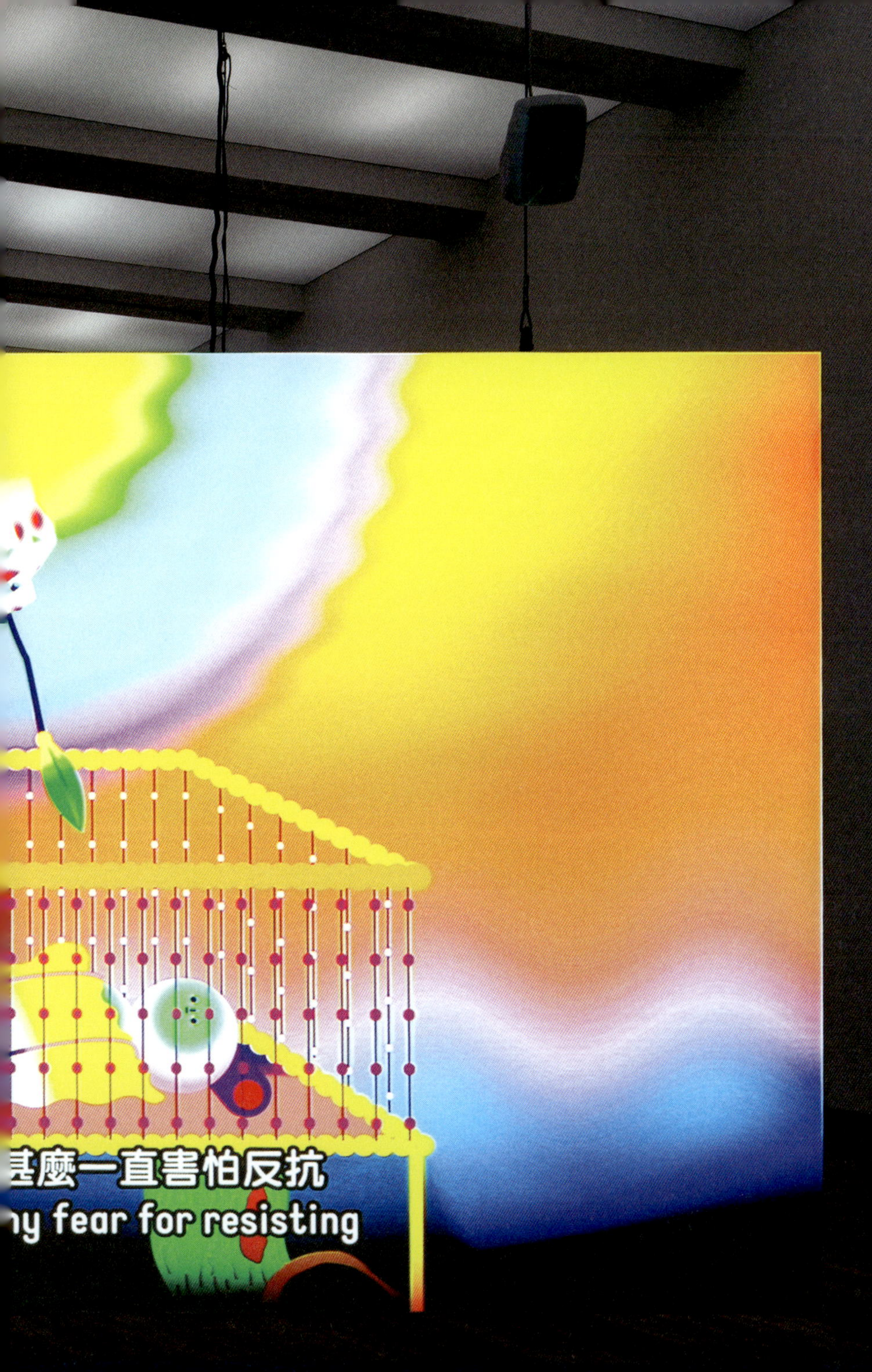
甚麼一直害怕反抗
hy fear for resisting

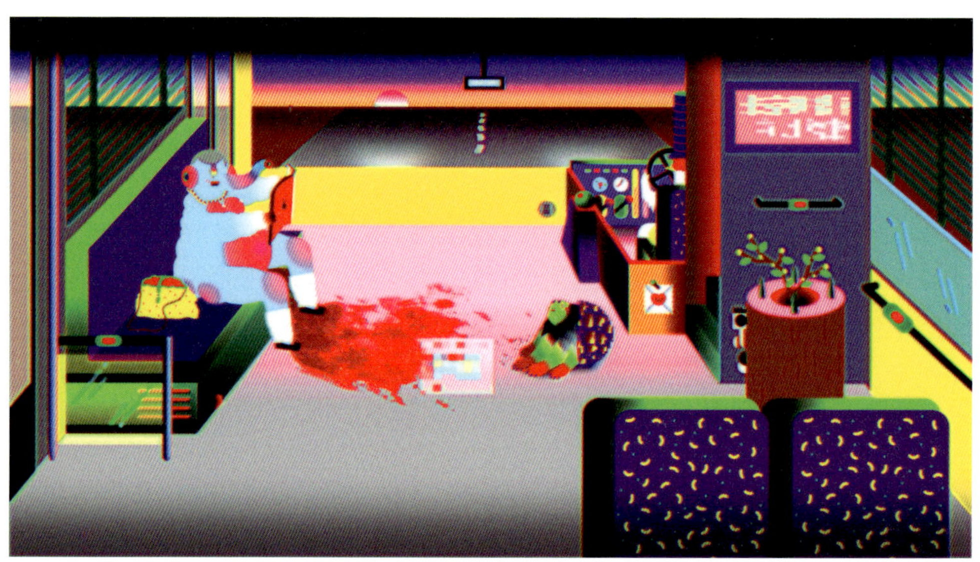

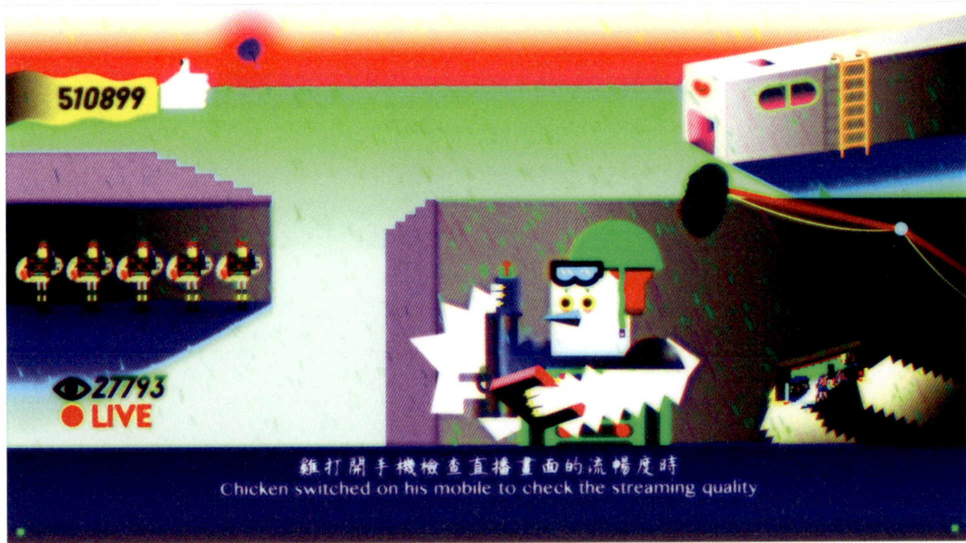

510899
27793
LIVE
雞打開手機檢查直播畫面的流暢度時
Chicken switched on his mobile to check the streaming quality

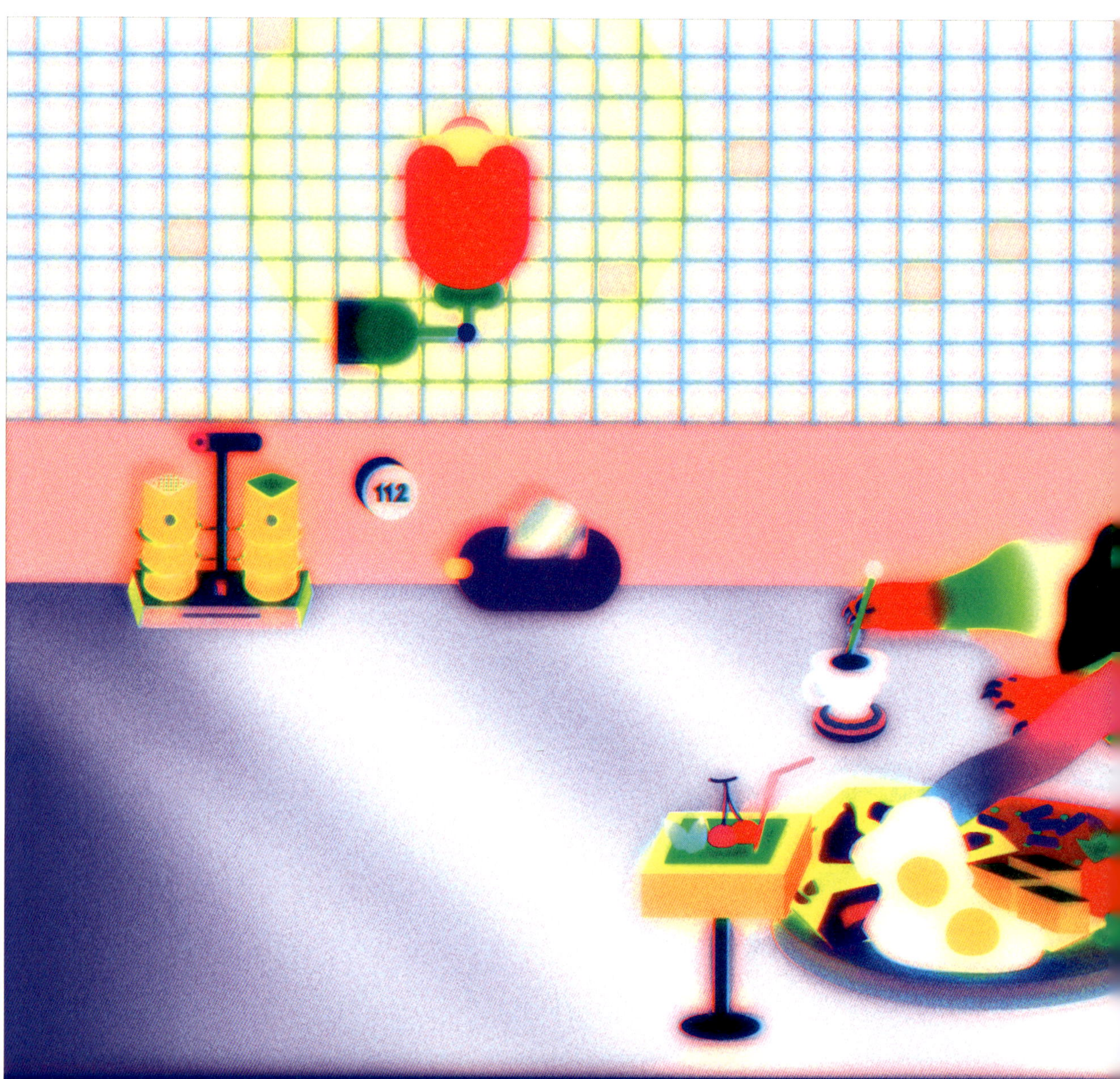

龜心想尼
Turtle thought, "Ho

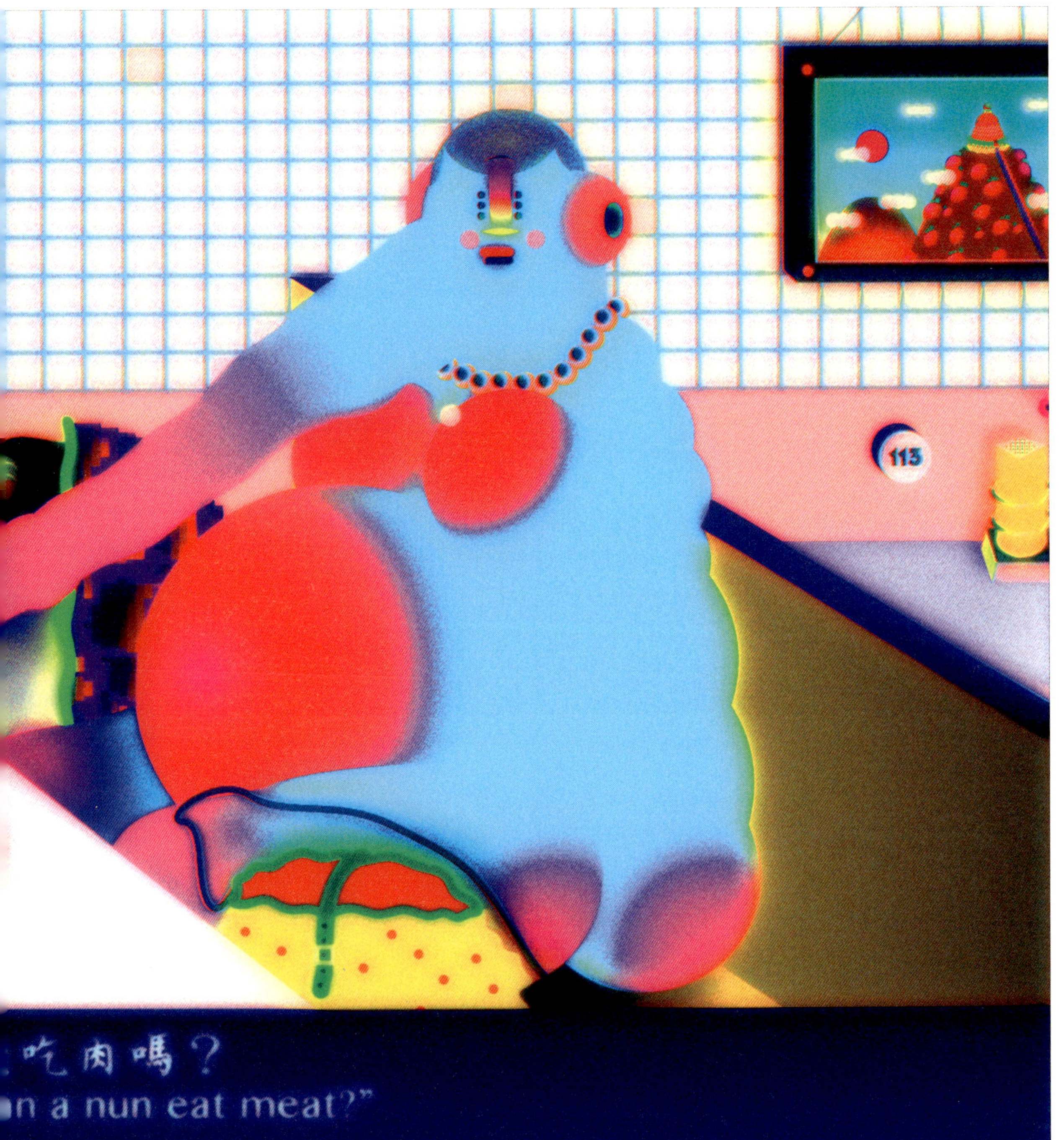
吃肉嗎？
n a nun eat meat?"

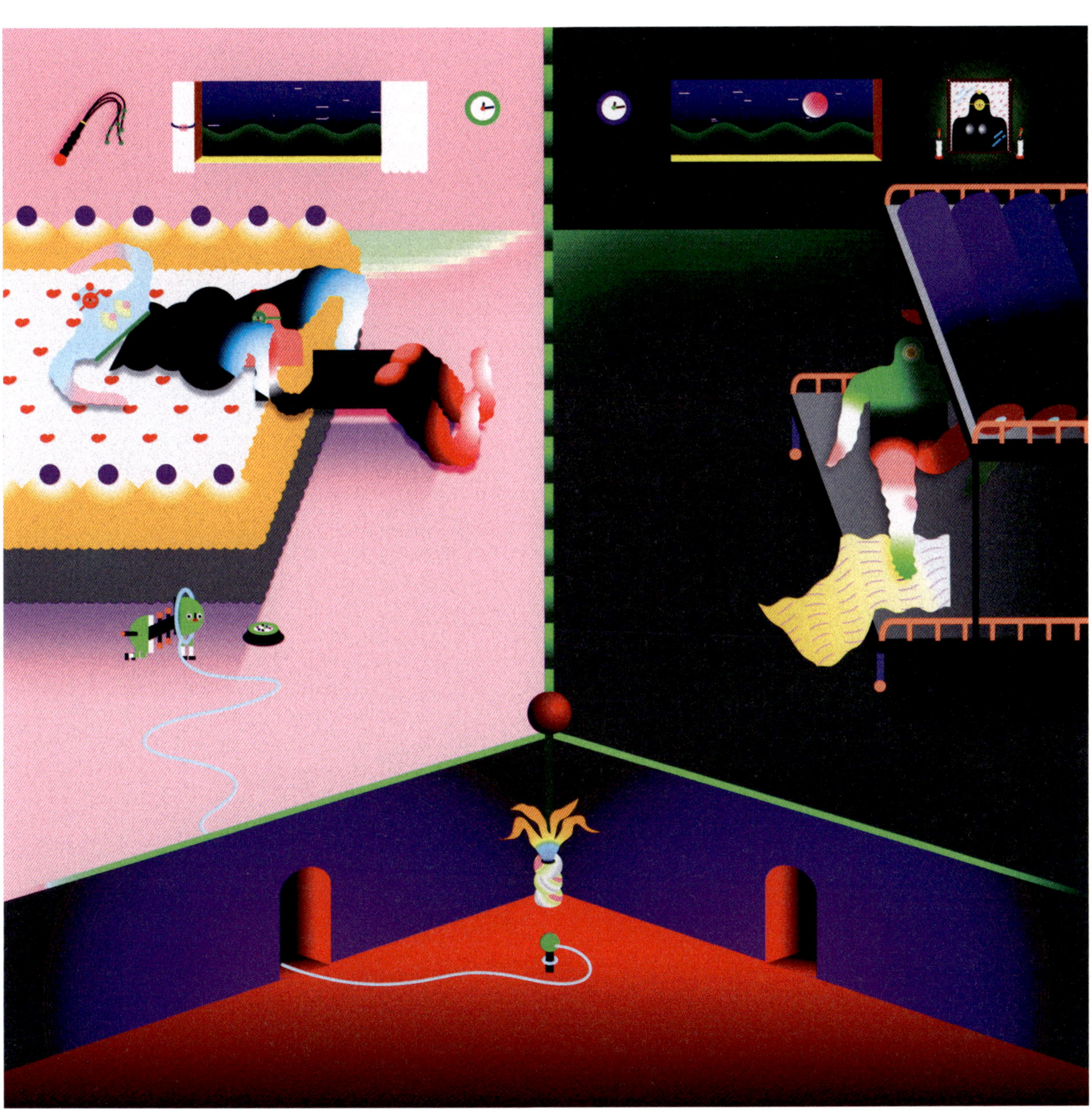

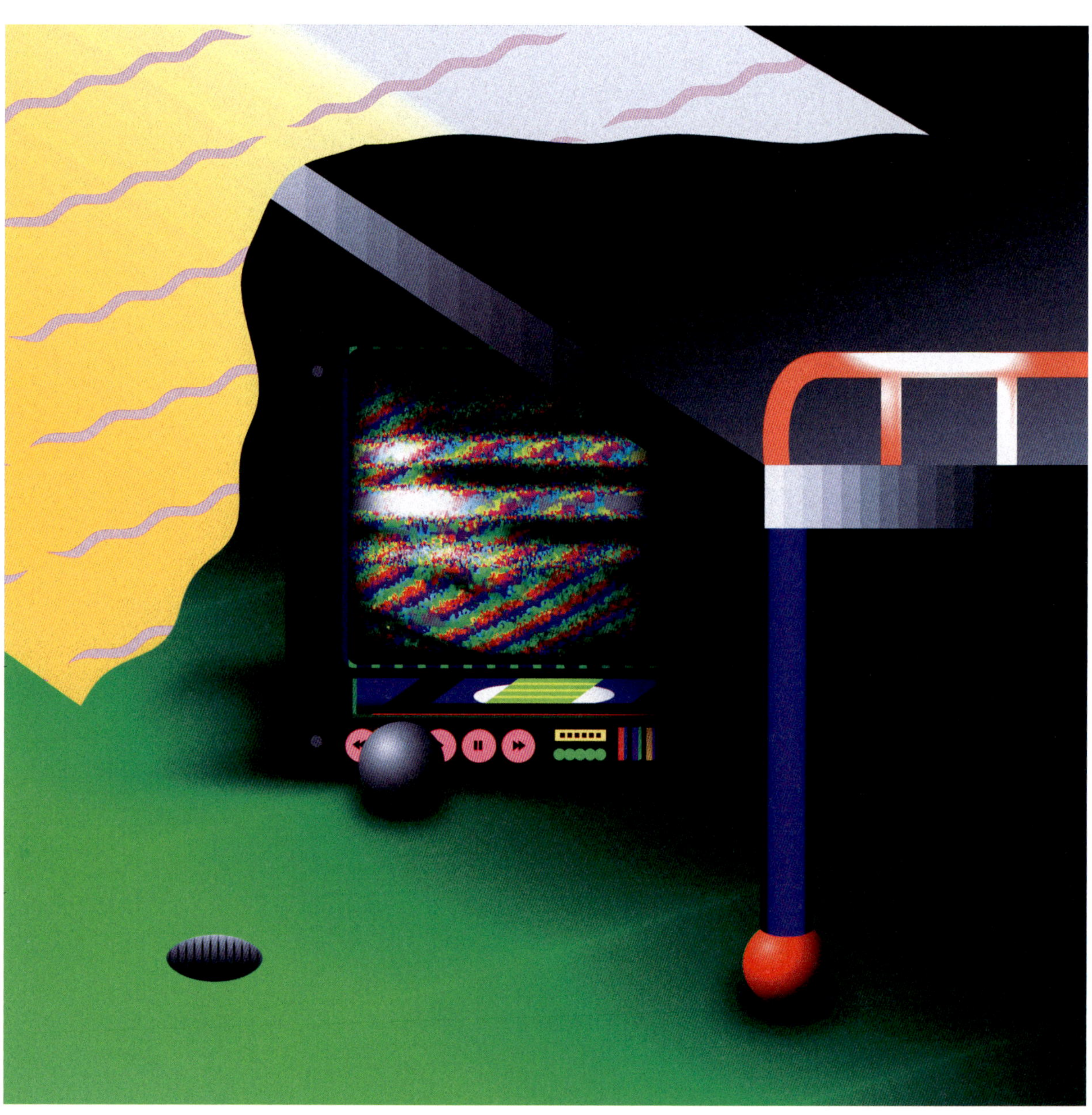

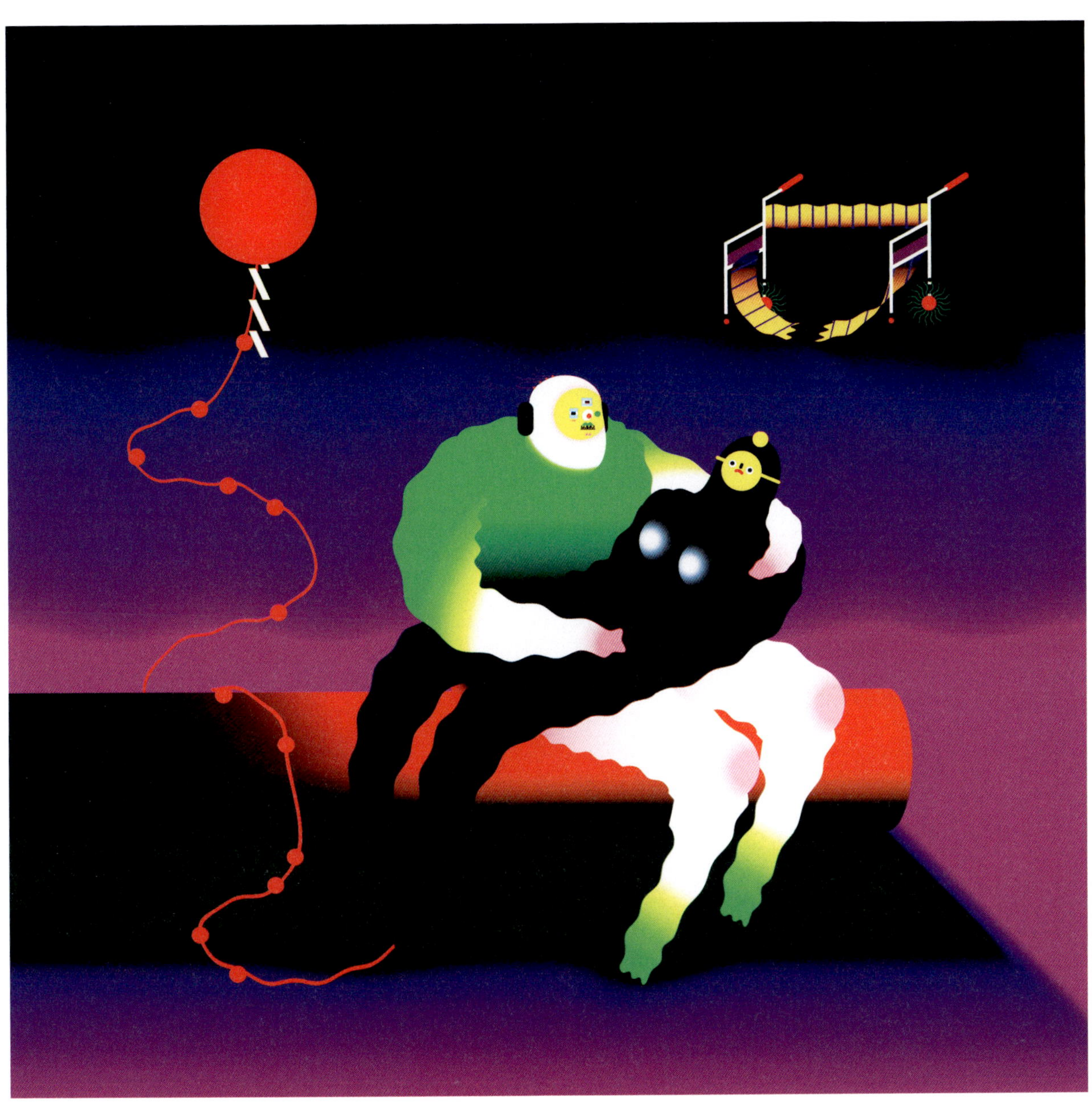

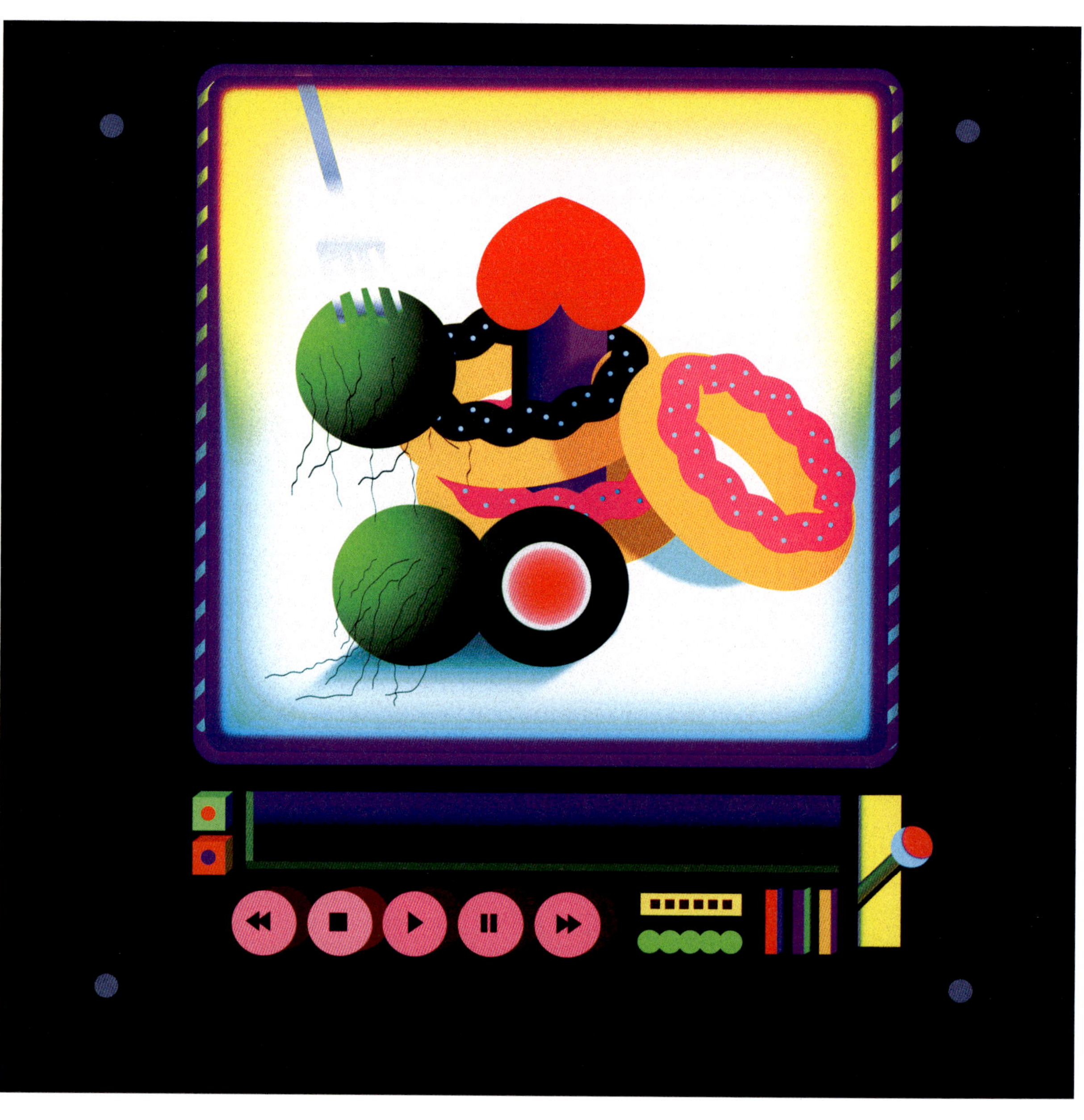

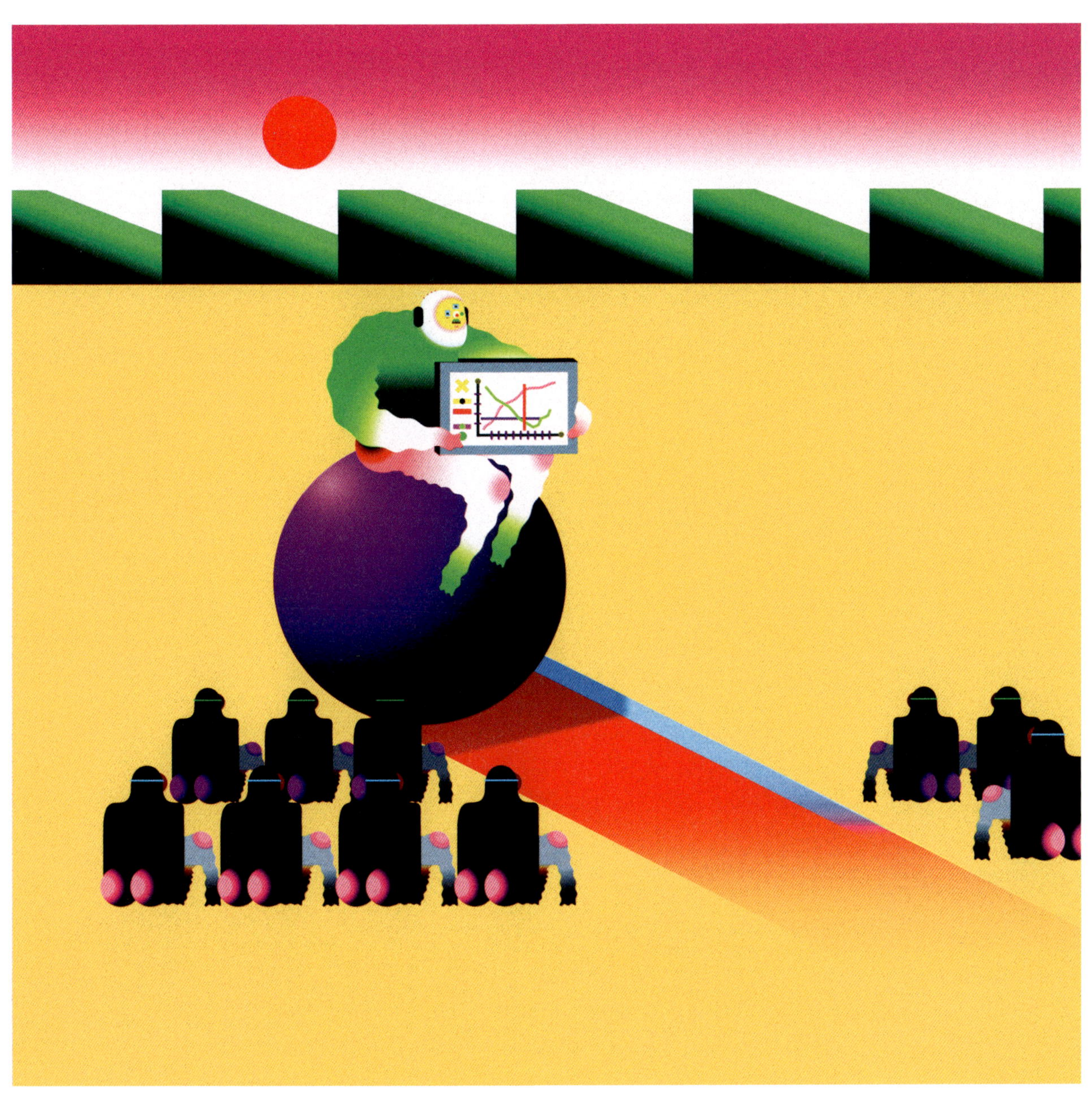

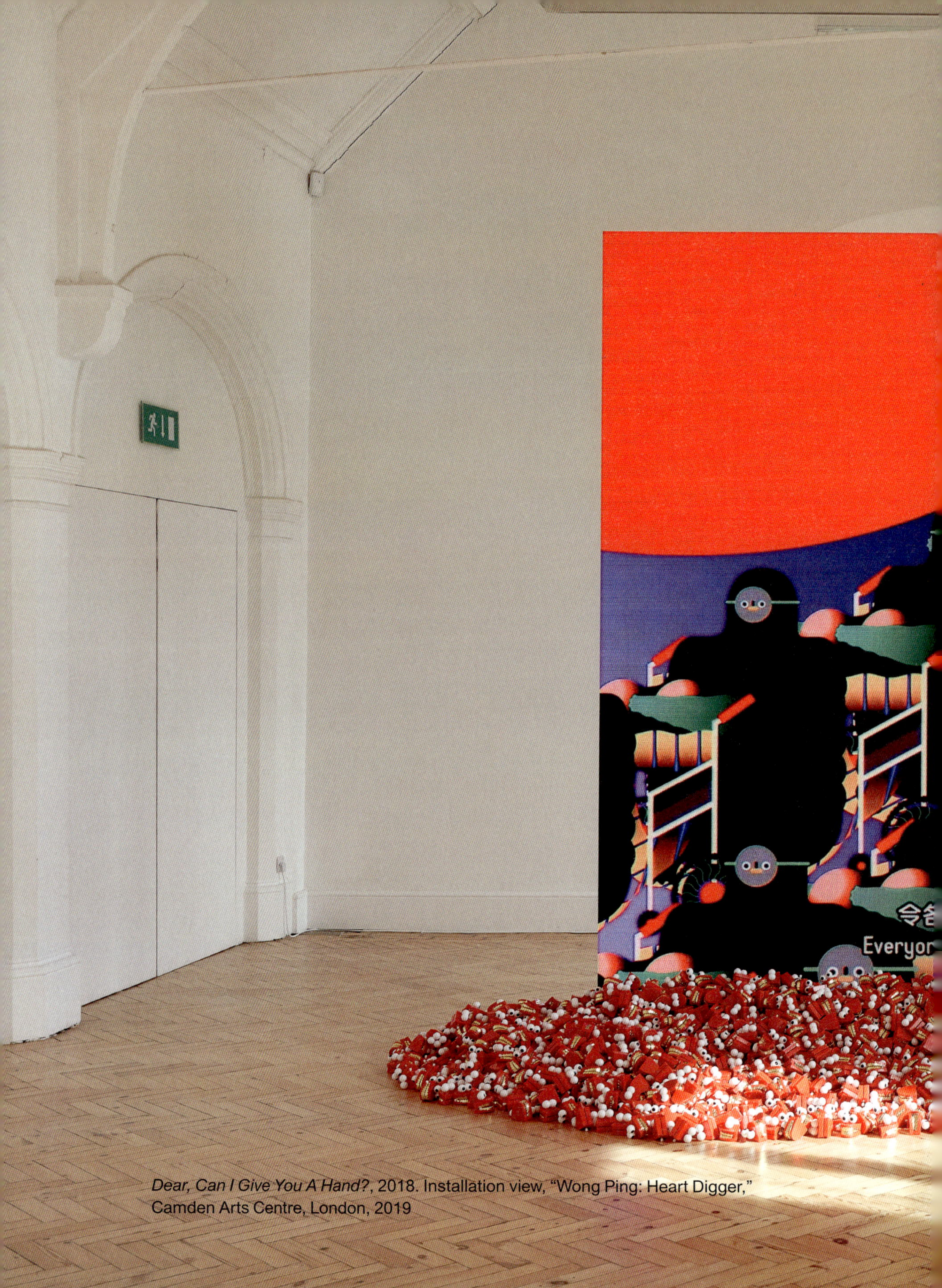

Dear, Can I Give You A Hand?, 2018. Installation view, "Wong Ping: Heart Digger,"
Camden Arts Centre, London, 2019

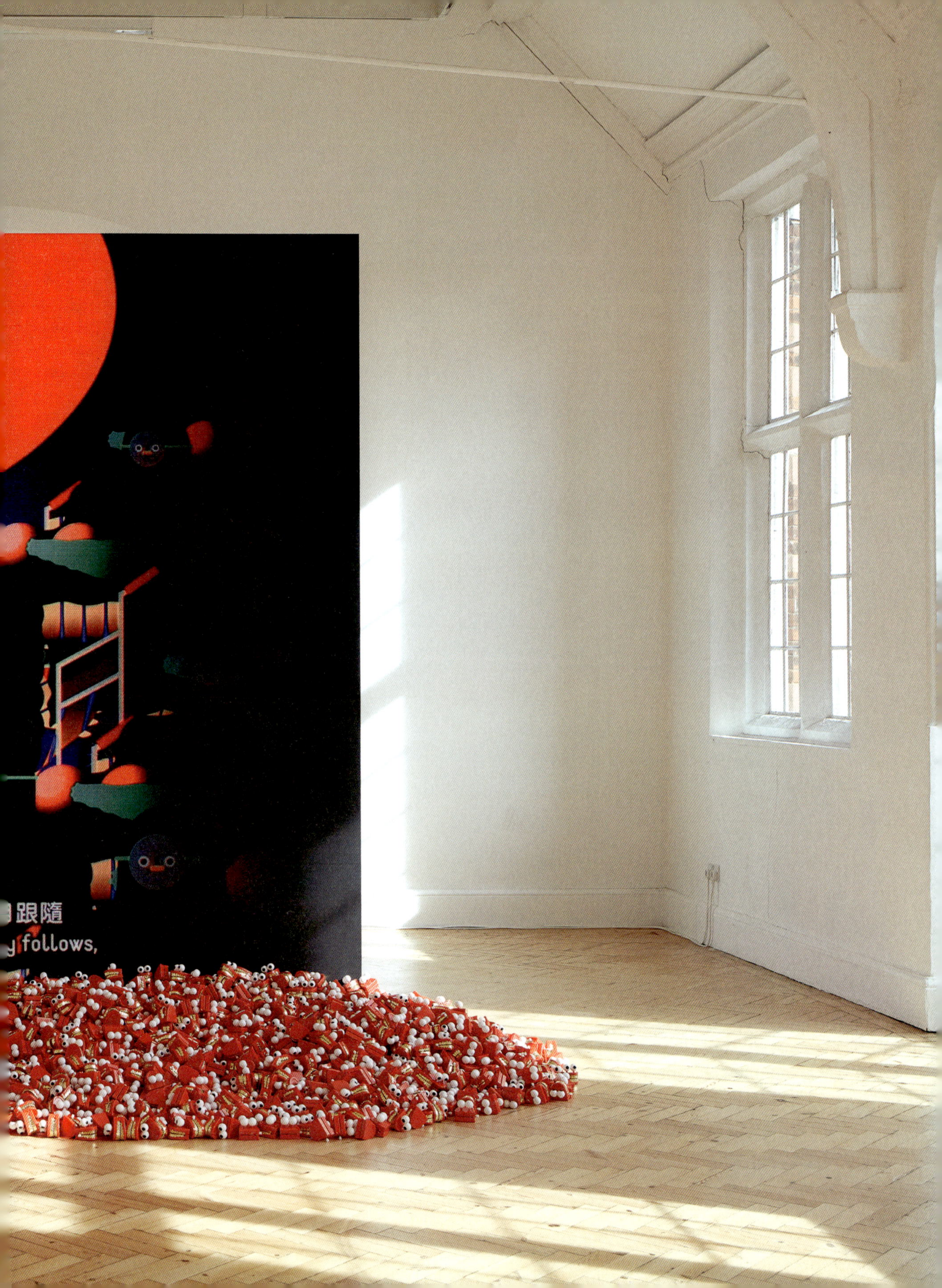
跟隨
follows,

Dear, Can I Give You A Hand?, 2018. Installation view, "One Hand Clapping,"
Solomon R. Guggenheim Museum, New York, 2018

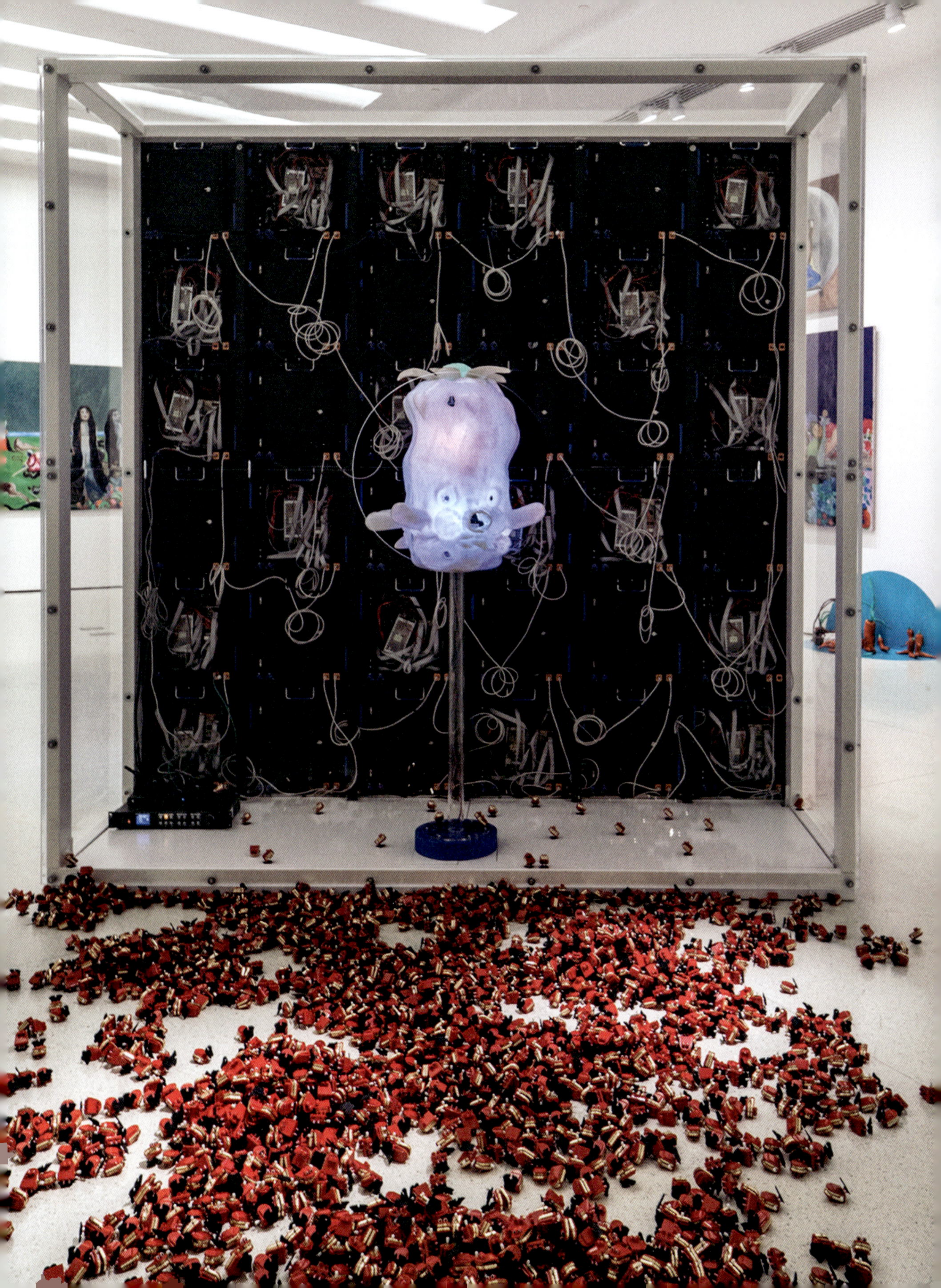

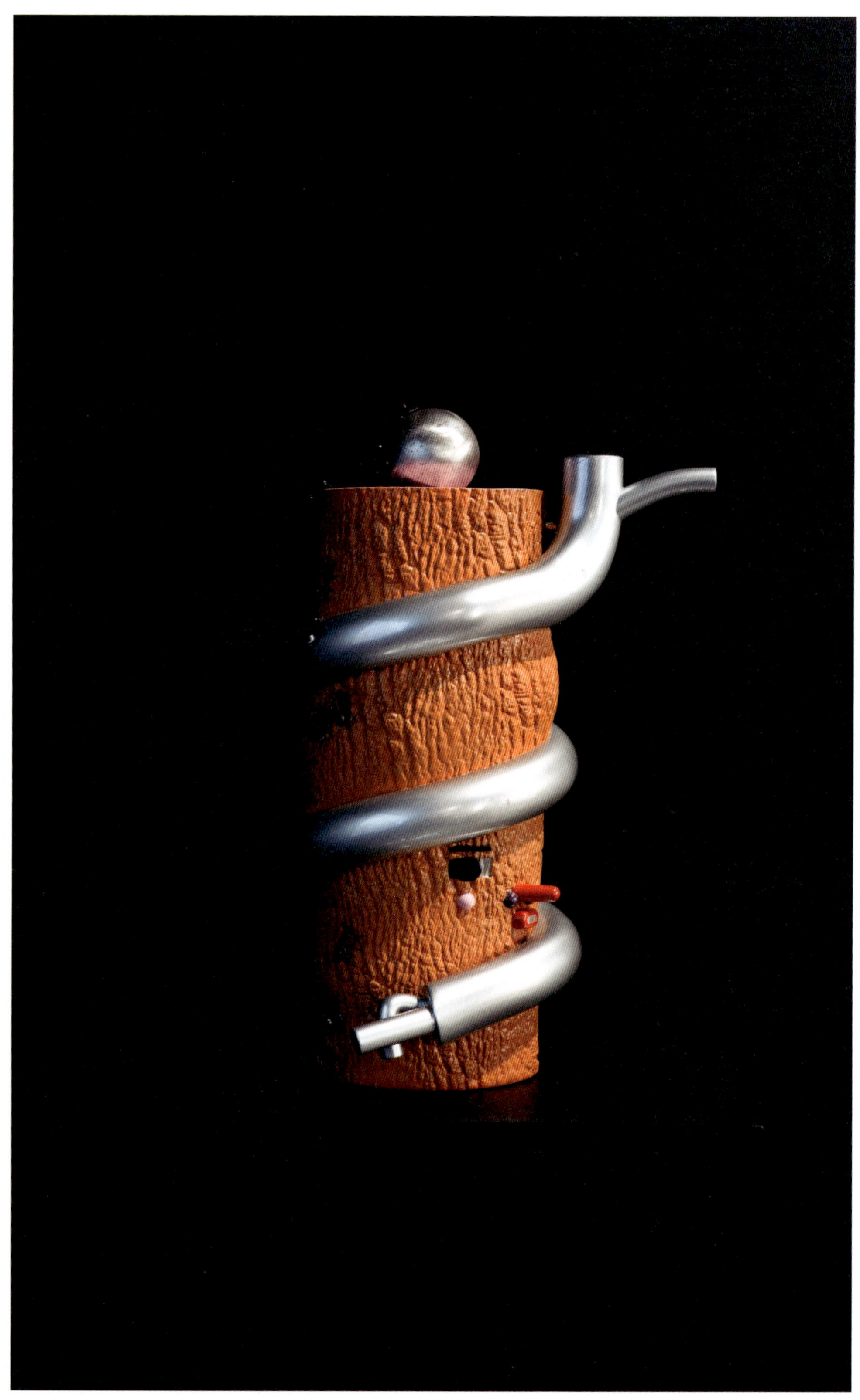

Tree takes on part-time body rental for Pole to do tree dance during his spare time, 2018

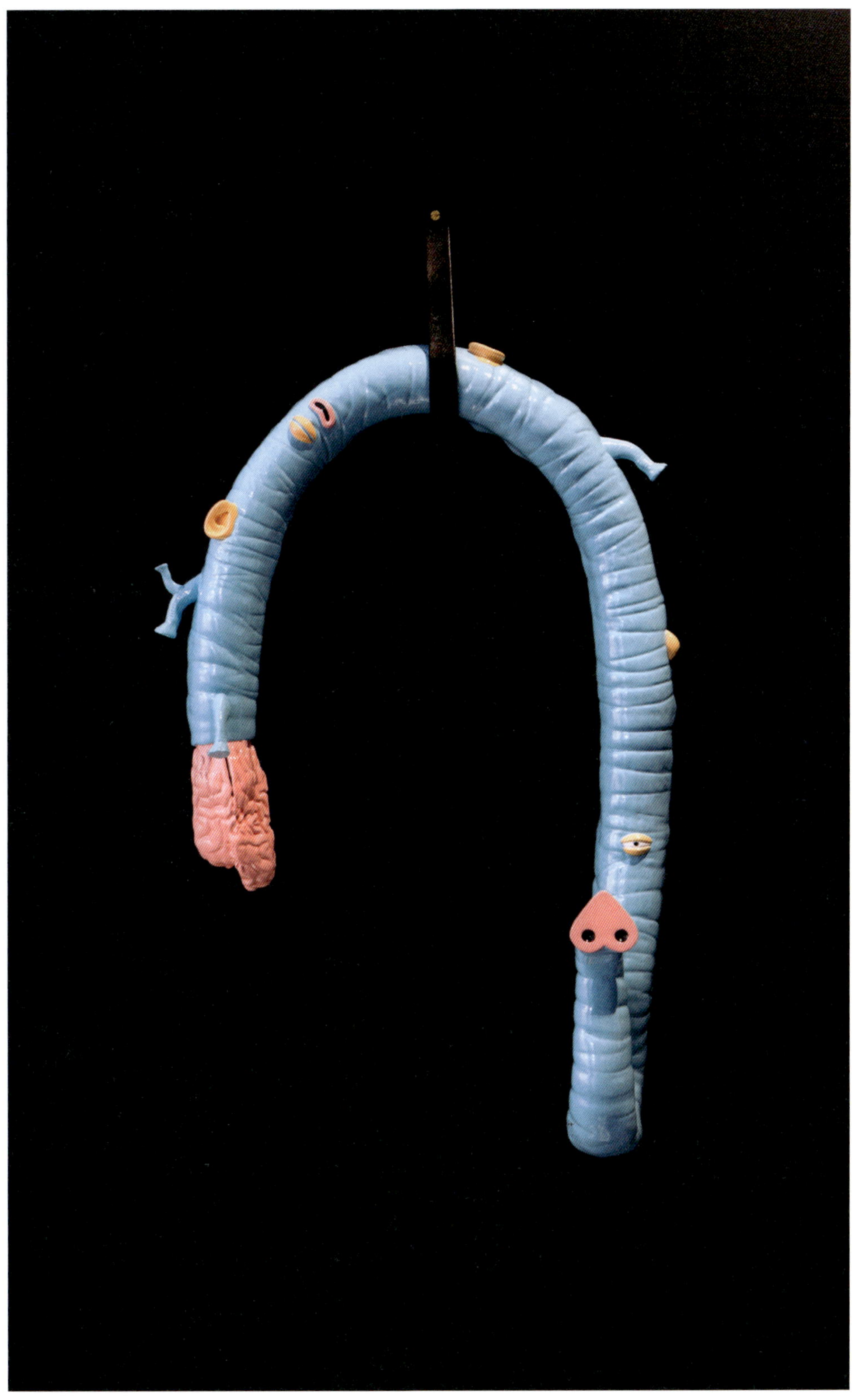

Premature Elephant, 2018

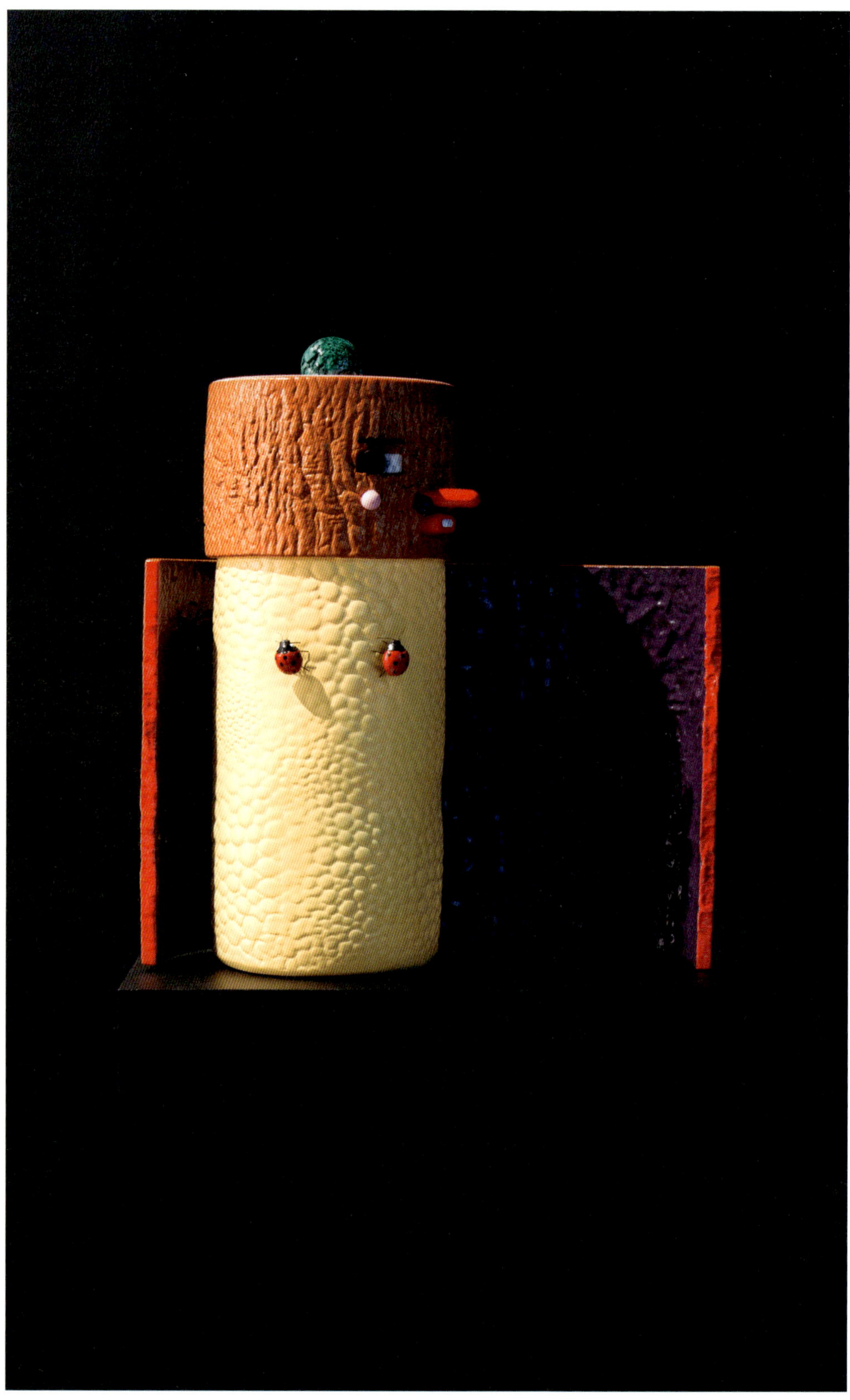

Tree takes on part-time nude life modeling during his spare time, 2018

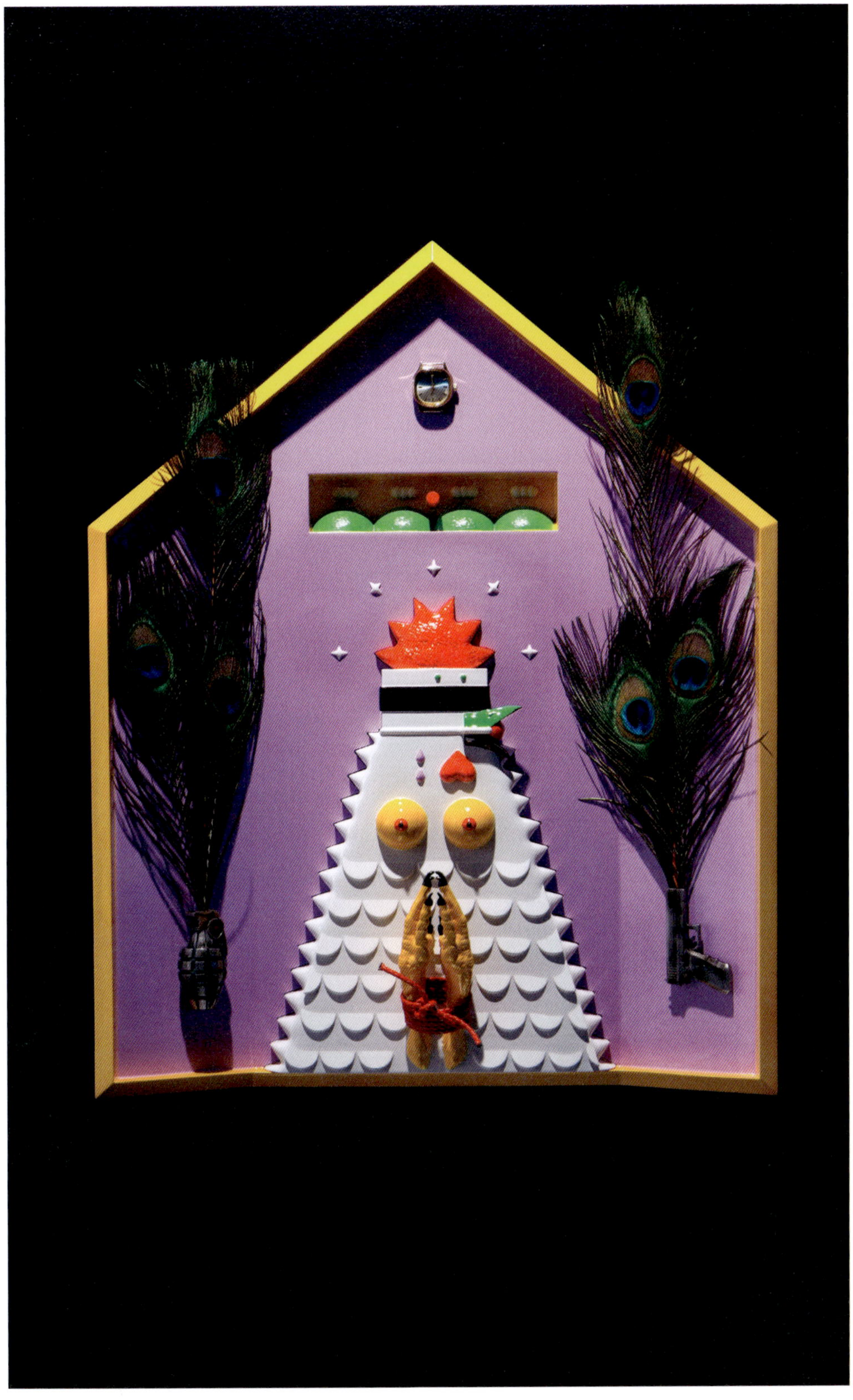

   Kidnapped Chicken feels guilty for his inability to crow before sunrise, 2018

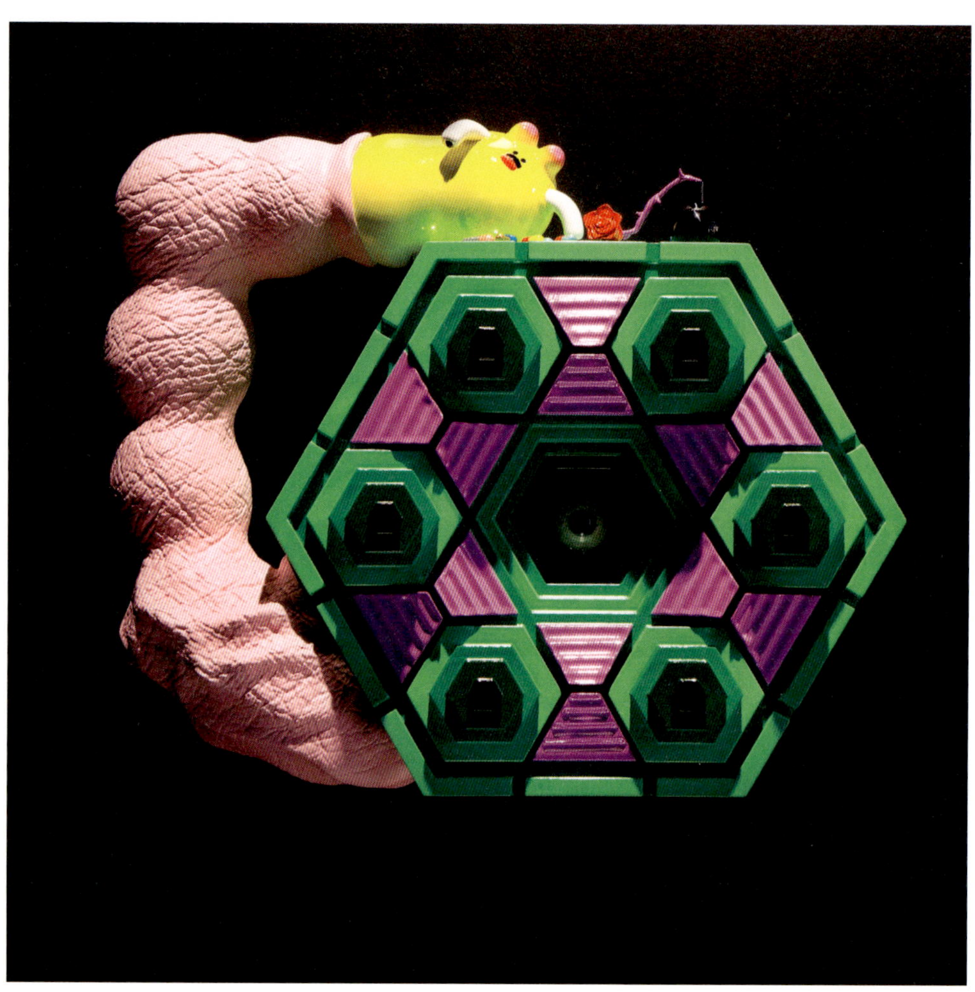

Turtle, who is often called by the name of penis because of his looks, suffers from severe depression and takes poison to commit suicide, 2018

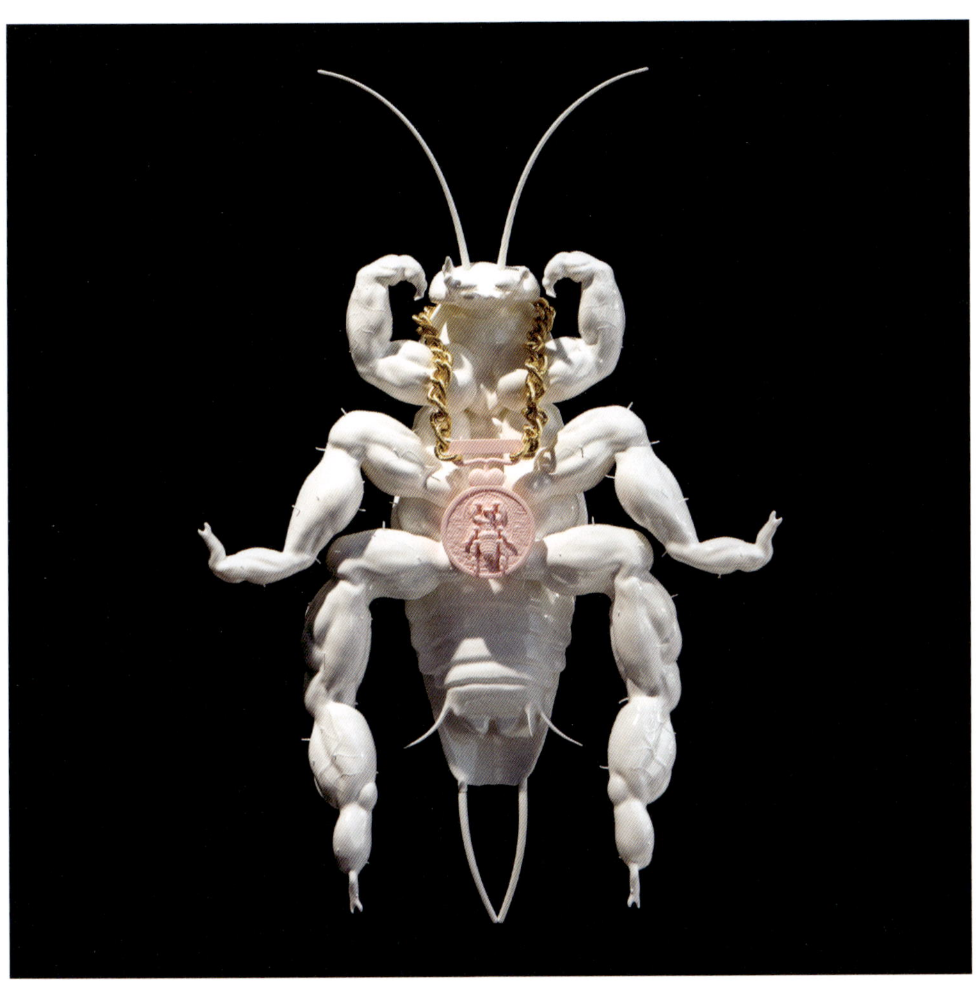

*Albino Cockroach becomes the lightest colour bodybuilding
championship winner in history*, 2018

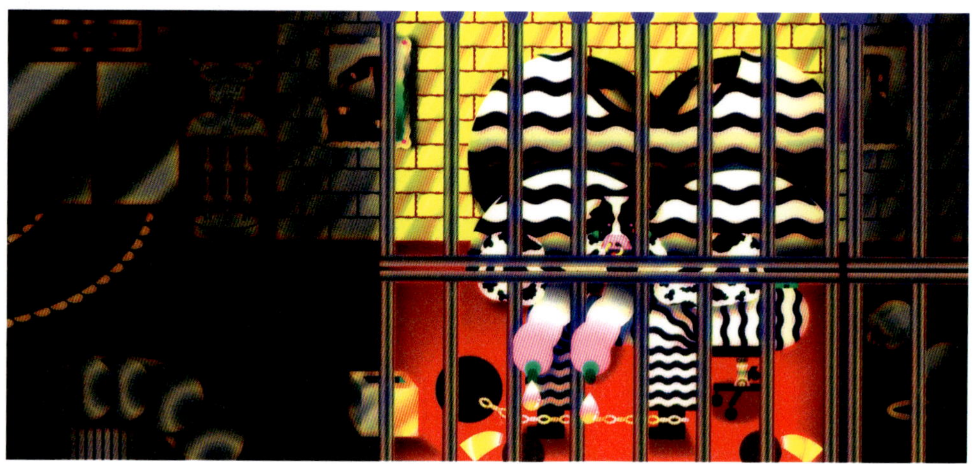

Wong Ping's Fables 2, 2019

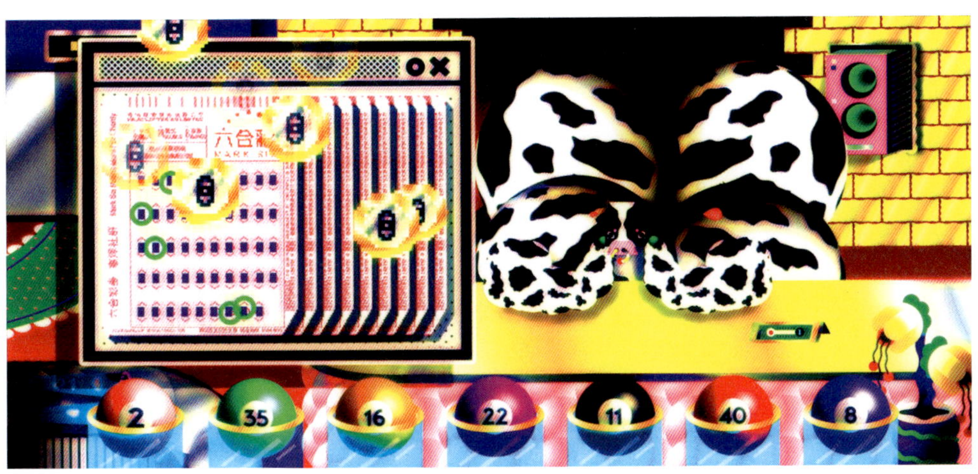
六合彩
2
35
16
22
11
40
8

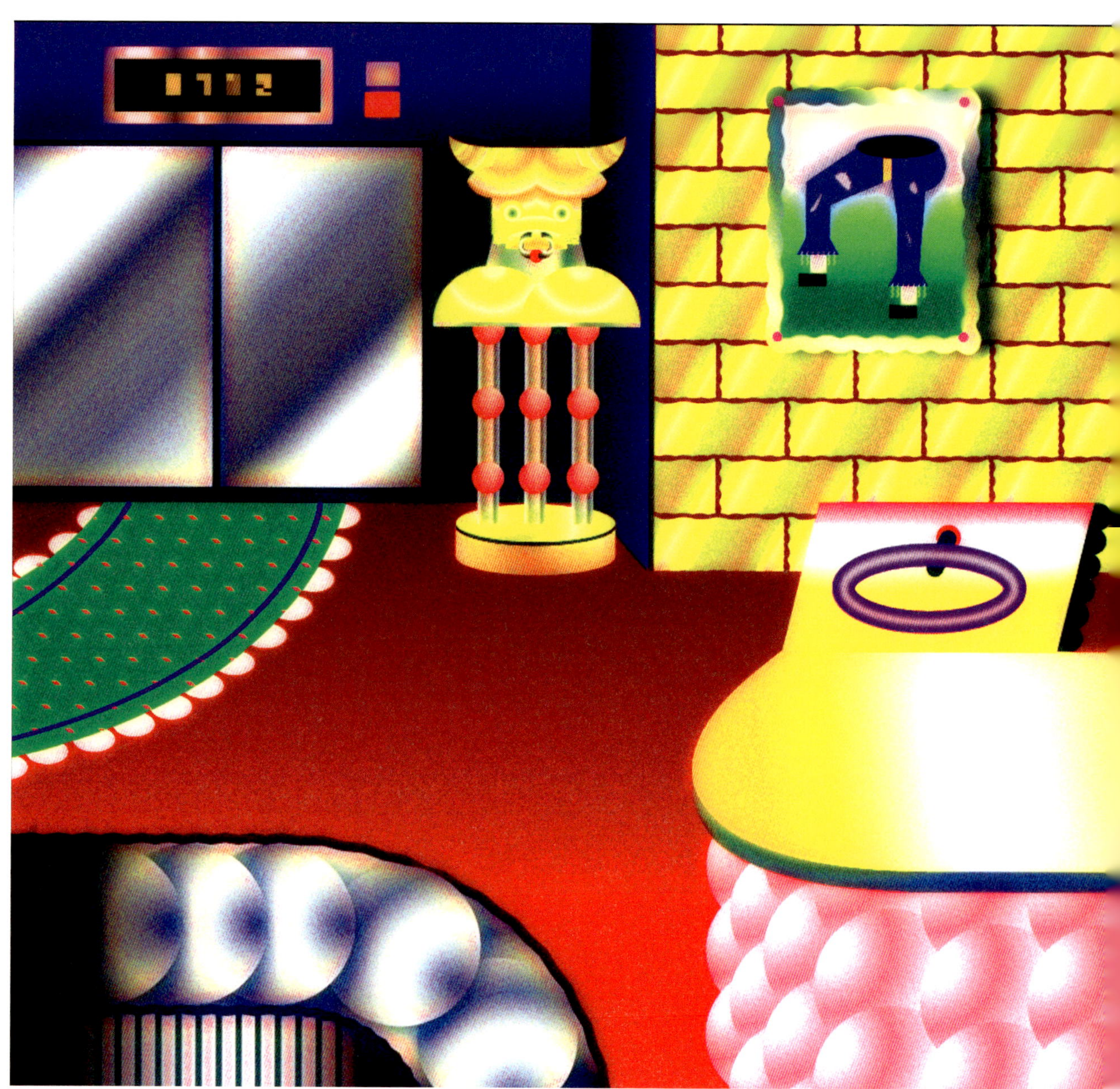

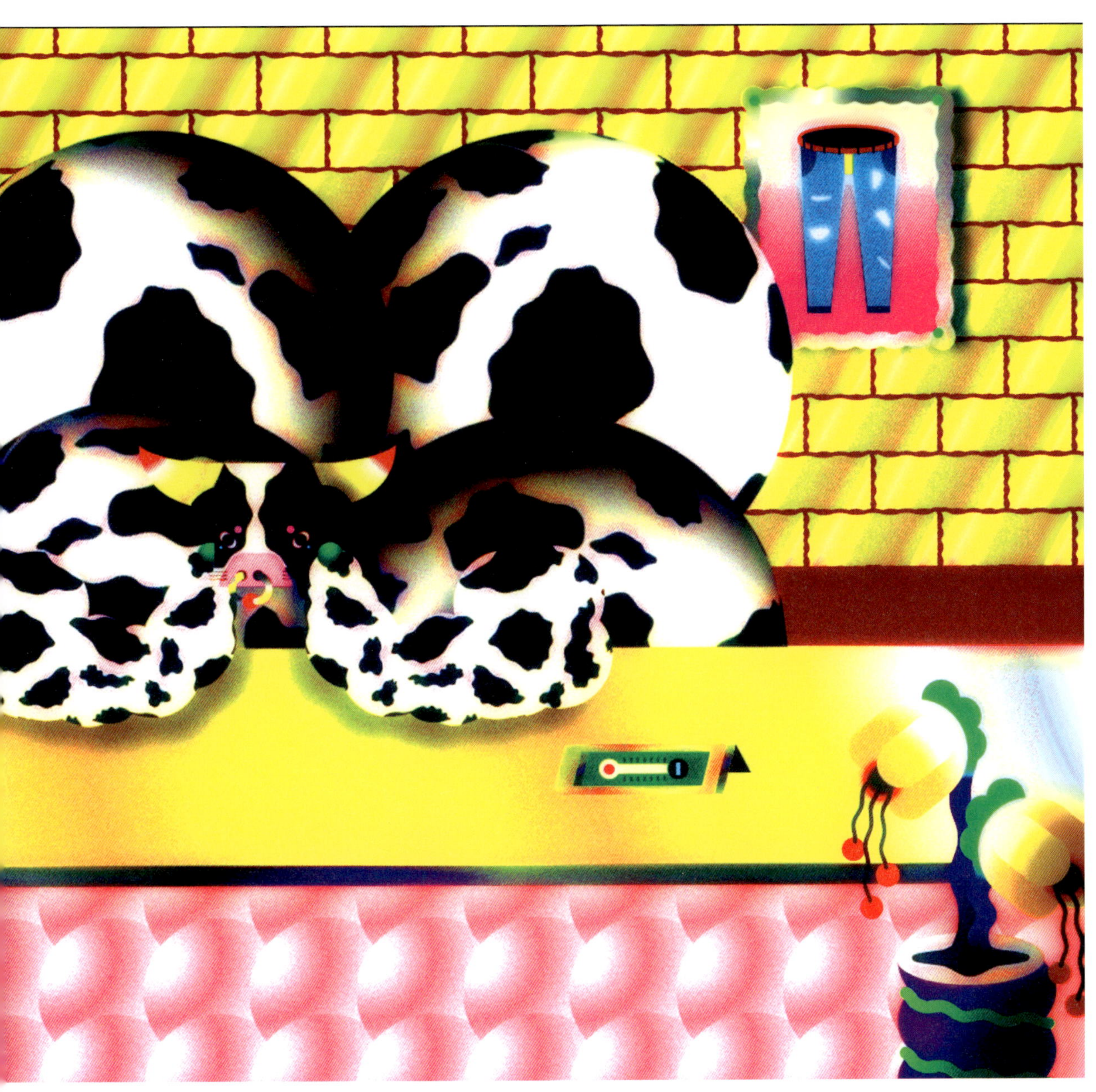

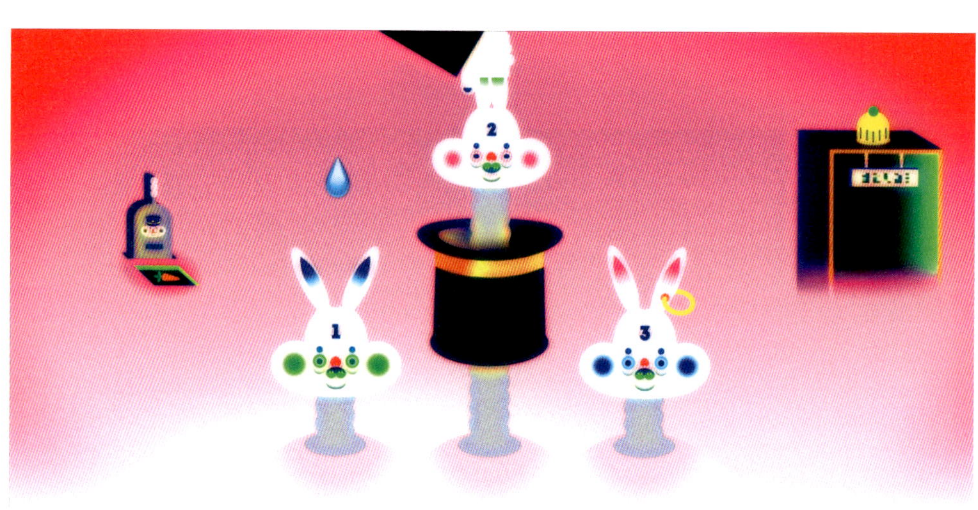

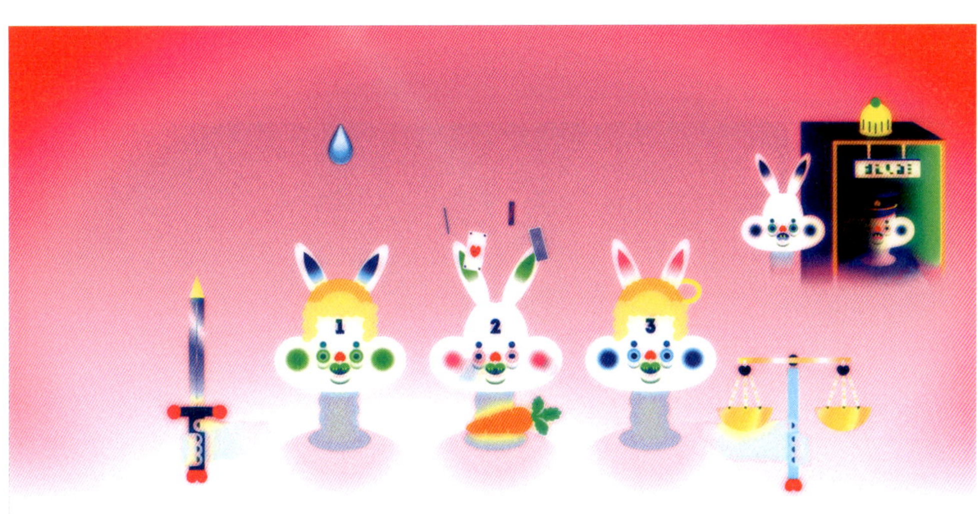

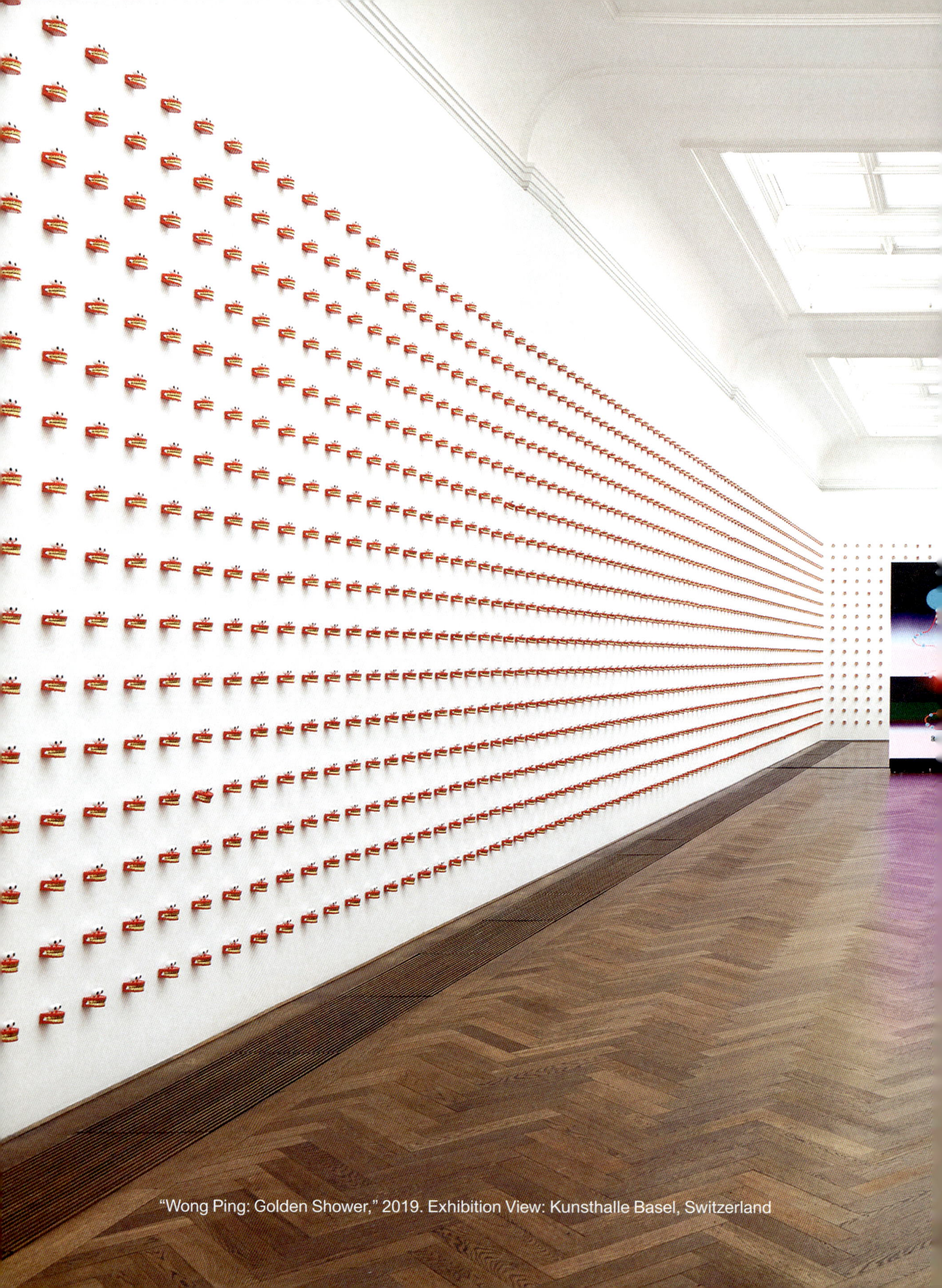

"Wong Ping: Golden Shower," 2019. Exhibition View: Kunsthalle Basel, Switzerland

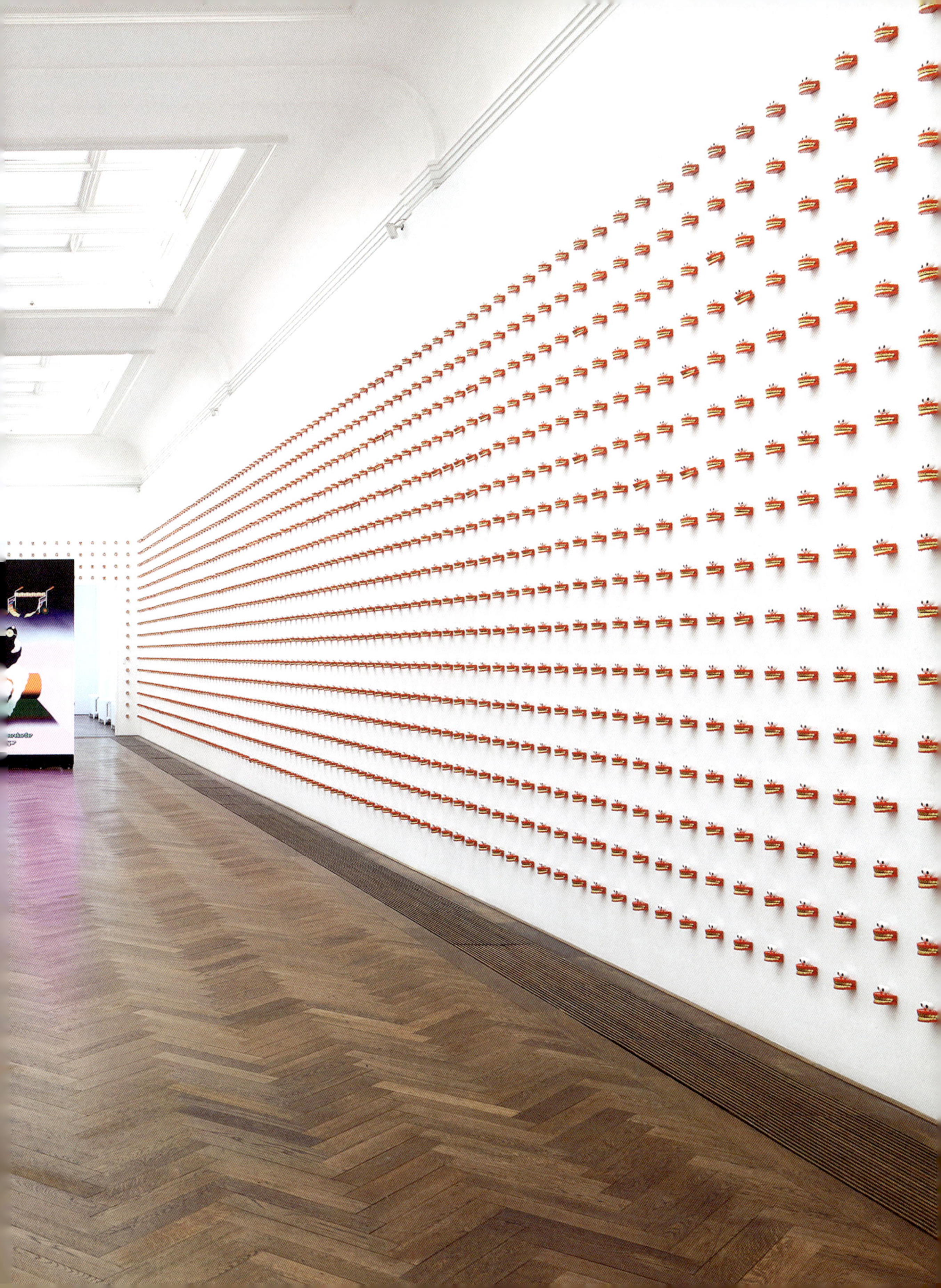

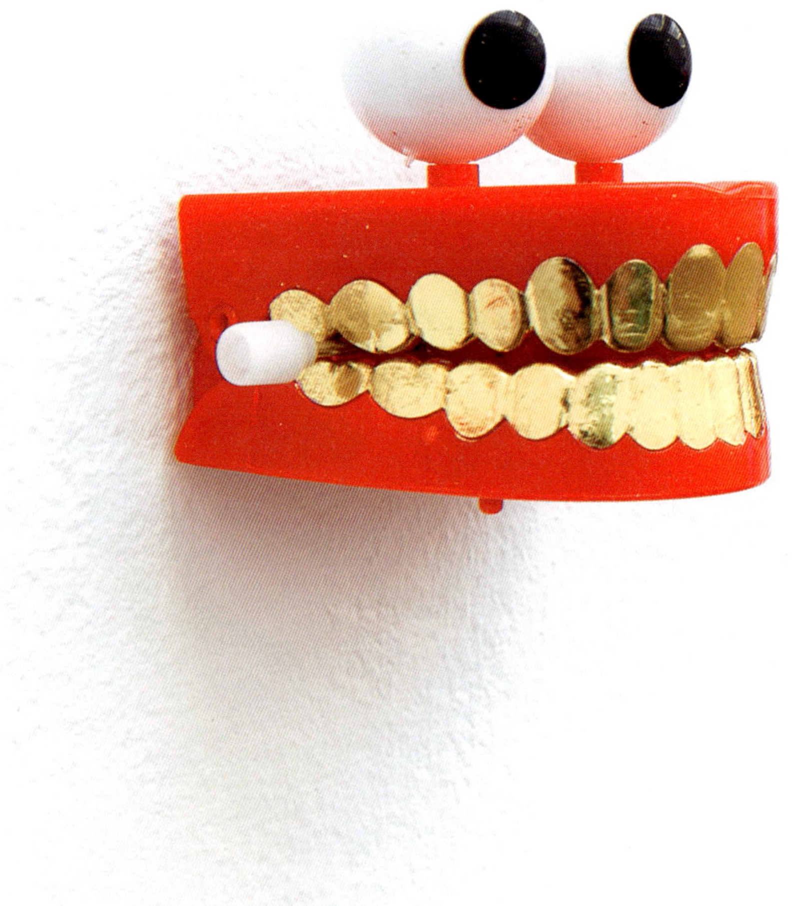

The Ha Ha Ha Online Cemetery Limited, 2019 (detail). Installation view, "Wong Ping: Golden Shower," Kunshalle Basel, Switzerland, 2019

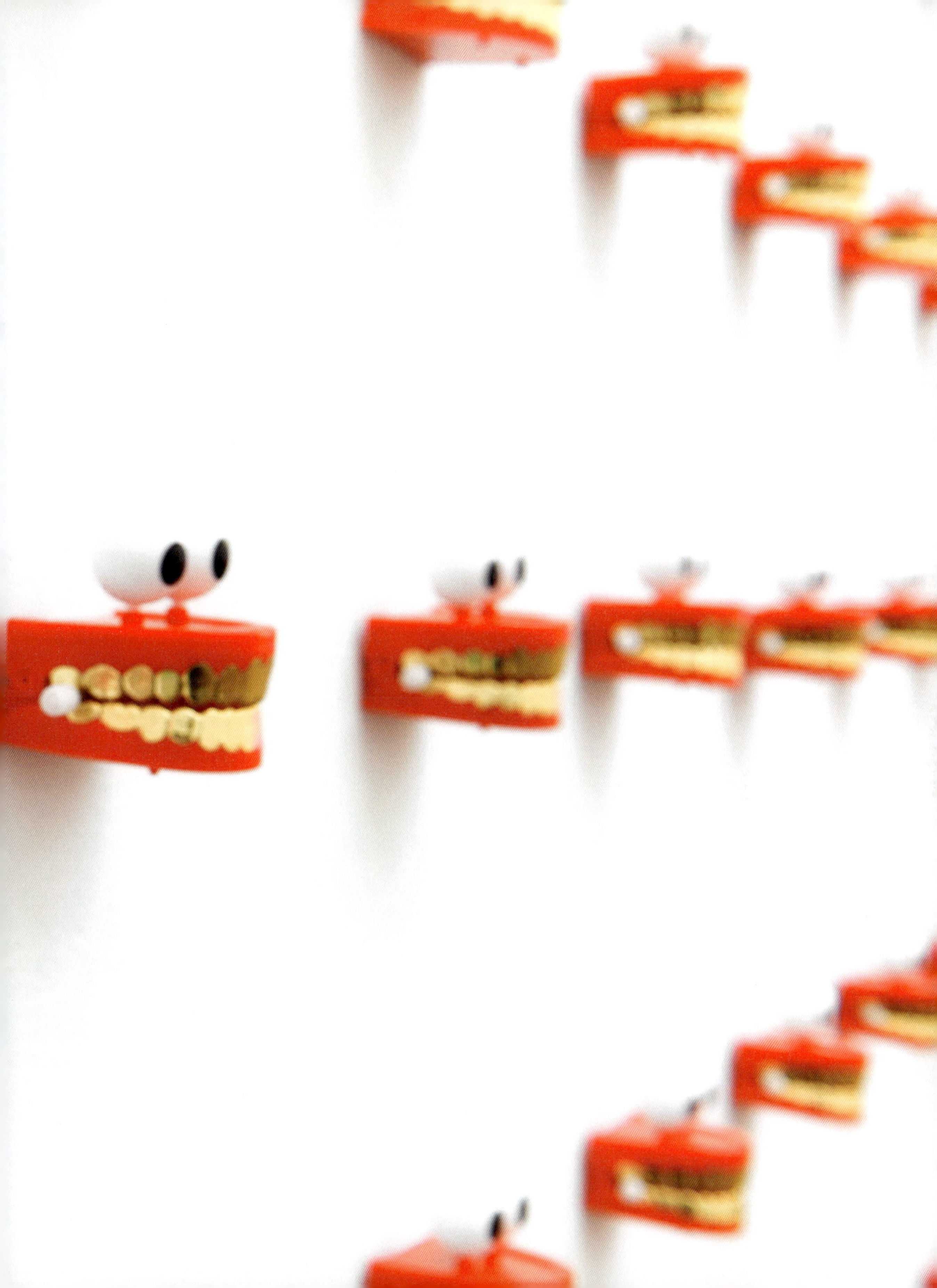

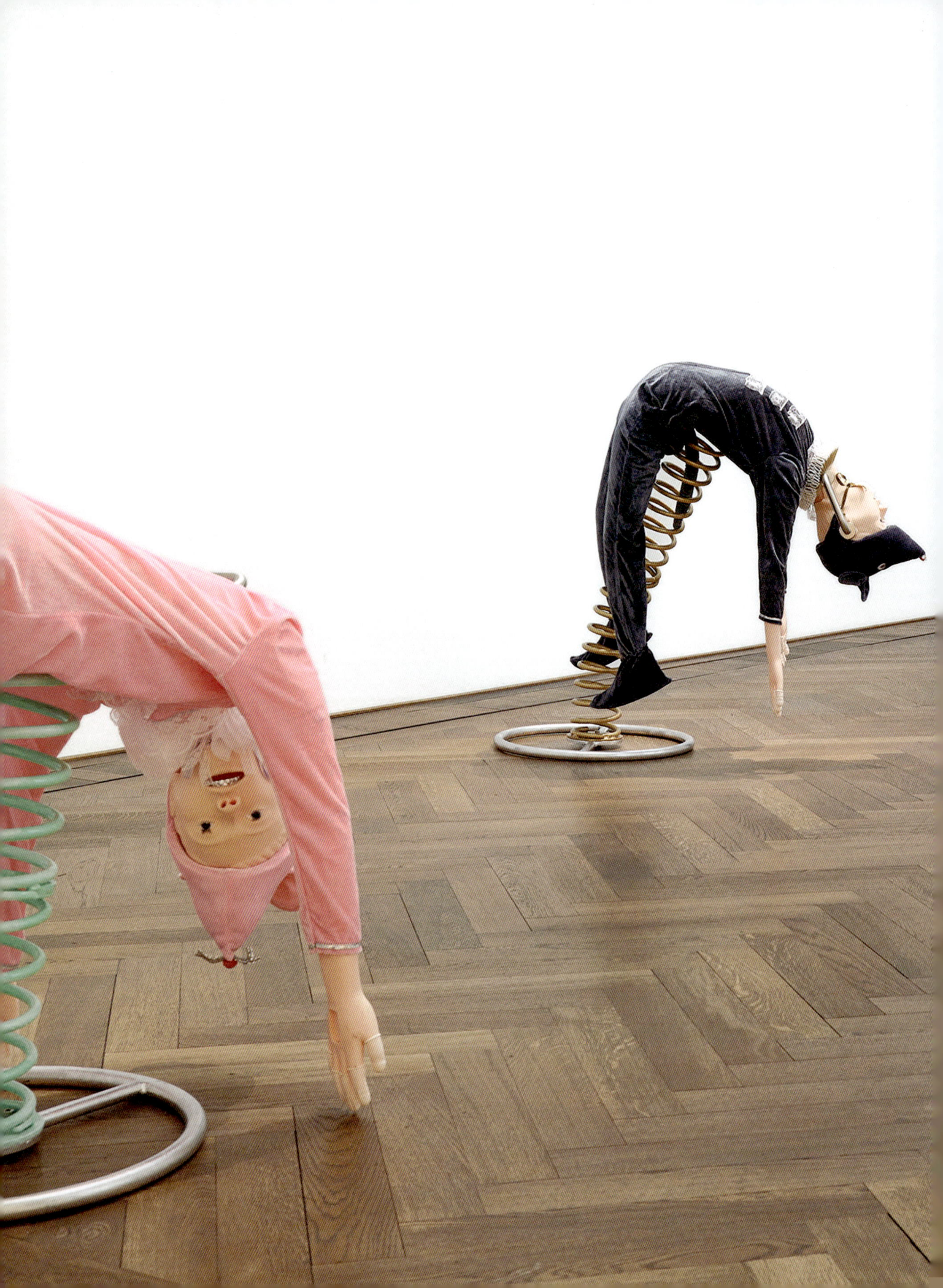

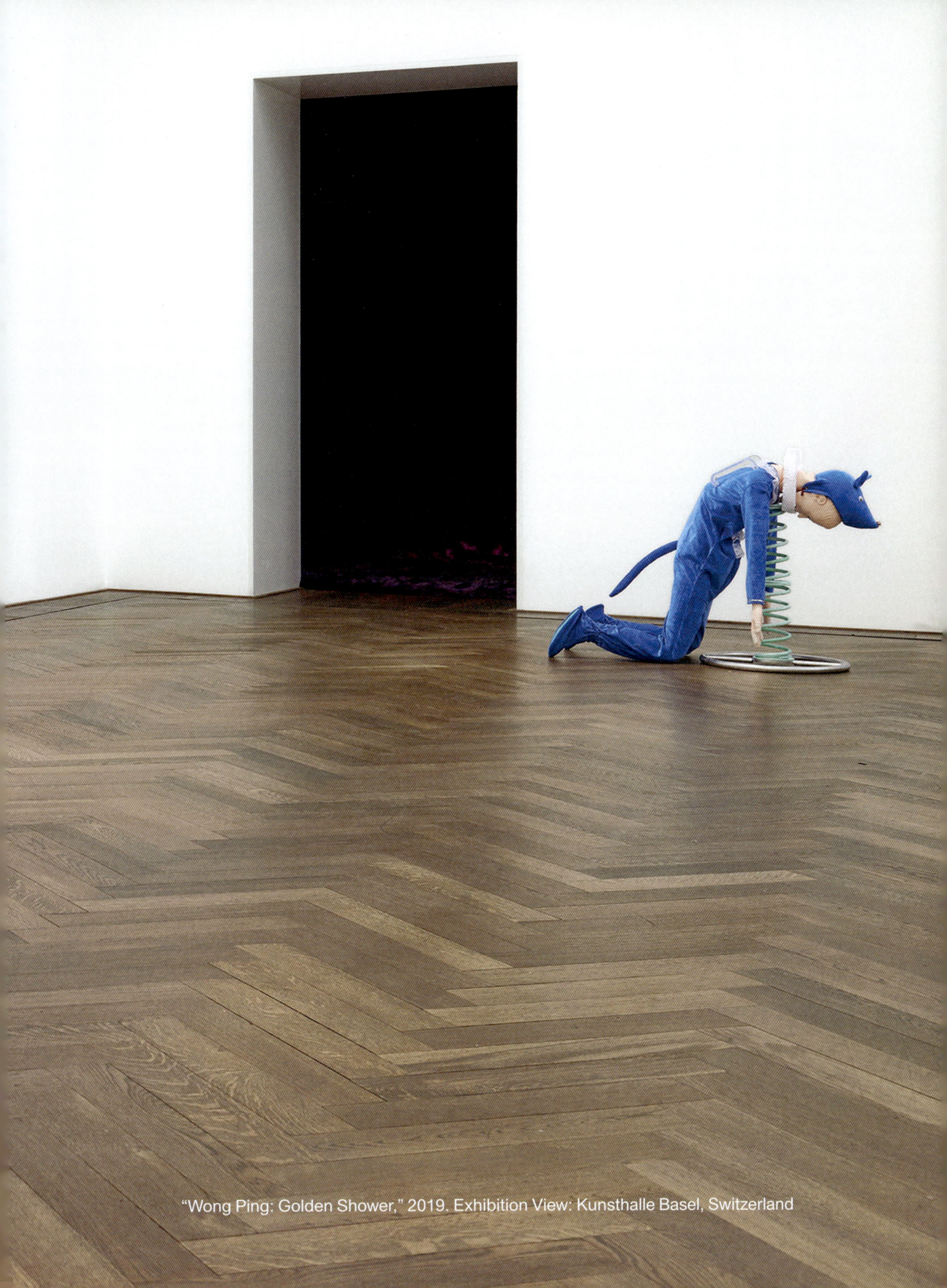

"Wong Ping: Golden Shower," 2019. Exhibition View: Kunsthalle Basel, Switzerland

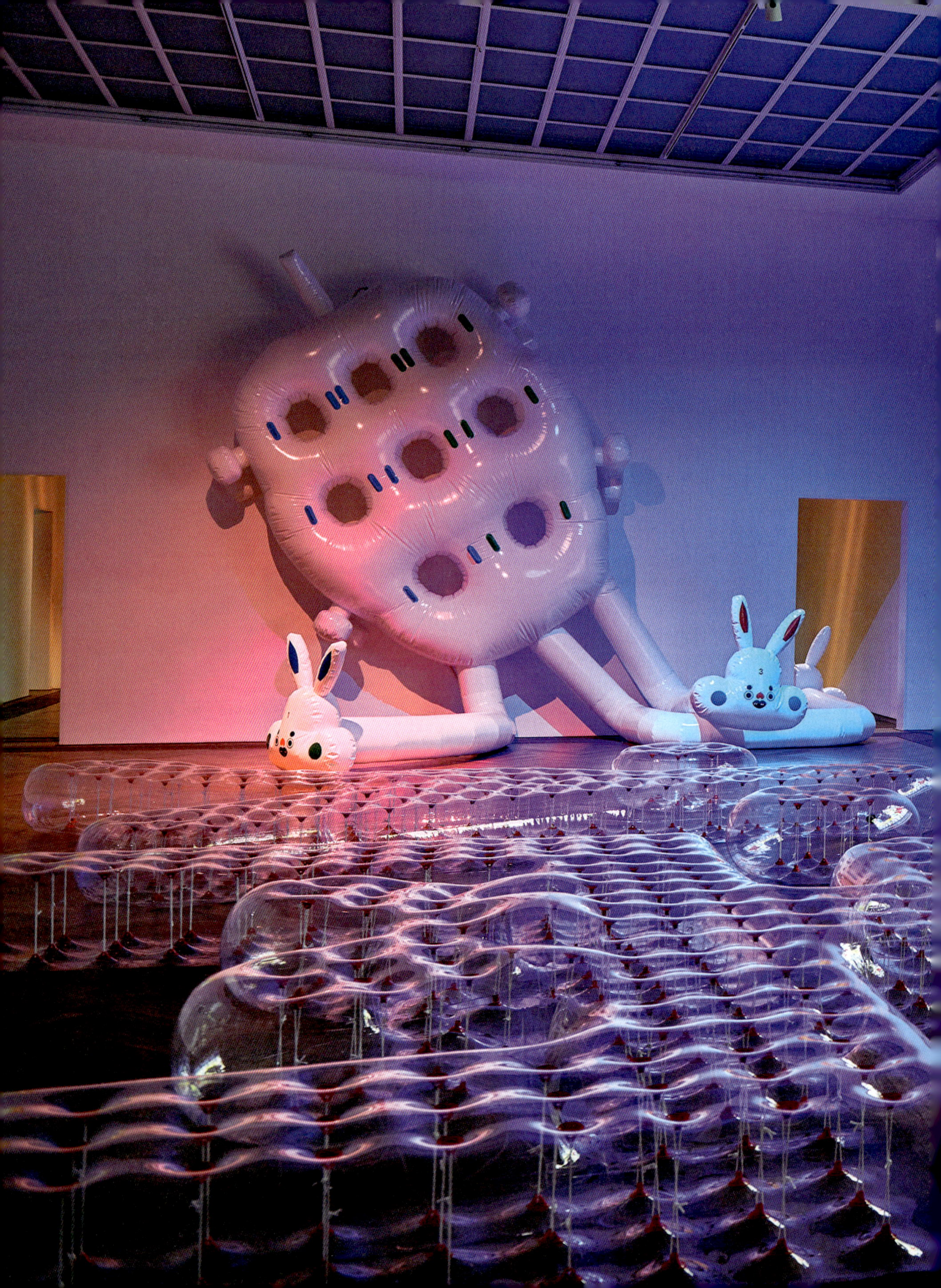

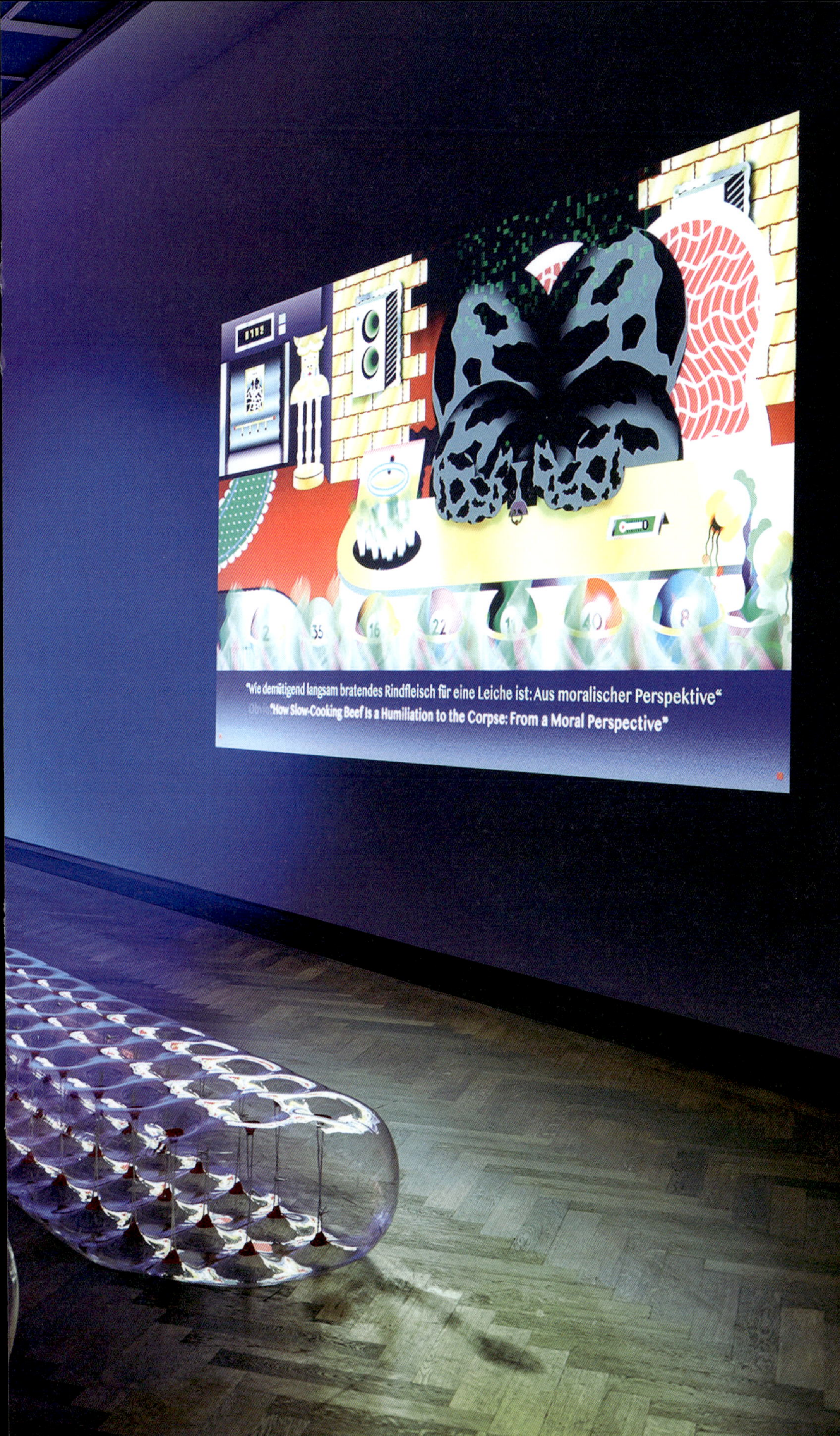
„Wie demütigend langsam bratendes Rindfleisch für eine Leiche ist: Aus moralischer Perspektive"
„How Slow-Cooking Beef Is a Humiliation to the Corpse: From a Moral Perspective"

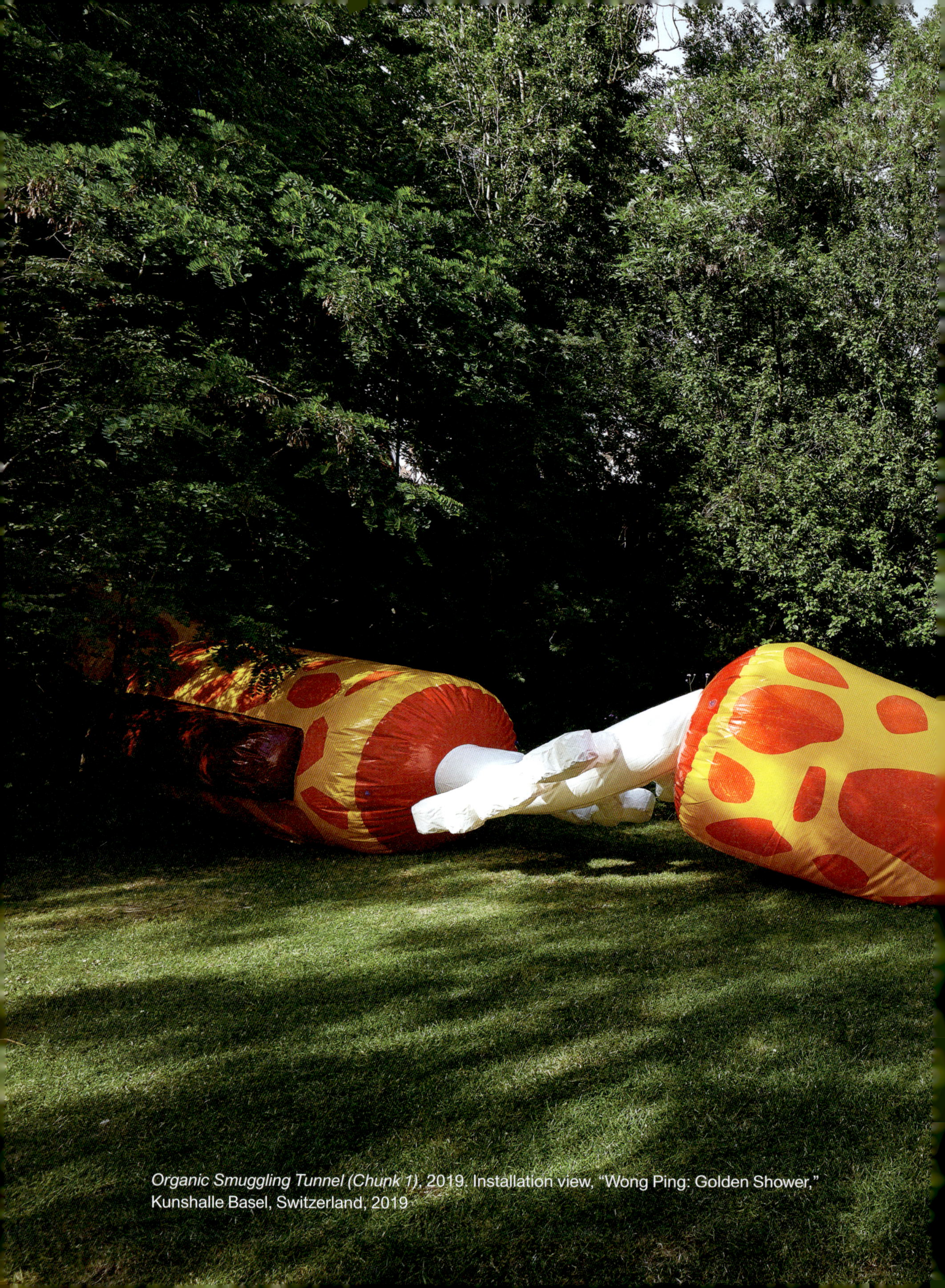

Organic Smuggling Tunnel (Chunk 1), 2019. Installation view, "Wong Ping: Golden Shower,"
Kunshalle Basel, Switzerland, 2019

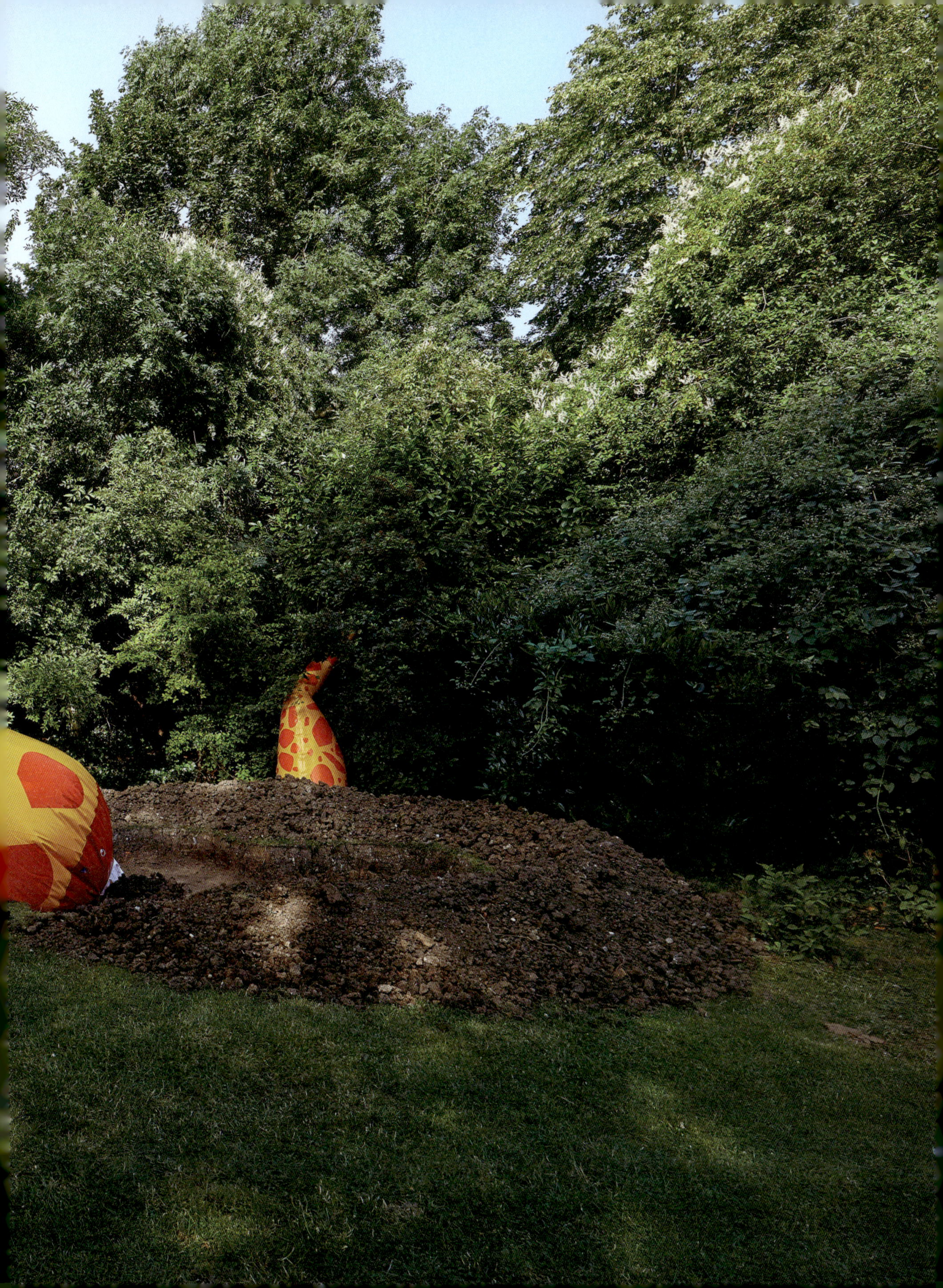

Brick Boner, 2019. Installation view, "Wong Ping: Heart Digger,"
Camden Arts Centre, London, 2019

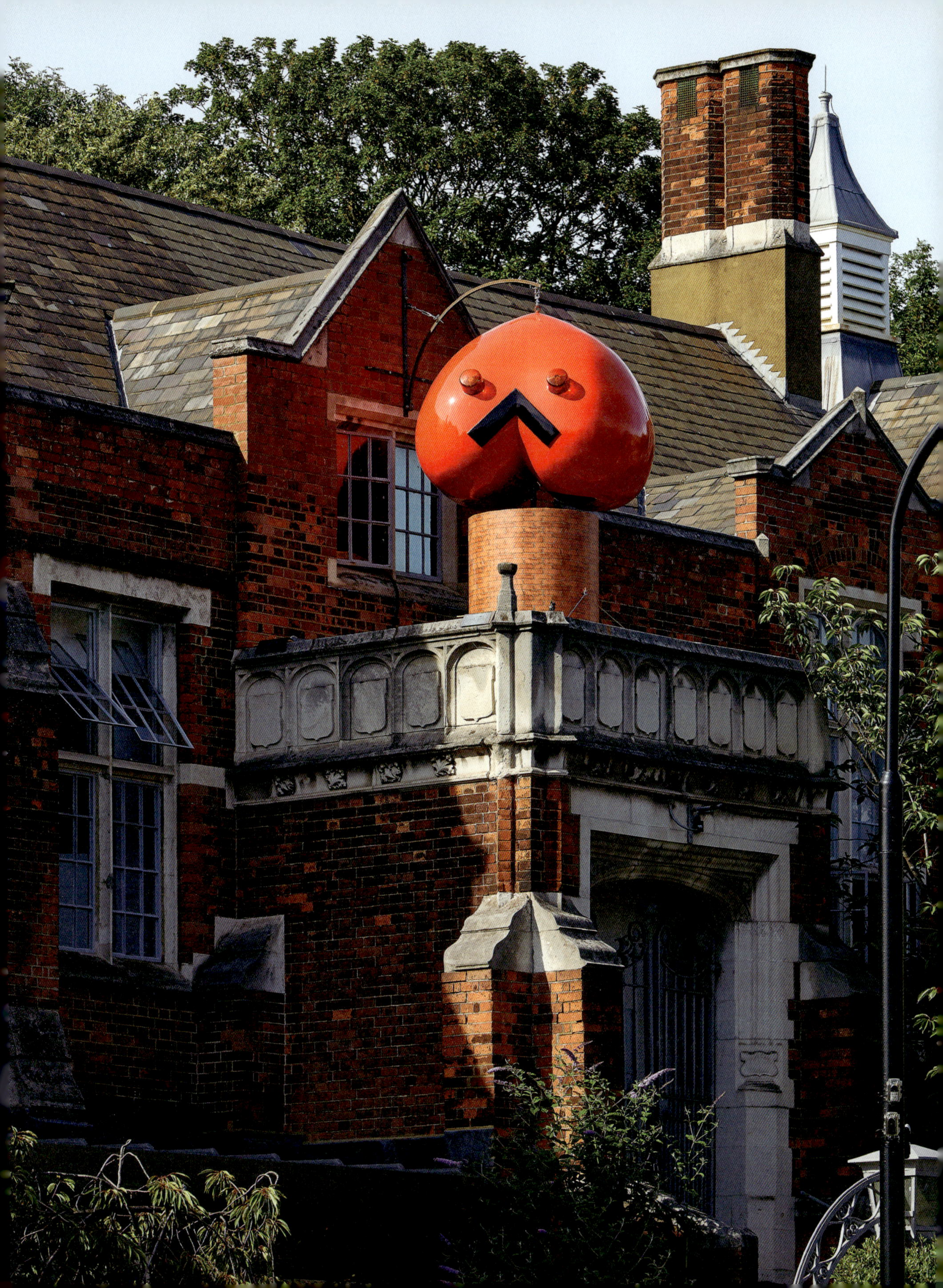

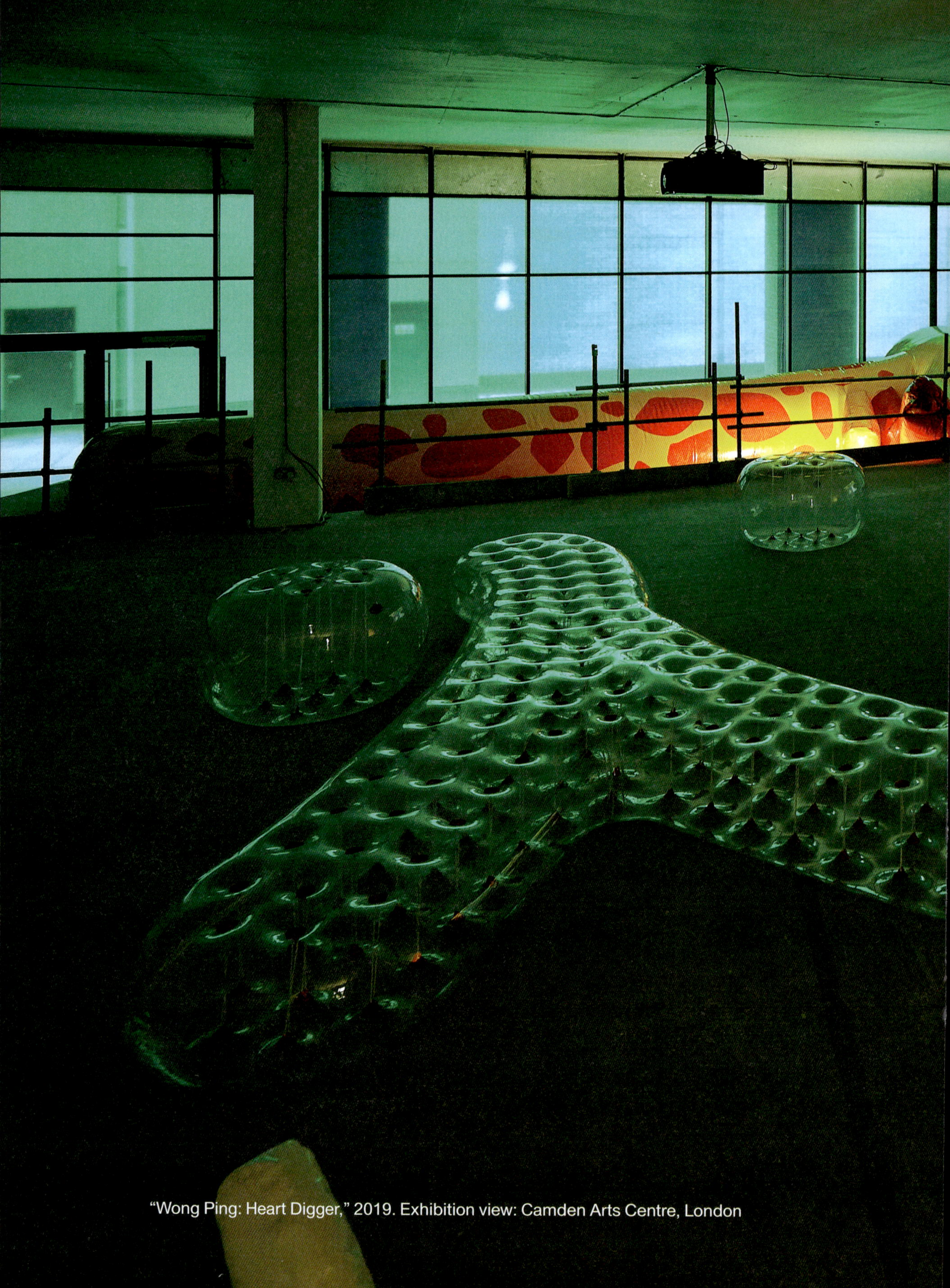

"Wong Ping: Heart Digger," 2019. Exhibition view: Camden Arts Centre, London

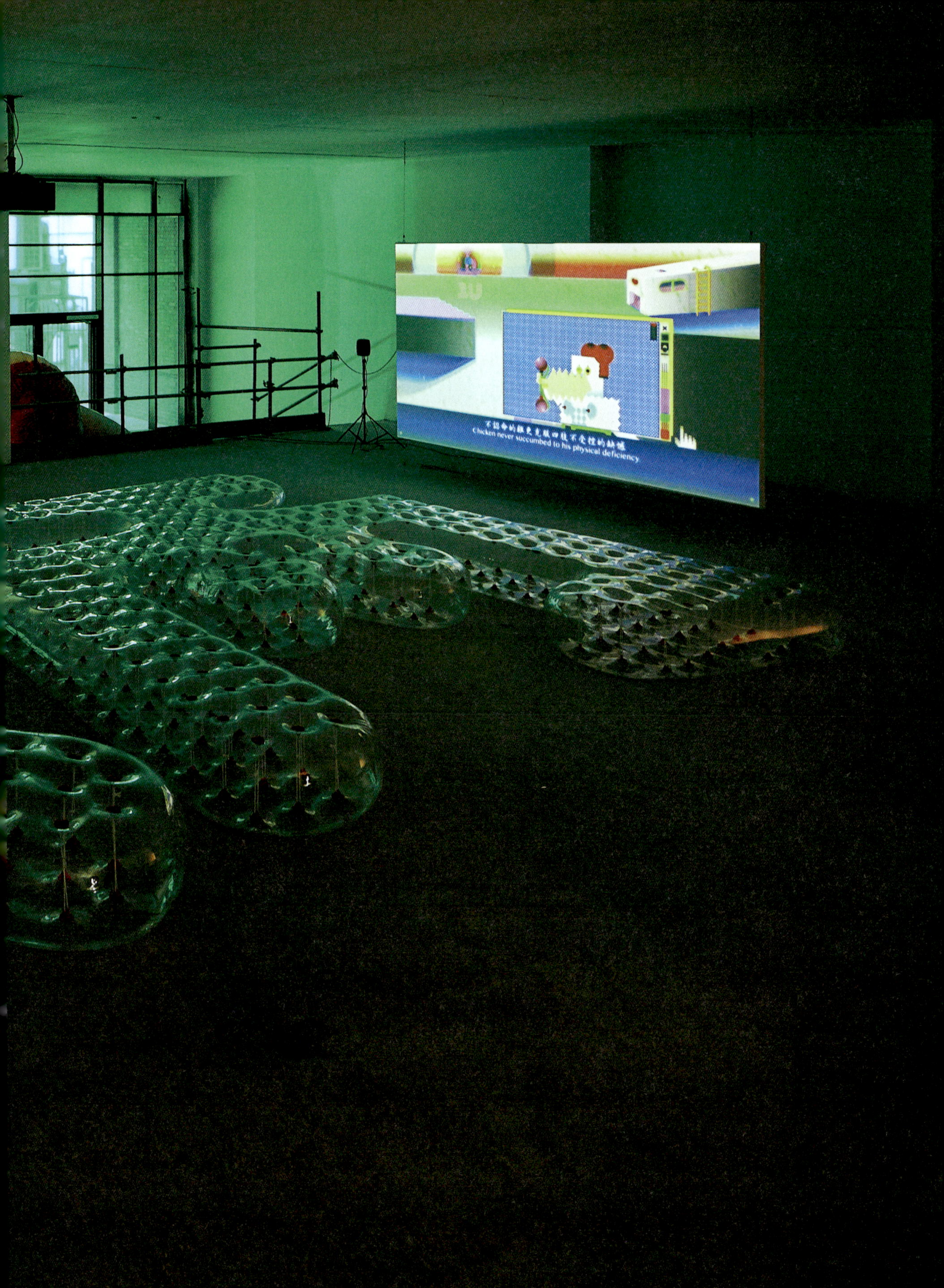

不認命的雞先克服四肢不受控的缺憾
Chicken never succumbed to his physical deficiency.

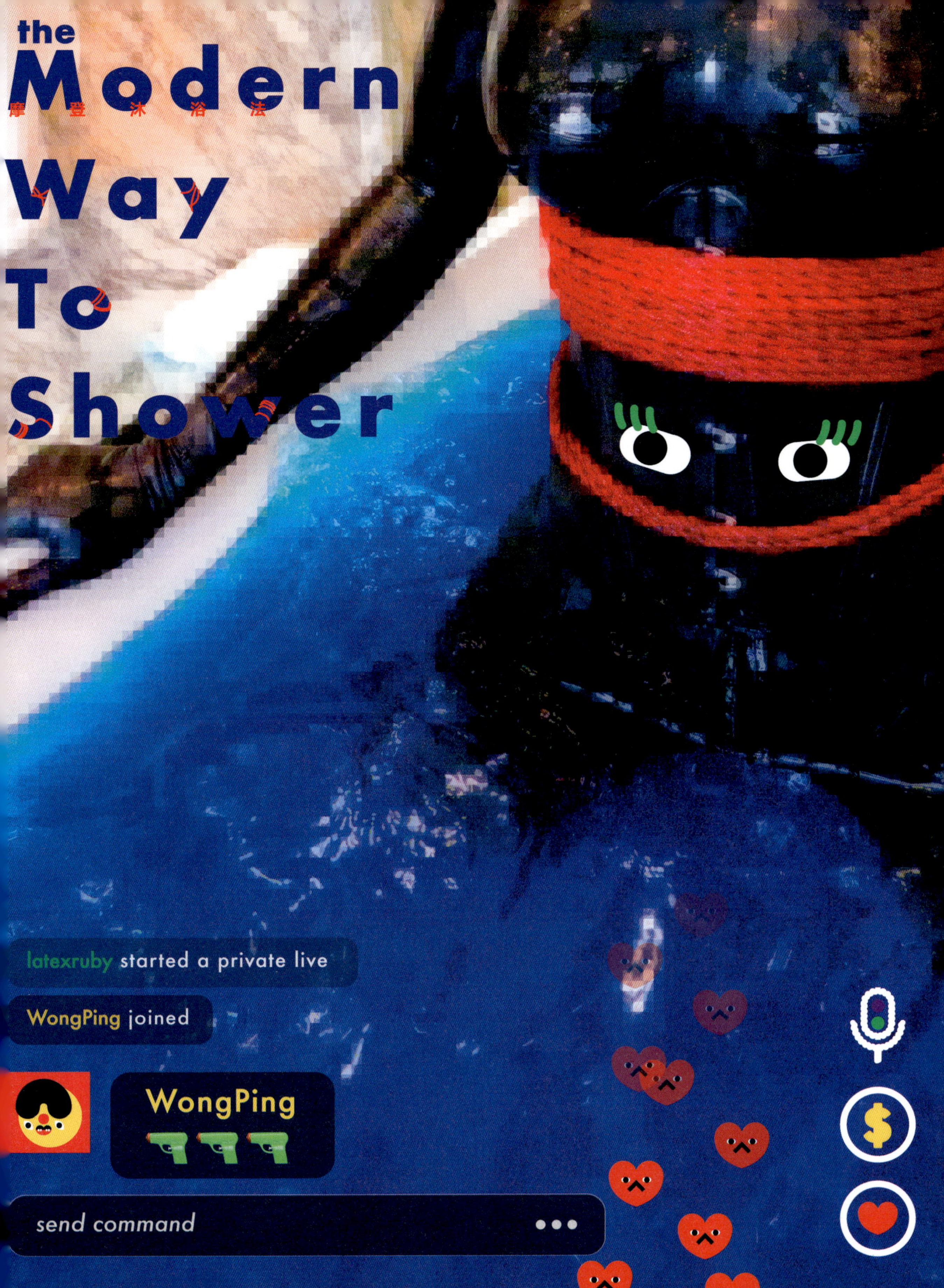
the
Modern
摩登 沐浴法
Way
To
Shower
latexruby started a private live
WongPing joined
WongPing
send command

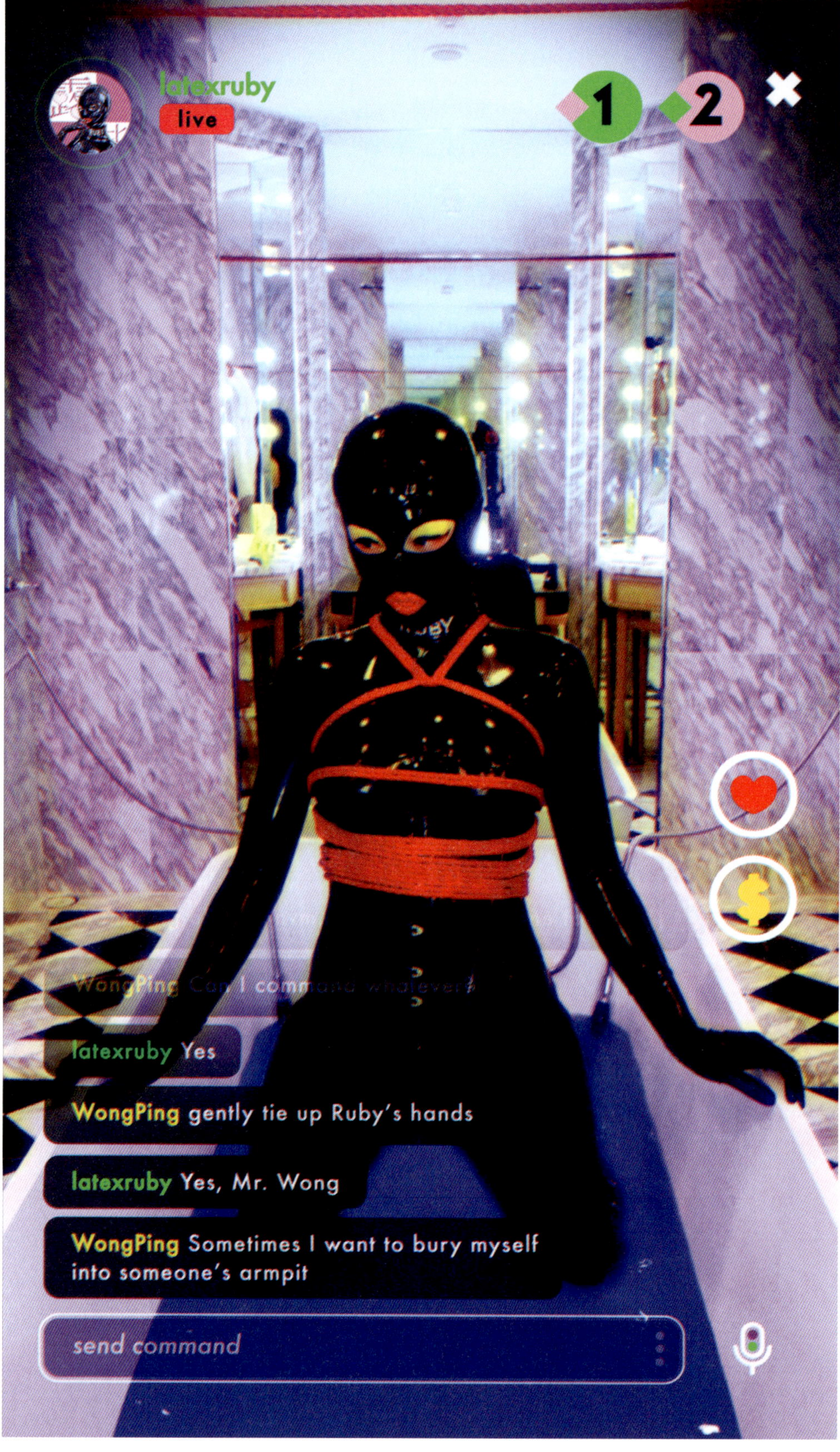

latexruby
live
1
2
WongPing Can I command whatever?
latexruby Yes
WongPing gently tie up Ruby's hands
latexruby Yes, Mr. Wong
WongPing Sometimes I want to bury myself into someone's armpit
send command

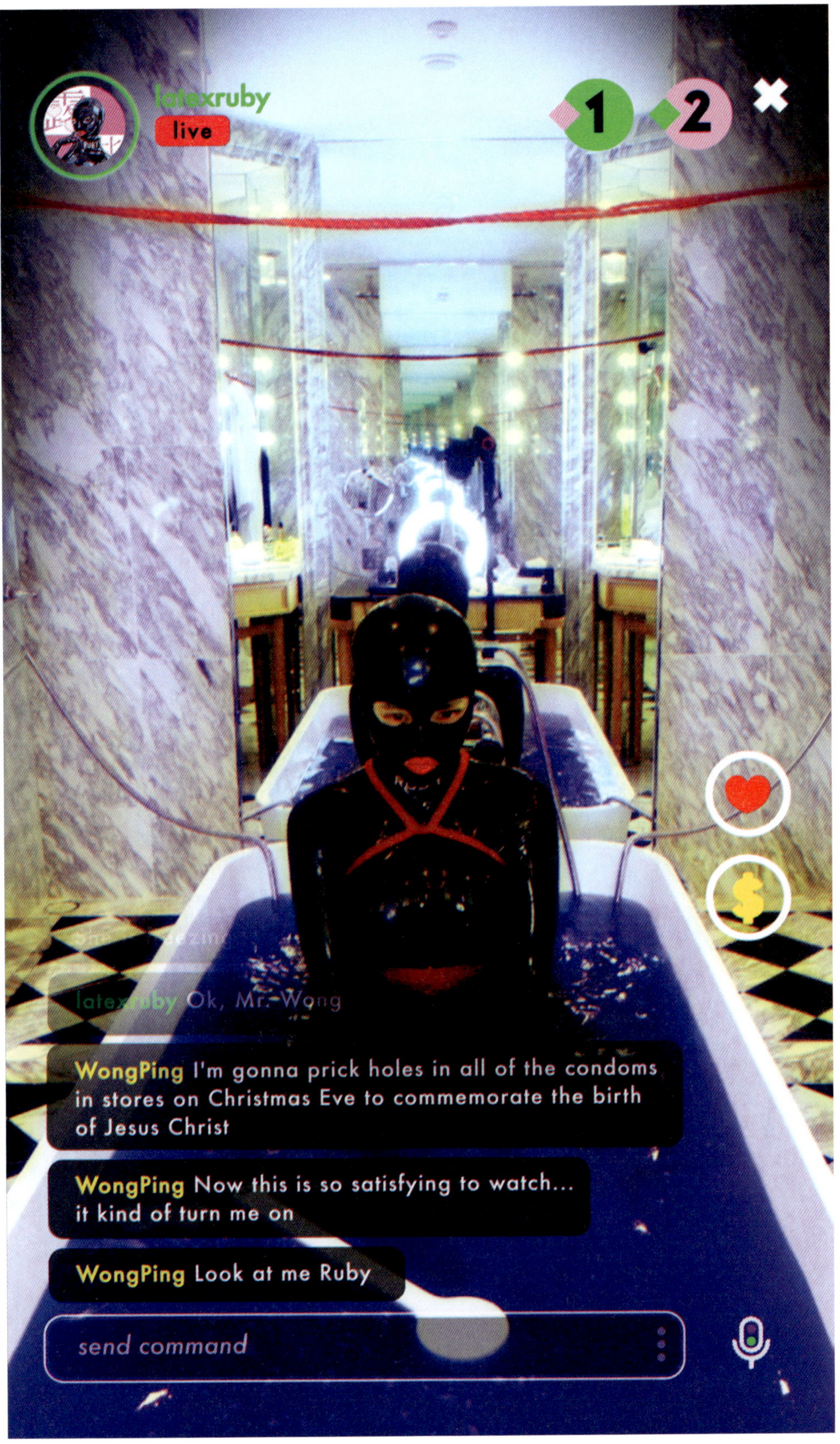

latexruby
live
1
2
latexruby Ok, Mr. Wong
WongPing I'm gonna prick holes in all of the condoms in stores on Christmas Eve to commemorate the birth of Jesus Christ
WongPing Now this is so satisfying to watch... it kind of turn me on
WongPing Look at me Ruby
send command

The Modern Way to Shower, 2019. Installation view, "Wong Ping: The Modern
Way to Shower," Institute of Contemporary Art, Miami, 2019

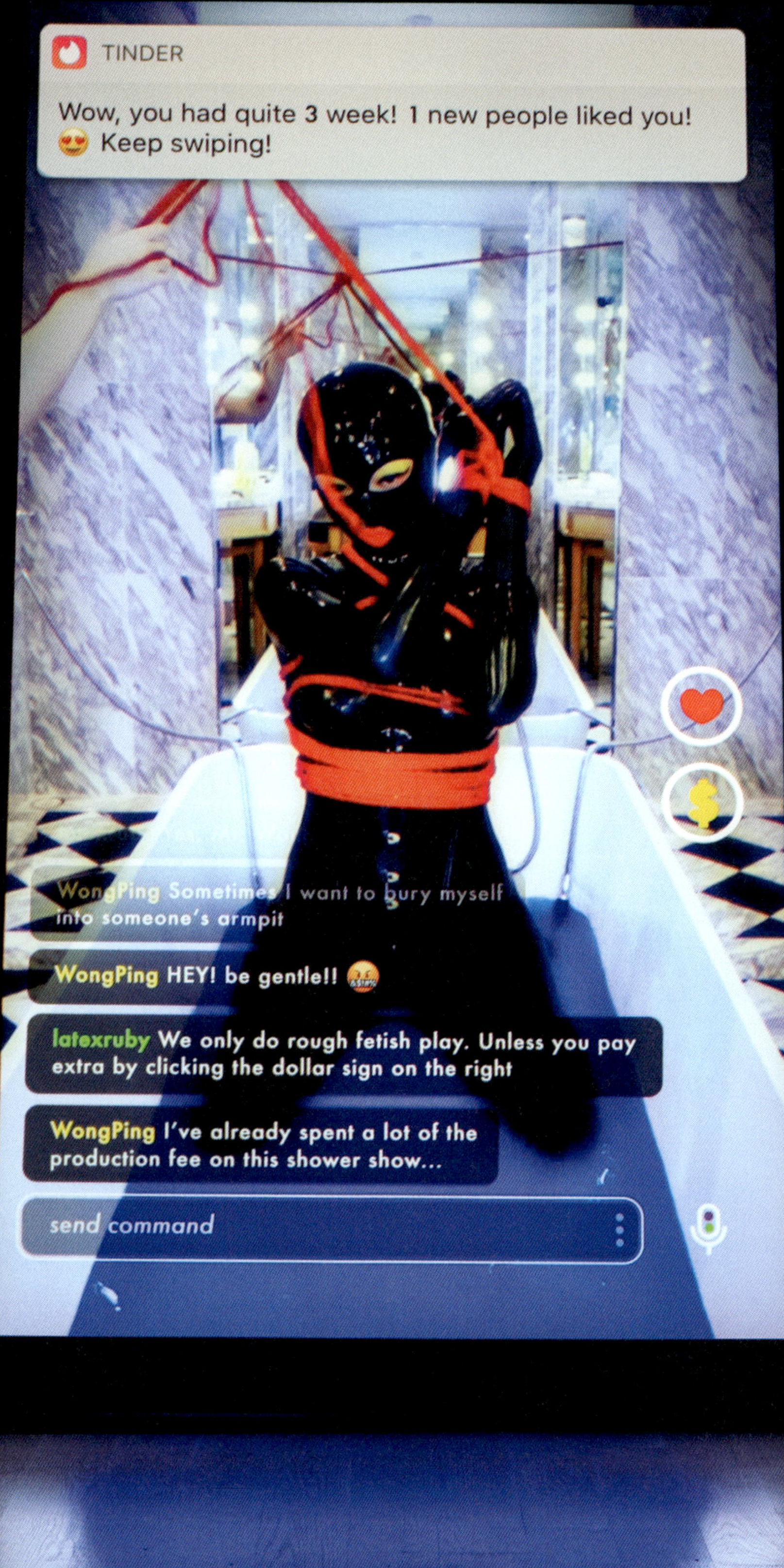

TINDER
Wow, you had quite 3 week! 1 new people liked you! 😍 Keep swiping!
WongPing Sometimes I want to bury myself into someone's armpit
WongPing HEY! be gentle!!
latexruby We only do rough fetish play. Unless you pay extra by clicking the dollar sign on the right
WongPing I've already spent a lot of the production fee on this shower show...
send command

List of Illustrated Works

p. 57
FRUITPUNCH – We Want More, 2010
Single-channel video, color, sound;
5:44 min

pp. 58–61
Under the Lion Crotch, 2011
Single-channel video, color, sound;
4:38 min

pp. 63–65
Slow Sex, 2013
Single-channel video, color, sound;
2:40 min

pp. 67–73
Stop Peeping, 2014
Single-channel video, color, sound;
3:48 min

pp. 74–75
Witch, 2015
Single-channel video, color, sound;
3 min

pp. 77–81
Doggy Love, 2015
Single-channel video, color, sound;
5:59 min
Commissioned by NOWNESS

pp. 83–89
The Other Side, 2015
Two-channel video, color sound; 8 min
Commissioned by M+, Hong Kong

pp. 91–99
An Emo Nose, 2015*
Single-channel video, color, sound;
4:23 min

pp. 101–113
Jungle of Desire, 2015*
Single-channel video, color, sound;
6:50 min

pp. 115–125
Who's the Daddy?, 2017*
Single-channel video, color, sound;
9:15 min

pp. 126–129
Wong Ping's Fables 1, 2018
Single-channel video, color, sound;
13 min

pp. 130–139
Dear, Can I Give You A Hand?, 2018
Animated LED video installation, color,
sound: 12 min
Solomon R. Guggenheim Museum,
New York, The Robert H. N. Ho Family
Foundation Collection, 2018. This video
was produced on the occasion of the
exhibition "One Hand Clipping" (2018)
presented at the Solomon R. Guggenheim
Museum, New York, and made
possible by The Robert H. N. Ho Family
Foundation.

p. 140
*Tree takes on part-time body rental for
Pole to do tree dance during his spare
time*, 2018
3D printing, ABS, malachite, clayed ants,
copper ball, plastic craft eyes
15 ¾ × 10 ⅝ × 7 ⅛ inches; 40 × 27 × 18 cm

p. 141
Premature Elephant, 2018
3D printing, ABS, varnish, black
leather band
15 ¾ × 24 ⅜ × 5 ½ in (40 × 62 × 14 cm)

p. 142
Tree takes on part-time nude life modeling during his spare time, 2018
3D printing, ABS, malachite, clayed ladybugs
16 ⅛ × 15 × 6 ⅝ in (41 × 38 × 17 cm)

p. 143
Kidnapped Chicken feels guilty for his inability to crow before sunrise, 2018
3D printing, ABS, stone, flower, watch, red leather rope, peacock feather
19 ⅝ × 25 ¼ × 4 ¾ in (50 × 64 × 12 cm)

p. 144
Turtle, who is often called by the name of penis because of his looks, suffers from severe depression and takes poison to commit suicide, 2018
3D printing, ABS, capsule, glitter powder, toy eyeball
21 ⅝ × 18 ½ × 8 ⅛ in (55 × 47 × 20.5 cm)

p. 145
Albino Cockroach becomes the lightest colour bodybuilding championship winner in history, 2018
3D printing, ABS, aluminum gold necklace, lace belt
26 × 15 ¾ × 6 ⅞ in (66 × 40 × 17.5 cm)

pp. 146–151
Wong Ping's Fables 2, 2019*
Single-channel video, color, sound; 13:30 min
Commissioned by Kunsthalle Basel

pp. 154–155
The Ha Ha Ha Online Cemetery Limited, 2019
Toy dentures with gold leaf, metal brackets
Dimensions variable

pp. 160–161
Organic Smuggling Tunnel (Chunk 1), 2019
Plastic inflatables
Dimensions variable

p. 163
Brick Boner, 2019
Mixed media
Dimensions variable
Co-commissioned and co-produced by Camden Arts Centre and Kunsthalle Basel

pp. 167–171
The Modern Way to Shower, 2019
Single-channel video, color, sound; 12:30 min
Commissioned by ICA Miami

All works courtesy the artist; Edouard Malingue Gallery, Hong Kong / Shanghai; and Tanya Bonakdar Gallery, New York / Los Angeles

* Works included in the exhibition

About the Artist

Wong Ping (b. 1984, Hong Kong) lives and works in Hong Kong, and founded the Wong Ping Animation Lab in 2014. He has had recent solo exhibitions at SCAD Museum of Art, Savannah, GA (2020); Institute of Contemporary Art, Miami (2019); Camden Arts Centre, London (2019); and Kunsthalle Basel (2019). His work has been included in group exhibitions at numerous venues, including Tai Kwun, Hong Kong (2019); 5th Ural Industrial Biennial, Ekaterinburg, Russia (2019); Today Art Museum, Beijing (2018); Times Art Center Berlin (2018); 6th Athens Biennial (2018); Changwon Sculpture Biennial, South Korea (2018); Sifang Art Museum, Nanjing, China (2018); Alt Space Loop, Seoul (2018); Solomon R. Guggenheim Museum, New York (2018); Haus der elektronischen Künste Basel (2018); and Arts Centre Melbourne (2017). His films have screened at many festivals and institutions, including London Short Film Festival, International Film Festival Rotterdam, Sundance Film Festival, Hong Kong International Film Festival, Kurzfilm Festival Hamburg, Centre Pompidou, and Artists' Film Biennial. Wong was the recipient of the inaugural Camden Arts Centre Emerging Arts Prize at Frieze in 2018.

Board of Trustees

Photography Credits

All images courtesy the artist; Edouard Malingue Gallery, Hong Kong/Shanghai; and Tanya Bonakdar Gallery, New York/Los Angeles unless otherwise noted

Photo: Philipp Hänger/Kunsthalle Basel: pp. 112–113, 152–159

Courtesy the artist, Tai Kwun Contemporary, Hong Kong, Edouard Malingue Gallery, Hong Kong/Shanghai and Tanya Bonakdar Gallery, New York/Los Angeles. Photo: Kwan Sheung Chi: pp. 122–125

Courtesy the artist, Camden Arts Centre, London, Edouard Malingue Gallery, Hong Kong/ Shanghai and Tanya Bonakdar Gallery, New York/Los Angeles. Photo: Luke Walker: pp. 136–137, 160–161, 163–165

Courtesy the artist, Solomon R. Guggenheim Museum, New York, Edouard Malingue Gallery, Hong Kong/Shanghai and Tanya Bonakdar Gallery, New York/Los Angeles. Photo: David Heald: p. 139

Photo: Fredrik Nilsen Studio: p. 171

Published by
New Museum
235 Bowery
New York, NY 10002
Newmuseum.org

On the occasion of the exhibition
"Wong Ping: Your Silent Neighbor"
June 30–October 3, 2021

Curators: Gary Carrion-Murayari,
Kraus Family Curator
Former Curatorial Assistant:
Francesca Altamura

Contributions by:
Tobias Berger
Gary Carrion-Murayari
David Horvitz
Shirley Lipner
Wong Ping

Design Template: An Art Service
Design Production: Nicholas Weltyk
Printing: SPC, Poland

Front and back cover: *The Other Side*,
2015. Courtesy the artist; Edouard
Malingue Gallery, Hong Kong / Shanghai;
and Tanya Bonakdar Gallery, New York /
Los Angeles

ISBN: 978-0-915557-25-7

The New Museum gratefully
acknowledges our Board of Trustees
and generous sponsors for their support
of "Wong Ping: Your Silent Neighbor."

Major support for this exhibition is
provided by the International Leadership
Council of the New Museum.

Support for this exhibition is provided by
the Toby Devan Lewis Emerging Artists
Exhibitions Fund.

Artist commissions at the New Museum
are generously supported by the Neeson /
Edlis Artist Commissions Fund.

Artist support is provided, in part, by
Laura Skoler.

We extend our special thanks to the
Friends of Wong Ping: Kiang Malingue,
Tanya Bonakdar Gallery, Nelson Leong,
Evan Chow, Andrew Xue, and Ruoqi
Amy Zhou.

Education and community programs
are supported, in part, by the American
Chai Trust.

Support for this publication has
been provided by the J. McSweeney
and G. Mills Publications Fund at
the New Museum.

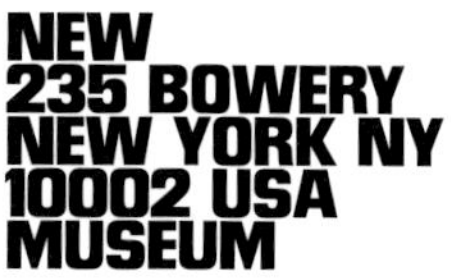